CW00905089

Bernard Who?

Bernard Who?

75 Years of Doing Just About Everything

BERNARD CRIBBINS

CONSTABLE

For Gill

CONSTABLE

First published in Great Britain in 2018 by Constable

3 5 7 9 10 8 6 4 2

Copyright © Bernard Cribbins and James Hogg, 2018

Unless otherwise specified all images from Bernard Cribbins's personal archive.

The moral right of the author has been asserted.

A CIP catalogue record for this book
is available from the British Library.

ISBN: 978-1-47213-016-7 (hardback)

Typeset in Bembo by Hewer Text UK Ltd, Edinburgh
Printed and bound in Great Britain by CPI Group
(UK) Ltd, Croydon, CR0 4YY

Papers used by Constable are from well-managed
forests and other responsible sources.

Constable
An imprint of
Little, Brown Book Group
Carmelite House
50 Victoria Embankment
London EC4Y 0DZ

An Hachette UK Company
www.hachette.co.uk

www.littlebrown.co.uk

Contents

CHAPTER ONE

The long drop

Well hello there!

Mr Bernard Cribbins here. Character actor, fisherman, former paratrooper, catwalk model and purveyor of the odd story. I expect that's why you're here, isn't it? To have me tell you a few tales? Well, you're in luck. Except this time, as opposed to me recounting somebody else's yarn, I'm going to be telling you my own, and in my own words. What a strange experience that's going to be. Cribbins on Cribbins.

It was only when somebody mentioned it to me the other day that I realised I'd been telling tales of one sort or another for over seventy-five years. SEVENTY-FIVE YEARS! That's quite scary, don't you think? After all, according to a pal of mine who's in the know, that's four and a half years longer than the worldwide average life expectancy, which means that while half the world has been popping its clogs, I've been rabbiting on!

What's been even more terrifying than the fact that yours truly has been acting the fool for over three-quarters of a century has been the task of trying to remember the details of what I've done. I'm not a diarist, you see, and the old memory's a bit up and down. I've been getting there gradually, though, I'm happy to say, but there's been an awful lot of toing and froing. Just when I think I've finished writing about a certain part of my life, something else springs to mind, and then something else. I haven't half got on my own nerves.

'Bernard,' I say to myself. 'You've forgotten that story about Peter Sellers during the making of *Two-Way Stretch*. And what about that thing Lionel Jeffries said to you during *The Railway Children*? That's not in yet. I ask you. Come along Bernard, my old son. Get a grip.' I sometimes think that if I had a brain I'd be dangerous.

By the way, in the interests of us all having a good time, I think we should keep the proceedings on the page, so to speak, quite warm and conversational, don't you? I want you to imagine I'm sitting in front of you with this very book, and I'm reading it just for you. Exactly like I used to do on *Jackanory*. Did you ever watch *Jackanory* when you were young? I expect some of you did. I hold the record for making the most episodes of that show and in my opinion that makes me one of the luckiest old codgers on earth. Why? Because I got to narrate some of the greatest stories that have ever been thought up by man or beast, that's why. Better still, I got paid for it! The only thing that might get a little bit lost in translation are things like accents, noises and silly voices, so I'll let you know when one's coming, OK? Then, you'll have to bring them to life. You can do that, can't you?

Do you know what I used to do just before we started recording an episode of *Jackanory*? I used to look straight into the camera lens and imagine that there was one little boy or girl

– just one – sitting patiently but expectantly waiting for me to tell them a story. Then, once I had that picture in my head, that's exactly what I'd do. Tell them a story. I've been doing something similar with this story, by the way, except the person I'm talking to is obviously holding a book. And, they're a bit older, of course. It might be a slightly odd way of getting your life story across, but that's how I've always prepared, you see. The *Jackanory method*, I call it.

Anyway, are you ready? Are you sitting comfortably, as the saying goes? Then I will begin. After all, we've an awful lot of ground to cover. And we're doing the whole thing, by the way, not just the career.

Where shall we start then?

At the beginning?

Well, it seems as good a place as any, doesn't it?

Here we go then.

I, Bernard Joseph Cribbins the first – and last, with any luck – was born in Oldham, Lancashire, on 29 December 19-something something. Oh, all right then. You've squeezed it out of me. I was born on 29 December 1928, almost ninety years ago. If that sounds depressing to you, imagine what it's doing to me.

One of the things people often ask me about when they meet me is my surname. Some assume it's just a stage name, but it isn't. Think about it: if you had to choose a new surname for yourself, you're hardly likely to choose Cribbins, are you? Not that there's anything wrong with it, although it is quite unique. I know there are one or two people called Cribbin knocking about but Cribbins seems to be about as rare as hen's teeth. That's good for an actor as people tend to remember you.

The name is Irish, in the first place, and I think it comes from the Gaelic name, McRoibin. Somewhere along the way it became McRibbin, then Cribbin, and then Cribbins. According to my mother the 's' was tagged on when it became a possessive. You know, 'That's Cribbin's cow,' or 'That's Cribbin's dog.'

For those of you who aren't familiar with the town of Oldham, it rose to prominence in the eighteenth century as a centre of textile manufacturing, or a mill town, as they were known, and although it's within the county of Lancashire it sits treacherously close to the People's Republic of Yorkshire. According to this pal of mine I mentioned who's in the know – or, I should say, who knows how to use a computer – other infamous Oldhamites include Tommy Cannon and Bobby Ball, Dora Bryan, who you'll hear about in a bit, Phillip Schofield, Brian Cox (the physicist, not the actor), the actor Jack Wild, who played the Artful Dodger in Lionel Barts's *Oliver!*, and a certain gentleman named Eric Sykes who you shall also hear a bit about later on.

The area of Oldham we lived in was and still is called Glodwick – pronounced Glod-ick – and our abode was a tiny little two-up-two-down that was one of thousands around the area. Anyone who hails from an urban part of the north of England will probably know what I'm talking about here, as almost every town or city has them.

The luxurious facilities at Chez Cribbins included a cold-water tap, a tin bath and an outside loo that we used to call 'the long drop'. Don't you think that's quaint? In a lavatorial kind of way. No cistern and a chain for us, thank you very much. We used to have to make our own entertainment. If you think your stomach can take it, I'll go into a little bit of detail about this as it's quite fun. Well, the long drop was literally a long porcelain tube that led from the bottom of our loo to a platform that used to tilt when a sufficient amount of 'material' had landed on it. Am I making sense, so far? Don't think about it too much, or you'll be there for ever. Anyway, whenever it rained heavily, which it does rather a lot in Oldham, some of the rain water would drain through grids onto this platform and when that happened the blasted thing would be tilting all night. CO-BA-DUNK, CO-BA-DUNK, CO-BA-DUNK, it used to go. I used to lie in bed listening to it and, if it hadn't been for the fact that I knew what else was falling onto it, it might have been quite cathartic!

In addition to having a rather primitive privy, we also had gas lighting in those days as opposed to electricity. Once, while in bed with a dose of flu, there was nothing else to look at so I started watching the gas mantle. As it burned I noticed there was a pulse in the flame and after a while I had to look at something else. Because I had a temperature my heart was beating quite heavily, and I think it just accentuated everything! What with that and the platform under the long drop going ten to the dozen, it's a wonder I ever recovered.

According to my mother, I was born 'between the lights', which I think means early in the morning. Don't you think that's a charming phrase – between the lights? I do. I think it's lovely. Apparently, I was a forceps baby, on account of me being a bit of a bighead, and although the doctor had to be called out both Mum and I were fine in the end. They made us hardy in those days. Bigheaded, but hardy.

Shall I introduce you to Mum and Dad? It'd be rude of me not to. My mum, Ethel, was short and had long dark hair. She was a weaver in a cotton mill and I was once told that her mother had paid half a crown a week to have her trained as a corduroy weaver. If you could afford it this was a good investment as it meant your child would earn more money.

How times have changed, eh? These days people send their kids to university to help them get on in life, whereas my old mum was trained to make cords!

Dad, who was known as Jack but had been christened John Edward, also had dark hair and, as well as being a bit on the small side, he was apparently a bit of a terrier. Professionally, Dad, who had served in the Medical Corps in the First World War, was a jack-of-all-trades and could turn his hand to most things, property repair being one of his main sources of income. He also sang in the church choir in his spare time, which he did with Mum – Dad had quite a pleasing tenor voice. He was also fond of amateur dramatics. *Ahaaaaah!* I hear you cry. *So that's why Bernard Cribbins is such a ruddy show-off. He got it from his dad.* Yes, you're probably right there. Well, at least you've got somebody to blame! The amateur dramatic society that Dad belonged to was attached to the church and, from memory, they used to put on a lot of shows by Gilbert & Sullivan. At the time that was meat and potatoes to your average am-dram outfit and Dad was a big fan. The reason Gilbert & Sullivan were so popular with these societies – in my opinion – is because they had a little bit of everything – music, drama, comedy – which meant the people taking part got to *do* a bit of everything. Perfect!

I also had a sister, by the way, called Veronica, who was about three years older than me. She and I both had fair hair, unlike Mum and Dad, so when the four of us went out together we looked like halves of two different families.

My earliest memory is going around to my Granny and Grandad's house. These were my mother's parents, by the way. Grandad was from Yorkshire and Granny was from Ireland – Queenstown, I think – and they were called Clarkson. It was Christmas and I must have been almost three years old, so we're talking 1931. Good grief! I've got to try and get used to this age thing, somehow. It's something I never normally think about, but at the moment I can't seem to escape it. It'll be the death of me.

What I remember is sitting at the table and seeing a huge black pot with a handle being brought in from the kitchen and put on the living-room table. Inside this pot was the Christmas pudding. Don't ask me why I know, I just do. The most vivid part of this memory is seeing lots of steam coming out of this pot, which in hindsight made it look like a witch's cauldron or a steaming cannonball! That's about it, I'm afraid. That's my memory. The most fascinating thing about it is the fact that it's almost eighty-eight years ago. I had no idea memories could last as long as that.

I never knew my dad's parents, by the way, as I think they went quite early. As far as I know, Dad's father had been a heavy drinker and I'm pretty sure he'd also been a clog fighter. Have you ever heard of clog fighting? This'll make you wince a bit! Clog fighting was a mill-town pastime that was used to settle disputes. It involved two blokes kicking each other's shins while wearing a pair of wooden clogs with irons on the soles. Their shins would be unprotected, of course, and whoever gave up or bled first would be the loser. A pleasant little pastime, don't you think? I could imagine it going down well on a Sunday afternoon on BBC1, just before *Songs of Praise*. There were also professional clog fighters, which is what my grandad might have been. This lot would travel for miles for a good clog fight and they could earn a very good second wage, apparently. I used to wear clogs when I was a child, although I swear on the Holy Bible that I never kicked anyone in anger! I had a pair of pit clogs first, which were lace-ups, with irons on the bottom. These were known as 'sparking clogs', as whenever you scraped them along the ground sparks would fly up. This is why some millworkers like my mother always had to work barefoot as a spark in the dusty environment of a cotton mill could easily cause a fire or an explosion.

Where on earth do I get all this rubbish from? Incidentally, do you remember that song from the 1970s called 'Matchstalk Men and Matchstalk Cats and Dogs'? It was a tribute to the Manchester artist L.S. Lowry. Well, there's a line in it that goes, 'He painted kids on the corner of the street that were sparking clogs.' I wonder if they were referring to me. You never know.

When I was about four we moved to 33 Smith Street, which is in between Greenacres Road and Huddersfield Road. That also had a long drop at the bottom of the yard next to the coal shed and, as before, we were back-to-back with the street behind. It was a tiny bit bigger, this place, so we must have been prospering somehow. Perhaps cords were becoming all the rage? Anyway, the reason I mention the move to Smith Street is because we were there for quite a while and a lot of things happened. One of the first events I remember is going to St Anne's Roman Catholic School for the first time, although I can't tell you much about what I did once I got there. Not a lot, most probably. The school was about half a mile away from home and most of the teachers were Irish. There was a Mrs Ryan, and her daughter who also worked at the school. Yes, I know, Ryan's daughter! Very funny. There was also a Mrs Kilcoyne, who was in charge, and then there was another one called Miss Gomez. I don't know how she got in there. There was also a Mr McMahon and a Miss Shannon. Mrs Ryan was quite small and round and used to carry a billiard cue in class, which she used either to point things out on the blackboard or to tap you on the noggin if she caught you whispering or thought you weren't paying attention. She did once turn the billiard cue around and drop the end of it on some lad's head. I remember thinking to myself, *For heaven's sake, don't get on her nerves!*

So, how do you think I fared at school then? Thick as muck, or bright as a button? I wasn't too bad if memory serves. I was good at picking things up and could apply myself quite well. I was good-to-average, I would say. I had lots of friends including a lad called Jack Rigby, who I used to play with a lot, and another lad called Francis Bradbury. Mark my words, he could have been a fantastic comedy actor or stand-up comedian. Even today, I remember him as being one of the funniest people I have ever met in my life, and I've met one or two over the years. Every class has its clown, of course, but there was something very special about Francis. I wonder what happened to him. I bet he became a priest or something.

The cock of our school was a lad called Frank Reid, who was in my class. Frank the tank is what we *should* have called him, but we decided not to chance it. I don't think I was scared of Frank, exactly, but because he was about the size of a small elephant he had the ability to squash you if he ever sat on you, so I was always a little bit cautious around him, just to be on the safe side. He had an equally large brother who also went to our school and the day I clapped eyes on him I remember thinking, *Oh crumbs, there's two of 'em!*

Going to a Catholic school meant there was never any shortage of altar boys, which was just as well as we were required to serve mass every ten minutes or so. OK, I might be embellishing the truth there slightly, but that's what it felt like. One of the priests, Father Horgan, was a friend of the family, which meant I was always expected to be first in line whenever he needed altar boys to serve mass. Father Horgan was a great big Irishman and when he used to knock on our door one of two things would happen. Sometimes he'd come straight in for a cup of tea, but occasionally, when Dad answered the door, Father Horgan would stay where he was and just touch his pocket. That meant he was carrying the Sacrament and couldn't say anything. Dad would then accompany Father Horgan to wherever he was going. It was usually to somebody who was dying.

Writing about Father Horgan reminds me of a story from when I was about eighteen months old. I know it's not chronological, but you don't mind me jumping back for a moment, do you? It's a good'n, I promise you.

Well, Dad was appearing in a show at the church hall for the local amateur dramatic society and one day Mum took me to one of the performances. I can't remember what show it was but as part of the proceedings he had to be tied up. As this was going on Father Horgan came up to me while I was sitting on Mum's knee and said in his lovely Irish brogue, 'What are they doing to your daddy now, Bernard? Oh, my word, would you look at that? They're tying him up. You should do something, Bernard. Help your daddy.' Apparently, I then stood up on my mother's knee and shouted, 'Let him go, you buggers!' I think we left rather quickly after that, Mum very red-faced!

Father Horgan was always trying to get a reaction out of me. And he nearly always succeeded. My sister and I had been down with chicken pox for some time when one day Father Horgan came to see us.

'How are you then, children? Are you feeling any better? Your mother says you've been bad with it now, so she does. Scarred for life you'll be, she says. Scarred for life.'

As he was leaving Father Horgan picked up an ornament of a horse – one of a pair – that was sitting on the sideboard.

''Ere,' I shouted. 'Where are you going with that?'

According to my mother, I chased Father Horgan right down the street and brought him to heel. Everyone was in stiches but me. Can you imagine that? A mini-Cribbins in his pyjamas covered in spots chasing a huge Irish priest down a street? The mind boggles. He was always winding me up, he was. He was a very naughty priest was Father Horgan.

Many years later, in the mid-1970s, he conducted my father's funeral and, while standing by the graveside afterwards, he said, 'Well, that's the end of Jack!'

The only time being an altar boy rankled with me was when I had to do early morning mass. Not because I didn't like getting up – I did – it was just quite boring. One of the priests at the church had a Basque name, which I can't remember, but we used to call him Father Franco, and he was a refugee from the Spanish Civil War. The nice thing about Father Franco was that if you did the very early mass, which started at 6.30 a.m., he used to give you a threepenny-bit or sometimes even a sixpence. That was a small fortune in our day, don't you know! Good old Father Franco. I used to like him.

As well as serving mass, I would do Benediction services at our church and for this the altar boys had to kneel down while holding a lighted candle. The candle was almost pure beeswax so when it had burnt down a bit I used to take a bit off, put it in my mouth and chew it. Yummy. Talk about the hungry thirties! Well, it was cheaper than gum.

My other job in those days, apart from chewing candles in a cassock and attending school occasionally, was as a paperboy. The shop, which was situated just around the corner from us, was owned by a Mrs Scanlon and her daughter, Lizzy. Tobacco, newspapers and sweets made up the majority of their stock and it was my job to deliver a not insignificant number of the news-papers. Now, I expect some of you reading this book of mine might have had a paper round at some point in your lives, but how many of you had two paper rounds a day – one before school and one straight afterwards? OK, you can start playing that music from the Hovis advert now. What is it, the New World Symphony? Dvořák? That's the one. DAA DAA DEE DA DAAA, DEE DA DEE DA DAAAA! Watch out, Cribbins is talking about how tough it was in the olden days. Get your violins out!

To be honest, it wasn't really that bad. Although I admit that getting out of bed at 6 a.m. on a cold and wet February morning with the prospect of having to cart a sack full of newspapers around the streets of Oldham didn't do much for my spirits. Off I used to trot, though, with my little clogs on, and at the end of every week I'd be handed six shillings by Mrs Scanlon. That's about thirty pence in today's money. During the winters, snow used to build up on the irons on the bottom of your clogs and this used to slow you down dreadfully. These build-ups were known as cloggy boggies and every so often you'd have to kick them off. The pavements and the roads were full of them when it was snowy.

Do you know what the best thing was about having a paper round or two? Being able to take back my money and hand it to Mum. That used to give me an unbelievable amount of satisfaction and Mum was always very grateful. What would I have been then? Eleven or twelve maybe? To be able to make a contribution to the family coffers at that age was a bit of a privilege and, without wanting to get too sentimental, it used to make me feel all grown up.

Despite handing everything over to Mum, she always used to give me a bit of spending money and, apart from buying sweets, I used to spend most of it going to the cinema. There was one at the bottom of Smith Street called the Savoy, and I used to go to what were called the Saturday Matinees there. Tales of us golden oldies attending the Saturday Matinees are many and varied, and the people telling the tales always tend to focus on things like *Flash Gordon* and *Buck Rogers*. They were great shows, don't get me wrong, but the one I remember most vividly was *The Clutching Hand*. I bet you haven't heard of that one, have you? Just like yours truly, *The Clutching Hand* pre-dates most movie serials by a few years.

The reason I remember it so well is because it used to scare the living daylights out of me! Each and every episode had to finish with a cliff-hanger, of course, and in those days, they didn't half know how to do 'em. That's what used to scare me the most, and, as Detective Craig Kennedy, who was the goody in *The Clutching Hand*, inevitably faced certain death at the hands of one of the baddies at the end of an episode, young Bernard would start sinking into his chair. By the time the credits began rolling I was virtually on the floor, but I was desperate to know what happened next.

During the Saturday Matinees, the cinema manager would have to come out to quieten everyone down as, when the kids got fed up with waiting, they used to start throwing things at the screen. Notice I said *they* started throwing things at the screen. I was far too well behaved. Ahem, he says, clearing his throat. Laurel and Hardy films used to make me laugh and other pictures I couldn't wait to see were the Tarzan films with good old Johnny Weissmuller, who became my first ever movie hero. I used to love swimming as a child, and I loved a bit of adventure. This chap ticked all the boxes. They were marvellous pictures and in my opinion they've aged very well.

Something else I enjoyed doing occasionally back then was 'birds' nesting' – climbing up trees to look in nests – which I don't think people do any more. I'd do it now if I could still climb trees, but I have to make do with watching them come and go from my front window. We've got a couple of bird feeders on our front lawn and some of the things you see are hilarious. The whole hierarchy thing has me in stitches sometimes. The food chain, I think they call it. The other day we had a couple of blue tits pecking away at some fat balls when all of a sudden a couple of starlings elbowed them out of the way. The blue tits thought about having a go back but in the end they flew off to a nearby tree. Two minutes later a magpie came along and elbowed the starlings out of the way. They tried to have a go back, but the magpie wasn't in the mood for sharing and told them where to get off. A couple of minutes after that a woodpecker flew in and the magpie didn't even stop to say hello. He was off! By this point I was absolutely fascinated and was wondering how high up the food chain we might get. Do golden eagles eat fat balls? Anyway, once the woodpecker had pecked enough fat, it flew off and within a few seconds the blue tits arrived once more and so it all started again. Isn't that just marvellous?

Birds' nesting was something I did very occasionally from the age of about twelve until the age of about fourteen, and the lad I used to do it with was called Ronnie Ashton. Ronnie and I were consummate climbers and regardless of how high a nest was, we could normally get up there. The only time I ever came unstuck while we were birds' nesting was when we went for a magpie's nest one day, which was up a hawthorn tree.

Because they like to collect shiny things, you never know what you might find in a magpie's nest. Without even thinking about it I was shimmying up this hawthorn tree like a good'n. The nest must have been about 15 feet above the ground and the trunk was fairly bare, which meant I could shimmy up quite easily and I managed to reach the nest without getting injured. Inside the nest were four eggs (no money, unfortunately) and so I put two of them in my mouth for safe keeping and started my descent. When I got to the trunk of the tree I started to slide down it, thinking I had the measure of where the thorny bits were. Well, it just goes to show how wrong you can be sometimes, because just when I was about halfway down the trunk I had an argument with a thorn that went right into the end of my . . . Now, what would I have called it back then? Ah yes, my willy. A thorn went right into the end of my willy!

Regardless of whether you have one or not, what's the first thing you do when you suddenly experience intense, searing pain? That's right, you scream your head off! Then, once you've done that, you start using words that you would never normally say in front of your grandmother. When that thorn suddenly infiltrated the end of my John Thomas, that's exactly what I started doing, except I still had two magpie eggs in my gob! Ronnie Ashton had no idea what was happening as he couldn't understand a word I was saying. Come to think of it, neither could I.

Once the pain had subsided slightly I made it down the tree as fast as I could and the first thing I did was open my mouth and retrieve the contents. Now, I suppose you think I ended up breaking those eggs while I was trying to scream and swear. Not a bit of it! I held out a palm, opened my mouth, leaned forward, and there in front of me were two intact magpie eggs. They might have been a little bit shaken – they weren't the only ones – but they weren't broken.

'What's up with you?' asked Ronnie, now finally able to communicate with me.

'A thorn went through the end of me dick,' I replied.

'Oooooooooh,' said Ronnie, wincing as if he'd suffered the injury himself.

I pulled my shorts down to have a look at the damage and sure enough, young Percy had been pierced.

'You'd best get your mum to have a look at that,' suggested Ronnie.

I'll let you guess what I said in return. I'll give you a clue, though. It ended with the word 'off'.

The other thing I used to do at that age was to try and catch tiddlers in a place called Hollow Brook. In order to get in to Hollow Brook, you used to have to squeeze through some old railings and that made it all the more exciting. We shouldn't have been in there, you see, so it was like breaking-and-entering for beginners.

Once through, I used to explore for a while and then fish for sticklebacks in the stream. If we couldn't afford a hook, which we used to attach to a piece of cotton thread, we'd tie the worms onto the line and sometimes, if you were lucky, you'd catch two fish at the same time. One would be trying to devour one end of the worm, with another fish at the other end of it. I think that must have been where I developed my love of fishing. Exciting stuff, eh!

The man who used to supply our milk in Oldham was called Mr Grinrod and he used to arrive on a little horse-drawn cart that had milk churns on the back of it. As the women queued up for milk the children would pet the horse and feed it bits of carrot or whatever they could pinch from the kitchen. When Mr Grinrod was done on Smith Street he'd let me and other children jump on the back of the cart and I'd go with him to the next stop. Once we'd arrived we'd jump off and walk back home again. Given what children play with nowadays that all sounds quite simplistic, but I promise you it was one of the highlights of my week, as was listening to 'Children's Hour' on the BBC Home Service. I think my favourite show was *Toytown*, which featured Larry the Lamb and Dennis the Dachshund. In my opinion, there's something very, very special about listening to the wireless, and whenever I'm lucky enough to be offered a radio play, I always leap at the chance. I think it's the fact that you can sit there, with your eyes closed, and be transported anywhere. It's like having your imagination massaged! There's nothing like it.

Every few weeks the wireless would stop suddenly and then panic would ensue. 'Mum, Mum, the wireless has gone off,' I'd shout. 'What are we going to do?' 'Quick, Bernard,' Mum would say, 'pop down to the ironmonger's and ask Mr Horrocks for a charged accumulator. Don't be long, though. *Toytown* starts in a few minutes.' Had they ever dished out medals for clog sprinting, I'm fairly sure I'd have won at least a bronze. Especially if there was an episode of *Toytown* at stake.

Something else from those days that you certainly don't see now is cattle and sheep being driven through the streets. Well,

I expect you still see it in the countryside from time to time, but never through the streets of Oldham. At least, I don't think you do. We never saw any pigs, by the way, just sheep and cattle. I think pigs are a bit too clever and independent for that. There was a Co-op abattoir about half a mile from us and, after being unloaded at Mumps railway station, they'd be driven through the streets and then slaughtered. The man who was in charge of driving these animals only had one arm and would shout at us kids to block off the side streets and alleyways as he went. 'You two lads, get that bloody side road blocked off now. There are three bullocks there eyeing an escape route!' It was great fun for us. A bit dangerous though, when you think about it. After all, it doesn't matter if you're twelve or twenty-five, if you've got two or three frightened bullocks charging at you at 10 miles an hour, there's only going to be one winner! Speaking of which. The only time I ever saw anything close to an accident happening during these runs was when a bullock made a break for it down one of those side roads one day and then went on a bit of a rampage. I had another sister by then, called Kathleen, and me and our cousin, a lad called John O'Connell, had to pick her up double quick and drag her out of the way. She scraped both her knees, bless her, but this animal was completely out of control and we only managed to move her with a second or so to spare.

Now then, how old would I have been when the war broke out? Let me think a moment. Dum de daaa. That's it. I'd have been approaching eleven years old. The reason I mention it is because this is when everything started happening for me so it's quite an important time. With regards to the war itself, Oldham wasn't really affected by air raids, although I certainly remember

19

hearing nearby Manchester getting a hammering. In December 1940 the Germans dropped over two thousand bombs on Manchester in just two nights. Isn't that dreadful? The whole thing was, of course. There were an awful lot of anti-aircraft guns positioned just outside Oldham and during the air raids they'd be going off every few seconds. Once the raids were over and it was safe to go out again, we kids would run around the streets, pick up all the shrapnel and then take it into school with us. I think every boy in every town and city must have had a box of shrapnel under his bed. After taking your new finds into school, you'd compare your collections in the playground. Trading bits of shrapnel was also incredibly popular and, together with sweets, it was the main form of currency.

'I'll tell you what, I'll swap you my nose cone for a bag of sherbet and your unexploded bomb.'

'Deal!'

My favourite shrapnel story happened not long after the war had started, so that must have been early 1940. We'd recently moved from Smith Street to a new council house in a place called Derker, which was on the edge of Oldham facing the moors. Across the valley from the estate was a so-called shadow factory where they were making something to do with the war effort. For those of you who aren't war historians or who are under the age of eighty, shadow factories were built at the start of the war to meet the urgent need for aircraft, and the reason they were called shadow factories is because they masqueraded as car factories. There's obviously a bit more to it than that, but that's the nub of it. Anyway, one day I spotted a German bomber flying towards this shadow factory. It was being shot at by an anti-aircraft gun and the moment I realised what was going on I ran into the house of some friends of mine called Mick and Eamon McEwan and shouted, 'Get your boxes, boys. There's a German bomber under fire.' Within seconds me and the McEwan brothers were chasing this plane for all we were worth and, as the other kids who were out and about realised what was going on, they started chasing it too. Before too long there was a great string of us running into the valley clutching cardboard boxes and looking skywards while this German bomber was being shot at. It sounds a bit like a wartime version of the Pied Piper, swapping Hamelin for Oldham and the piper for the plane. It got away unscathed in the end, but there was shrapnel lying absolutely everywhere and we went back to our homes slower, but a lot happier.

Come to think of it, that's something else you don't see much of in Oldham any more: German bombers flying overhead. What with that, horse-drawn milk floats, and lots of cattle and sheep roaming the streets, it's a wonder we didn't all die of excitement!

CHAPTER TWO

Why don't you offer that lad a job?

How are you getting on then? Everything OK so far? I must say, I'm finding this quite a joy, to be honest. You see, despite being as old as the hills, I've never really done any in-depth interviews before, so this is the first time I've gone into detail about anything to do with anything. It feels like I'm taking a history lesson, except I'm also the pupil. 'What have you got today then, Bernard? English Language, Maths, PE and Double Cribbins!' Anyway, I expect we'll be getting onto the acting stuff soon, so just you sit tight.

Sometime at the beginning of the Second World War, the British government started a fundraising campaign called Warships Week, during which lots of civil communities within the British Isles were encouraged to adopt a warship. A community would sponsor a ship by purchasing government bonds, which were paid for via a programme of local fundraising events. Throughout the duration of the war, well over a thousand Warship Weeks were organised, raising a total of £955,611,589. That's about £40 million in today's money! Other campaigns included Wings for Victory Week, which raised money to purchase bomber planes, Spitfire Week, to purchase fighter planes, and Tanks for Attack Week, to purchase – yes, you guessed it – tanks.

In February 1942, my town of Oldham held its own Warship Week during which we raised money to adopt an O-class destroyer and flotilla leader named HMS *Onslow*. As part of the fundraising activities, a drama festival was organised featuring all the schools and this was held at the Coliseum Theatre, which is on Fairbottom Street. I know you didn't need the address, but I rather like it.

Over the course of the week, each school had to perform a one-act play – twice, I think – and because I was a good mimic and a bit of a show-off I decided to volunteer. Now, I'm afraid this is where my brain fails me a bit, as I can't for the life of me remember what the play was. While I was making my dramatic debut in whatever the heck it was, sitting in the audience was the theatre's resident producer, a lovely chap named Douglas Emery. Now, don't ask me why coz I never asked him, but Douglas must have thought I had a modicum of talent as after the festival had finished he approached my mum and dad and asked them if they'd be willing to allow me to perform with the Oldham Repertory Company, as and when any boy's parts came up. The first thing Mum and Dad did was ask me if I was interested, which I most certainly was, and so they went back to Mr Emery and told him I was in.

During the rest of 1942, I played two or three roles with the Oldham Repertory Company, the first one being in a play called *Lavender Ladies*, in which I appeared as a cheeky grocer's boy. I must have fared OK in the role as I got a very nice review in the *Oldham Chronicle*. As payment I received a guinea, which was worth a pound and a shilling, and a present, which would have been a book or a Dinky toy or something. Look at that, eh? Money, gifts and adulation! Not bad for a boy of thirteen.

Shortly after we broke up for Christmas in 1942 my mum and dad received a letter from the school informing them that I wouldn't be required to come back after the holidays. I bet you're thinking, *What's he been up to then? Kids don't leave school at thirteen!* Well, by the time term started again I was fourteen and, in those days, unless you were from a rich family or were particularly gifted, which I wasn't, that's when you left school. The education system was quite basic in those days, so you never did things like French or chemistry. It was all based around the three Rs: reading, writing and arithmetic. That said, everything we did at school was very thorough, so despite leaving early we weren't necessarily stupid. Daft, yes, but not stupid.

One of the first people to hear about my enforced retirement from full-time education was Douglas Emery and, before you could say, 'Why don't you offer that lad a job, he's obviously a star of the future,' he offered me a job! As an assistant stage manager first, with a starting salary of fifteen shillings a week. As you'd expect, I was absolutely over the moon about this. After all, theatre was already my passion, and so to work in it full-time was the start of my dream come true. I say the *start* of a dream come true, because I didn't actually know what I wanted to do at the time. I never thought that far ahead. All I knew is that I loved working in the theatre and if somebody wanted me to do it full-time for a bit, why not?

The only thing that miffed me slightly about becoming a pro at fourteen was that I had to take a pay cut. A significant pay cut! As a cherubic amateur I'd earned a guinea and a gift per show, as you well know, and, with each show lasting about a week front to back, that was a good return. Now, as a professional assistant stage manager, I was earning six shillings less and the gifts were nowhere to be seen. What's more, instead of just attending the rehearsals and the shows before taking a bow and then popping home to bed, I was now required to work – wait for it – a seventy-hour week for fifteen shillings!

Despite the long hours, there were one or two immediate benefits to working full-time in the theatre, and one of those was being able to go to the cinema for nowt. I think there must have been a reciprocal arrangement between the theatre and all the cinemas, so on a Wednesday afternoon, say, if I didn't have any lines to learn, I could pop along and watch Johnny Weissmuller or Laurel and Hardy. You might be wondering if I had any ambitions to appear in films at this age. To be perfectly honest with you, I probably didn't. I was just enjoying myself.

So, what on earth does a fourteen-year-old assistant stage manager do during his seventy-hour week? I hear you ask. Well, it was all based around something you don't see any more called weekly rep, as in repertory theatre. Looking back, which is something I've been doing a lot just recently, this was an excruciating discipline and if you don't already know what weekly rep entailed you might find it a bit hard to believe. Ready? Right then. We used to open with a new play every Monday evening, and that afternoon we'd have a dress rehearsal. Because I was stage management I'd be in at the crack, and my entire morning would be spent polishing furniture, setting things up, and helping to hang pictures and the like. Over the years Douglas Emery had built up a huge stock of props and furniture, so we were always well equipped. It all needed looking after, however, and that was also part of my job.

The following morning, prior to the Tuesday matinee, the actors would come in and read the following week's play. Now then. Can you imagine that? You've just opened in a brand-new production lasting at least a couple of hours and, as well as having to perform it twice the following day, you also have to read through the play you're doing next. Does that sound doable to you? On Wednesday during the day the actors would learn their lines while the stage management assembled props for the new production. On Thursday, you'd rehearse act one of the new play and then read through the rest. On Friday you would rehearse whatever you hadn't done yet and then on Saturday, during the day, you'd rehearse the whole thing – twice, sometimes – and then do a matinee and evening performance of the current play. On Sunday, you generally slept – all day – and then on Monday you'd have a dress rehearsal during the day before performing the play at night, and then the whole thing would start again. It was, without fear of overstatement, a continuous cultural conveyor belt and despite certain aspects becoming second nature to you, it was still terrifying. But I was only stage management, of course. Imagine being one of the leading actors or actresses. How they did it, I do not know. Even the thought of it gives me the heebie-jeebies. I'll tell you what, let me give you an example, shall I?

In February 1943 the Oldham Repertory Company produced four plays: *The Good Young Man* by Kenneth Horne, *Wuthering Heights*, which was obviously based on Emily Brontë's only

27

novel, an American play called *Too Young to Marry* by a chap called Martin Flavin and, finally, a Jacobean play called *The Witch* by Thomas Middleton. These days, you might find a programme like that spread over a season, but certainly not a month. It's quite a mixture, don't you think? How we did it all I'll never know.

Incidentally, the only member of that company I joined in 1943 who went on to become famous was a blonde girl called Dora Broadbent. She was about six years older than I was and about a year or so after I joined Oldham Rep she went off to London with hopes of becoming a star. A few years later, while appearing in a Noël Coward play, it was suggested to Dora by the man himself that she ditch Broadbent and take a stage name. Taking the Master's advice, she changed her surname to Bryan and later became a big star. I expect you'd already guessed it was her, hadn't you? Years later, during an interview, Dora claimed that I'd turned up on my first day at Oldham in the snow wearing short trousers and newspaper around my legs. My poor mother was mortified by this; partly because it wasn't true, but mainly because it made out as if she couldn't look after me. So much for poetic licence, eh?

I may not have had time to get to know Dora that well, but I made some marvellous friendships at Oldham Rep. So, not only did it take care of things professionally for me, but it sorted out my social life too. A lad called Jim Cassidy was probably the best friend I made there. He and a few others had been drafted in from the Oldham Arts School to play extras for a production, and we just got chatting one day. Jim was tall, artistic, very Lancashire, but also devoted to Ireland. He also enjoyed hiking, and not long after getting to know each other he invited me out for a trek on the moors. This would have been a Sunday, which was usually a rest day, but after spending so many hours in the theatre I couldn't wait to get out there. I was also a young lad, you see, so for all my blether about working a seventy-hour week I had more than enough energy for it.

It became a regular thing and so as soon as my eyes opened on a Sunday I'd get up, put on my big hiking boots, grab my rucksack, and we'd be off into the hills. Actually, that's not true. We'd usually get a fourpenny bus ride up to the moors and then take off from there. We'd explore the Pennines, and take in places such as Saddleworth Moor, Blackstone Edge, Alphin Pike and Chew Valley. Anyone who's ever walked across these areas will know how wild it can be in the winter. Come to think of it, anyone who's ever driven on the M62 from Leeds to Manchester should have a good idea. It's about 1300 feet above sea level up there, and if you are daft enough to go when the weather's a bit dodgy you'll probably need a few distress flares and some good thermal underwear!

As the word started to get out among Jim's friends at the Arts School and mine at the Rep about our Sunday expeditions, we started receiving requests from people who wanted to join us. In no time at all we'd gone from two to around fifteen, and so in the end we decided to form a group. We called ourselves the Pennine Rangers, and we even got ourselves a hut – or, *t'hut*, as we used to refer to it. We used to rent *t'hut* for about two shillings a week and inside we had a few old chairs and a Primus stove. The Primus stove was mainly used for warming up baked beans, which was the staple Sunday diet of your average Pennine

Ranger. The only issue we ever had with *t'hut*, apart from it being rather rickety and a bit draughty, was the fact the roof seemed to contain rather a lot of soot. Don't ask me why, it just did. This meant that even the slightest movement from a Pennine Ranger could result in a torrential sooty downpour and if there were ever beans on the Primus, which was often, they'd be covered within seconds.

The worst experience we had in that hut was when one of the Pennine Rangers came in *t'hut* after having a tinkle and the wind slammed the door shut so hard that the beans fell off the Primus stove onto the floor and we all got a right sooting! Jim and I ended up writing a song about this called 'Three Pennine Rangers' and we used to sing it every time we went there. Now, if you'd have asked me a month ago what the lyrics were to that song I'd have told you not to be so flaming daft! After all, it was over seventy years ago. Then, my pal in the know – the one with his finger on the inter-thingamabob – managed to find a clip from my appearance on *This Is Your Life*, which took place back 1981. I'd completely forgotten about this but the producers managed to track down the surviving members of the original Pennine Rangers and as part of a little film they made for the episode they re-enacted 'beangate' and even sang the flipping song! How about that then? They even managed to get a very famous folk band called the Oldham Tinkers to accompany them, and then afterwards, as was often the way when they staged one of these tributes on *This Is Your Life*, all the people involved walked through those big double doors and said hello in person. Because of all the laughter I could only make out the opening lines, but here they are anyway.

> Three Pennine Rangers went up to the hut,
> the beans were on the Primus, cov-er-ed in soot,
> one Pennine Ranger went to shut the door,
> the beans fell off the Primus and cov-er-ed the floor.

That brought back some memories, I can tell ya.

Until recently I've always been quite fearful of technology, my excuse being that you can't teach an old dog new tricks. Especially one as old as me! Now I know what the possibilities are I think I'm coming around to the idea and am even considering learning how to use a computer! Or maybe an abacus.

Again, this was Jim's influence, but after we'd finished walking on the moors for 20 miles or so, we'd get on another bus to Manchester and go Irish dancing. Jim used to know this little Irish club there and they used to have the most marvellous cèilidh band, or céilí, as they were Irish. You know the kind of thing – tiddly adle-udle-adle-udle-adle-adle-ee! It was all tin whistles and things. In fact, I've still got one. It's in a box somewhere among all my old stuff. Is it me, or am I starting to sound like an Irishman? I do have Irish blood on both sides, but the dancing was down to my mate Mr Cassidy, so it was more social than cultural. That man was more Irish than Éamon de Valera and, because he was a few years older than me, I used to look up to him. It was certainly a lot of fun, though. There you go then, that's the Pennine Rangers. Happy days!

As much as I enjoyed my Sundays, it was just a bit of fun, and meanwhile the amount of time I spent at work still mirrored the amount of enthusiasm I had for the theatre. As well as being the assistant stage manager I also got to act quite a bit. After all, that was how Douglas had discovered me, and had I been restricted to polishing furniture and sweeping up floors the lustre of the greasepaint may have waned somewhat. The parts I played were small, generally – two lines and a smile – but between them and the stage management I received an across-the-board viewpoint of exactly how a theatre works. It was just like my formal education – condensed yet comprehensive – and I consider myself to be a very lucky boy.

The only time we ever made the national headlines at Oldham Rep, at least while I was there, was, alas, because of a tragic accident that happened, rather spookily, during a production of the 'Scottish play', *Macbeth*. It was January 1947, which meant I'd just turned eighteen. There's a rather sad irony here as the three months leading up to that accident had been some of the best months of my life, and certainly the best I'd had in theatre.

In October and November 1946, we'd done a tour of West Yorkshire, playing a programme that included *Portrait in Black*, a three-act play by Ivan Goff and Ben Roberts, George Bernard Shaw's *The Devil's Disciple* and *A Man About the House*, which had been adapted from a novel by Francis Brett Young by John Perry and was later made into a film. Bearing in mind we were from the wrong side of the Pennines, not to mention the fact that Yorkshire folk have both a talent and a reputation for speaking their minds, we were expecting, at best, a bit of a rough ride from the West Riding. We were, however, in for a bit of a surprise. We played all the main theatres there, such as the Grand Theatre in Halifax and the Theatre Royal Huddersfield – both long-since demolished, unfortunately – and the very first notice we received, which was in the *Yorkshire Post* for a performance of *A Man About the House* in Huddersfield, was bordering on being complimentary. It was pure Yorkshire really: short, to the point, and memorable. It read, 'Douglas Emery's production of *A Man About the House* is given a satisfying all-round performance by the Oldham Repertory Theatre Company this week. Antony Oakley is outstanding in his characterisation of Salvatore Ferraro.' That was it. Less is more, lad, less is more!

Well, when we read that, you could have gone to the foot of our stairs. We very nearly did.

A few nights later in Halifax, the same person from the same newspaper must have come again, as the next day there was *another* review in the *Yorkshire Post* for the same play. This one was bordering on being longwinded, and read, 'John Perry's dramatic play, *A Man About the House*, adapted from the novel by Francis Brett Young, was given by the Oldham Repertory Theatre Co. last night. The performance was studded with excellent characterisations, notably Ferraro, the Italian majordomo, by Antony Oakley, and the portrayal of the two English sisters by Muriel North and Janet Cameron, while Brenda Hogan's Maria was an admirable cameo.'

The only thing they didn't mention there was me. The great Yorkshire puddings! To be fair, I'm fairly sure the roles I played in these productions were tiny and I was mainly confined to the backstage area. Regardless of which, we had a great couple of months over in West Yorkshire, and every review we received after those two was a corker.

Then, in December, and for the first time since I'd been there, the company produced a pantomime. Don't ask me why, but the custom at Oldham Rep had been to present a play over the Christmas period, and when it was announced that we'd be swapping that rather untraditional tradition for something more seasonal, we were all thrilled. Cock-a-hoop, in fact. The panto in question was *Aladdin* and Douglas himself played Widow Twankey, Muriel North played the principal boy, and Harold Norman played Abanazar. Even Dora Bryan came back for this show, putting in a great little turn as Abanazar's daughter. I think the whole of Oldham benefitted from the decision to put on a panto because as well as playing to packed houses the atmosphere was just terrific. I'm pretty sure the entire company spent the whole month laughing – *and* we got tremendous reviews – again.

You don't mind if I quote one of them, do you? The best I've found is one from the *Stage*, which is the trade newspaper for us theatrical types. I wish I could namecheck the journalist who wrote this review because I'm very grateful but unfortunately they're not listed. It's under the headline Provincial Pantomimes, and features a headshot of Douglas in costume. It reads, 'Following a custom of some years' standing, the members of the Oldham repertory company, instead of presenting a play during Christmas time, produced a pantomime. There is an outstanding performance by Douglas Emery, the producer, as Widow Twankey. His invigorating humour is infectious, and he is a favourite with audiences.' Isn't that lovely?

About two-thirds of the way through the run of *Aladdin* I had my eighteenth birthday, so I'd leapt into 1947 full of the joys of spring. Or winter, in this particular case.

As a young aspiring actor, I suppose I took theatrical

superstitions quite seriously – you know, saying 'break a leg' instead of good luck, etc. – and so, when I was told that we'd be producing the Scottish play I adhered to all the rigmarole that went with it. Just in case you're not au fait with all that stuff, you're not supposed to mention *Macbeth* by name in the theatre prior to a performance because it is reckoned to be cursed, and if you do, you HAVE to perform a ritual to break the curse. Sound daft to you? Well, that's because it is. You wait till you hear about the ritual. Or, should I say rituals. They tend to vary according to local custom and include leaving the theatre, spinning around three times, spitting, swearing and then knocking to be allowed back in. It is, of course, a complete load of old cobblers but we acting folk are superstitious types, and in January 1947 I was not looking forward to the Scottish play one little bit. Harold Norman was playing Macbeth, Muriel North was playing Lady Macbeth and Antony Oakley, who'd played Ferraro in *A Man About the House*, was Macduff. I had a small part and believe it or not my dad was also in the cast. He too only had a small role and as far as I can remember it was the first and only time he appeared with Oldham Rep. He was certainly there on merit though and I remember being quite proud of him. I always was.

Now, I'm not trying to add any credence to the whole superstition thing (especially after just dismissing it), but Harold North, who had been with the Savoy Theatre Company in Belfast prior to landing in Oldham and who was very highly thought of, named the play openly during rehearsals and rehearsed his lines out loud, which is another no-no. This had made quite a few people wince, I can tell you. But, just like me

– well, now, at least – he didn't go in for all that. 'It's rubbish,' he used to say. 'Let's just get on with it.'

For those of you who aren't familiar with the play – which is a tragedy, by the way – there's a fight scene at the end between Macbeth and Macduff, which ends with Macduff killing and then beheading Macbeth. Actually, let's change that to a bloody tragedy! Believe it or not, it was normal then to use real swords during fight scenes. Fake ones were prohibitively expensive in those days and with every theatre in the land having several in their props room, it made sense to use them. That's health and safety, 1940s style! Even so, I'd never heard of any accidents before and because the fights were always well rehearsed nobody batted an eyelid.

The production opened on Monday 27 January and, if memory serves me correctly, it was very well received by the audiences. Three days later, during the fight scene between Harold and Antony, in Act III, Scene III, I was waiting in the wings for the show to finish when all of a sudden Harold crawled off into the wings and said, 'I've been stabbed.' Douglas was standing next to me and said, 'Nonsense, Harold, you've been winded. Now get back on that stage.' A second or so later we realised that Harold was bleeding from his stomach and so the curtain was immediately dropped. Because it was so close to the end of the play the rest of the cast went on and took their curtain calls, and the audience, who obviously thought it was part of the proceedings, applauded wildly. After a few minutes they started calling for Harold to take a curtain call, which is when my boss, the stage manager – a dear old chap named Mr Arthur Hall – went on and explained that there'd been an accident. Poor Harold had taken about four inches of sword in his guts and was immediately taken to Oldham General Infirmary where he was operated on twice.

The following day it was all over every paper in the land and after his operations it seemed like Harold was going to make a full recovery. That too was widely reported in the press and so as the nation breathed a sigh of relief, we at the theatre readied ourselves for Harold's return. On Tuesday 25 February Harold unexpectedly contracted peritonitis and he died the following morning.

Naturally, the entire company was devastated, but especially poor Antony. An inquest was duly held and on 12 March 1947 a verdict of accidental death was recorded by the coroner. Antony had said in a statement to the police that during the fight Harold had twisted his wrist too far forward (moving him closer to Harold's sword) and fell on his weapon before it could be turned outwards. Before he died, Harold told his wife that dangerous weapons should not be used again in the theatre, and as far as I know that was the catalyst for them being replaced – although it happened very, very slowly.

About five years later, in the early 1950s, I was seconded over to Liverpool to appear in a production of William Shakespeare's *Cymbeline* at the Liverpool Playhouse. That used to happen occasionally – people filling in at other repertory companies – and I was all for it. During that play there's a battle scene between Ancient Brits and Roman soldiers, and the lads who were playing the Roman soldiers were using real Roman short swords. Seriously. These things had big brass handles and something like a twenty-inch steel blade. Within this scene, in which

I appeared as one of the Ancient Brits, I had to fight somebody who was a lot bigger than I was. The fight had been arranged and rehearsed beforehand, of course, and it was supposed to be quite straightforward: two upstairs – bang, bong – two downstairs – bang, bong – and off I went. Exit Cribbins. During one performance, the actor who I was fighting went totally bonkers and started swinging his blade all over the place. I actually had to block some of these swings otherwise I'd have been done for. In the end I grabbed his wrist, kneed him in the balls as hard as I could and then dragged him off stage. What an absolute bloody fool!

As well as me and this other idiot we had some students from Liverpool Art School taking part in this scene and one of them got a cut on the hand and another a nick on the face. Imagine what *could* have happened? Anyway, in the end, another actor called William Lucas, who played Dr Gordon in *Black Beauty*, and me decided to rearrange all the fighting and, with a couple of rehearsals, we got it down to something simple but, most importantly, safe!

I remember watching some fabulous fight scenes in films starring Douglas Fairbanks and Errol Flynn. The old swashbucklers. Each and every one of those would have been worked out meticulously by a professional stunt arranger and then rehearsed for hours on end. That, boys and girls, is the only way to do it, so if any of you reading this are aspiring to become actors or actresses and you end up doing a fight scene using weapons, please make sure it's been arranged properly and always *stick to the plan*. If you don't, you'll get my foot where it hurts!

Onwards and upwards.

CHAPTER THREE

Acting, walking and shooting

Having been at the Oldham Repertory Company from the age of fourteen to eighteen I was then called up to do National Service. Obviously, I was keen to do my bit, but since becoming a teenager the vast majority of my life had belonged to the theatre and so the prospect of a complete about-change didn't exactly fill me with joy. Even so, there was absolutely nothing I could do about it and I think the sense of adventure I possessed, which had been stimulated by my walks across the Pennines and by theatrical secondments to the far reaches of West Yorkshire via Huddersfield and Wakefield, had rendered me with a sufficient amount of wanderlust to make the prospect of a long trip away exciting rather than forebidding.

Strangely enough, just as I was about to leave Oldham Rep in March 1947 to do my basic training before joining the Army, a young actor and writer who was about five years older than me and who'd served with the Royal Air Force during the war was about to join Oldham Rep and make his first professional performance. Eric Sykes, for t'was he, had only been a writer up to then after being discovered by Bill Fraser just after the war. His first performance as an actor in a professional capacity

39

took place at the Oldham Coliseum on 31 March in a play called *All This Is Ended* in which he played an American called Michael O'Brien. Anyway, that's enough about the great Mr Sykes for the time being. He'll be back soon enough, bless him.

For my basic training I was sent to a place called Dunham Park near Altrincham in Cheshire. There are three things I remember clearly about that time: the weather, which was biblically Baltic, a boxing match, and the fact that I had to eat my first ever meal in the Army using just my fingers. It was steak and kidney pie and nobody could find a knife or a fork for love nor money.

The winter of 1946–7 was, according to my chum with the worldwide whatsit at his fingertips, one of the harshest winters ever recorded in the United Kingdom with the worst of it taking place from 21 January until the end of March. There were multiple deaths, I remember, and as well as snowdrifts 10 feet high we had to endure blocked roads, food shortages and fuel shortages, and thousands upon thousands of farm animals were lost. Even in those days, when the winters were a lot harsher, we still weren't prepared for anything so extreme, and when the thaw eventually came at the end of March thousands of homes were flooded. It was chaos!

Not surprisingly, a large proportion of our armed forces had to assist in keeping the country moving and the effect this had on us trainees was that we were all sent home for a minimum of one week. More, if the weather persisted. I think I'd only been doing basic training for a few days and if it hadn't been for the fact that we'd almost died of hypothermia in our hut, I'd have been asking to stay rather than go home. Everyone had been very kind to me and, because I was an active sort of chap and was house-trained, I'd done well. Physically, the training had ticked a lot of boxes for me and I looked out of the windows at home praying for the weather to turn. Incidentally, just to put the effect of this cold snap into perspective, the eventual cost to the nation, both in terms of damage to amenities and the effect it had on the economy, was the equivalent to about £15 billion in today's money, and on top of that over 25 per cent of the entire sheep population was lost. It took the country several years to recover, but recover we did. The Second World War hadn't finished us, and neither would this.

When we were finally called back to Dunham Park I packed my bags and caught the first train to Altrincham. It was still cold, but I couldn't wait to get there. Having been at Oldham Rep since childhood I was used to being part of a company and, although this was obviously different to the theatre, there were a lot of similarities. Camaraderie, for one thing. That was something I'd thrived on in the theatre and had experienced something similar with the Pennine Rangers. In fact, this was a more active version of that, in a way, with less singing, fewer beans and no women.

Back in those days, one of the things I enjoyed listening to most on the radio was boxing. This was still a good few years before television, and unless you could get a ticket to the Empire Pool at Wembley, Bell Vue in Manchester or the Royal Albert Hall, which is where a lot of the big fights took place, you'd have to rely on the dulcet tones of radio commentators such as Raymond Glendenning. The United Kingdom had a lot of talented boxers in those days, people like Freddie Mills, Bruce

Woodcock and Don Cockell, and the biggest stars in the country would turn up to watch them box. The matches were real events.

Without wanting to sound too sentimental, just hearing the name Raymond Glendenning is enough to send a shiver down my spine and make me grin from ear to ear. You see, these wizards of the wireless didn't simply accompany the action on screen like they do today, they brought it completely to life: the setting, the atmosphere, the build-up. And the fight, of course. My word, did they do a good job. We're back to the joys of radio again, I suppose. It was all so magical and evocative. Somebody once said that they preferred radio to television because the pictures were better! Isn't that a terrific little saying.

Around this time, on Tuesday 15 April, 1947 – that's etched on my memory for evermore – the aforementioned Bruce Woodcock was taking on the American fighter, Joe Baksi, for the World Heavyweight Championship at the Royal Albert Hall. Together with some of the boys I was training with I listened to the fight on a wireless in our hut. The excitement was just incredible, and it was all thanks to the commentator: Raymond Glendenning. He set the scene for the fight and told us who was there. I forget the rollcall, exactly, but I remember picturing the scene in my head: the film stars turning up in their finery and the lights dimming prior to the fanfares beginning and the Master of Ceremonies introducing the fighters. We might have been a bit colder than usual, but my word we were entertained! Joe Baksi won the fight, more's the pity, but that didn't spoil it for me. I was completely lost in the event.

Right then, let's get into these weapons. During this primary training we were taught how to use a gun and young Cribbins here turned out to be a pretty good shot. I'd already shot an air rifle a few times so I wasn't a complete novice, but for some reason I took to it like a duck to water and I ended up winning a certificate. We were on the two-two range, and I'd got a full house. I'm pretty sure that was the first prize I'd ever won for anything and I was presented with my certificate by the local mayor. I was so chuffed. Not a bad skillset: acting, walking and shooting. I've got a photo of me receiving this certificate from the mayor so I'll see if I can dig it out. If it's in, I've managed to do just that.

Just prior to that, we'd been visited one day by a recruiting officer from the Parachute Regiment. He'd come in full of brass and bullshit with his nice red beret, and he had all the patter. He kept going on and on about the *esprit de corps* of being in the Paras and the fact it was a great life but the only bit I really listened to, and the thing that ultimately swung it for me, was the fact that you got two-and-six a day extra once you'd done your jumps. I thought to myself, *Ethel could probably do with another seventeen-and-six a week*, and so, once the officer had finished extolling the virtues of *esprit de corps* and what have you, me and four others put our name down. A few days later we all went through the selection process for the Parachute Regiment, and the only one who was accepted was me. Subsequently, when it came to our passing out parade at Dunham Park a few weeks later, there were twenty-five lads all waiting to join the Service Corps on one side, three or four waiting to join the Manchester Regiment on the other, and in the middle was me.

I did have a bit of a scare when the regimental sergeant major called my name out as I thought he'd referred to me as an ACC, which stands for Army Catering Corps. Fortunately it was a mistake, but I remember being mortified momentarily. I didn't want to become a cook! A few minutes later when an officer came over to inspect me and say well done, he stopped right in front of me, smiled and said, 'Army Air Corps, eh?'

'Yes, sir,' I replied, somewhat relieved.

'Gooood,' he said. 'It's a short life but a sweet one.'

And then he buggered off! Suddenly, the Catering Corps seemed quite attractive. What did he mean by a short life but a sweet one?

A few days later I was sent to the Army garrison at Aldershot to begin thirteen weeks of intense square bashing and weapons training before being sent to a place called Upper Heyford where I learned how to jump. The training at Aldershot was extremely physical and I was quite taken aback. One of the men who'd been charged with getting us all physical was called Drake and he was from Huddersfield. He was about 6 feet 2 or 3 and he had the longest feet I'd ever seen in my entire life. Not that I tend to look at people's feet when I meet them, but when you're presented with an outsized pair they do demand your attention somewhat. Surrounding these enormous plates of meat of his were the shiniest boots I have ever seen too. They were immaculate. This made his feet look like two giant black mirrors and you know what they say about large angry Yorkshireman who have giant shiny feet, don't you? Whatever you do, don't get on the wrong side of them.

One day, while on parade, a fellow private of mine called Haddert did just that and it resulted in the entire platoon very nearly having our backsides kicked. For some reason Private Haddert just couldn't get anything right that day. He reminded me of Corporal Jones from *Dad's Army*, in that everything he did was about a second out. The longer this went on the more incandescent with rage Corporal Drake became, until eventually, to save himself from throttling the poor private, he leaned right over him and screamed, 'IF YOU DON'T GET THIS RIGHT, PRIVATE HADDERT, I'M GOING TO CLUB YOU TO DEATH WITH A SWAN VESTA!' It might well have been a funny line, but Corporal Drake certainly wasn't playing for laughs and the fact that we were all aware of this made it almost impossible for us not to laugh. As the giant Drake continued threatening Private Haddert with matchsticks, we all began shaking like washing machines and after a few seconds the corporal realised what was going on and suddenly stopped dead in his tracks. It was one of those moments when you genuinely have no idea what's going to happen next and it was almost going to be life or death. I think what saved us was the fact that Corporal Drake had used this line on a great many occasions and it had almost become his catchphrase. We were therefore laughing with him, as opposed to at him, so as we all stood there shaking, a grin started infiltrating his usually inscrutable countenance. The only person who wasn't laughing was Private Haddert. I think he was too busy shitting himself.

We used to go on these cross country runs that seemed to last for ever. We would run to a cantilever bridge that crossed the Basingstoke canal but once, instead of being allowed to cross the canal using the bridge, as you might have thought sensible, we had to use one of its thin girders. In those days very few people could swim, and I remember crossing that canal very gingerly. I felt like P.T. Barnum! A few days later we did the same run again except this time we were in full uniform wearing helmets and were carrying guns. When we got to the bridge we were blocked from using the girders. 'Get in the water,' said the sergeant major. I was just about to say, 'You are joking, aren't you?' when I saw the look on his face. His expression said something like, 'You argue with me, sunshine, and I'll make your life a misery,' but probably with one or two swearwords thrown in for good measure.

As I stood by this canal and stared at the dark, uninviting water, I thought to myself – and you'll have to excuse the language here, boys and girls – *What a complete load of bollocks this is*. Fortunately, it wasn't too deep and with it being a canal there was hardly any current. Even so, the water was definitely quite wet, and I was not looking forward to trying to extract myself. One thing I haven't mentioned yet is the fact that on this particular run we'd been spilt into teams and so in addition to having to get in, across and then out of the canal, there'd be a trainee paratrooper or two who'd be trying to stop me. Happy days! My word, what fun we were having. Just as I reached the other side of the canal a fellow trainee ran up, stuck his boot out and tried to kick me back into the canal. Luckily for me I spotted him in time and managed to lower my head and took the blow on the helmet. I say luckily for me. At the time, I considered myself to be anything but lucky and as my head re-emerged from the water I started cursing myself for not grabbing his size-eleven boot and pulling the rotten bar-steward in with me.

Even just thinking about that thirteen weeks makes me feel absolutely exhausted. The parade grounds there were quite enormous and one day, after being accused of being idle on parade (me?!), I was ordered to put my rifle above my head and double around the parade ground until I was told to stop. After a lap or so the regimental sergeant major, a formidable chap named J.C. Lord, called me over to him. Sergeant majors often have very high voices, which helps them carry.

'That man, come here,' he shrieked.

'Yes, sir.'

'What is your crime?'

'Idle on parade, sir.'

'Idle on parade, eh? Well, you're no good to me standing there. Get that rifle back above your head and carry on at the double. Left, right, left, right, left, right.'

Something else we did a lot of was inter-company boxing. I used to spar with a lad from Liverpool called John Conway, who was a bit handy, and he and I used to get along very well. When it came to the actual contests, I was classed as a welter-weight – about ten-stone-six – but because there were no welterweights in the other platoon I had to fight somebody from my own, which was just ridiculous. The chap's name was Danny Williams and as well as being a pal of mine he was a much more experienced boxer. I think I lasted three rounds when we fought and managed to land one solitary punch. He murdered me! We'd been dancing around to begin with, as we didn't want to hurt each other, and after a round or so the instructor, who was also a company sergeant major, decided that enough was enough. 'This is supposed to be a boxing match, not a foxtrot.' After that it became serious and two rounds later I was on the canvas.

One highlight from the thirteen weeks was that my company managed to win the coveted drill cup. There's obviously something quite theatrical about people doing things in unison, and the sound it makes it just fantastic. Sixty pairs of boots hitting the concrete at exactly the same time – bang!

After the training at Aldershot, my fellow trainees and I were then sent to RAF Upper Heyford in Oxfordshire where we attended parachute training course number 221B. I'm pretty sure we arrived at RAF Upper Heyford on 19 July 1947 and we were there for about a month. On arriving we were immediately introduced to our instructor, a Yorkshireman called Jack Marlborough. He was one of the most delightful people I had ever had the pleasure of meeting and I have to admit that over seventy-one years later nothing at all has changed. You often hear stories about soldiers being treated unsympathetically by their colleagues or commanding officers. Well, when my fellow trainees and I started out parachute training we experienced nothing but care and attentiveness. We weren't mollycoddled. That doesn't happen in the armed forces. We were simply treated like human beings, and that made a big difference. Why? Because most of us were bloody terrified, that's why! If you've ever been daft enough to jump out of an aeroplane travelling at about 100 miles an hour – sometimes they'd throttle back to 90 – and at a height of about 800 feet you'll know exactly what I mean. Makes you squeak a bit, doesn't it? Especially when questions such as, *What if my parachute doesn't open?*, enter your head. For the sensible among you, I'll try and bring what it's actually like to life.

We began our training in a great big aeroplane hangar where, with the help of lots of ropes, harnesses, scaffolding and mats, we learned how to jump and land, and how to control our parachutes while descending. We were also taught how to carry out emergency measures, such as untwisting our lines, or what we should do if we collided with another parachutist. Despite it being quite fun, that did tend to lull you into a false sense of security and when it came to us doing our first jump we were reminded very quickly about the reality of what comes in between jumping and landing. Some of the views were nice, especially the ones that were in front of me and down a bit. It was the ones directly below me that I had a job getting used to.

Our first two jumps were out of a cage underneath a barrage balloon before doing six from an aeroplane. Complete all eight, and you got your wings, if you hadn't died. Actually, that's not strictly true, as if you died that's exactly what you *did* get. In a biblical sense. Please don't think I'm being flippant, by the way. In those days you had just one parachute, so if it didn't work, barring a miracle such as a fellow jumper who was skilful enough to rescue you or the sudden appearance of a giant blancmange, you were a goner. It was, as we used to say, shit or bust. These days you have a reserve parachute, which, while not eradicating the prospect of the Grim Reaper making an appearance, at least cuts it in half.

I've often asked myself if the luxury of having a reserve parachute would have made a blind bit of difference to how I was

49

feeling prior to my first jump, but I doubt it would. You're not quite yourself in that situation and if it hadn't been for the calming yet confidence-inspiring Jack Marlborough, I doubt whether any of us would have gone ahead with it. As it was, I was as raring to go as you can be under those circumstances and when the barrage balloon that was carrying us began floating upwards I think I was actually looking forward to it.

This balloon, by the way, which was lifting a cage containing five jumpers and Jack Marlborough, was tethered to the ground by a steel cable and it looked like a small Zeppelin. We only went up about 700 feet, but that still gave us sufficient time to jump out and land safely. The point being that because we were closer to the ground, less could go wrong.

Without wanting to bang my own drum, I was the most confident of the five jumpers and so Jack Marlborough asked me to go first. 'Come on then, Private Cribbins,' he said cheerfully. 'Show 'em how it's done.' It sounded like he was asking me to do a soft-shoe shuffle or something, not jump out of a balloon! Even so, he was the one who'd helped me to build that confidence, so I was more than happy to oblige. 'Yes, Corporal!' I said.

The next thing I remember is falling through the air and then feeling my parachute open. There's nothing to pull, by the way. While you were training the parachutes were on what are called static lines and it was actually your weight after you jump that opened them. The only emotion I felt was elation and, after rolling over on landing, I got up, picked up my parachute and ran away as instructed. I obviously didn't run too far as I'd have been collared for desertion, but after stopping and then looking up at where I'd jumped from I don't mind admitting that I felt quite pleased with myself. Well done, Private Cribbins! Not bad for a young thespian from Oldham.

Incidentally, shortly before we went up for our first balloon jump Jack Marlborough called us over. 'There's an instructor friend of mine called Corporal Sweeney going up first with five trainees,' he said. 'He'll be the last one to jump, and I want you to watch him very carefully. Don't try and copy him, though, whatever you do.'

Naturally we were intrigued so, as Corporal Sweeney and his trainees ascended underneath the barrage balloon we all watched on agog.

'What's he going to do then?' I asked.

'Just you wait and see, lad,' said my instructor, grinning.

After the five trainees had jumped, Corporal Sweeney suddenly appeared but instead of jumping feet first like the rest, he took a running jump and then swallow-dived out of the balloon. That wasn't it, though. Once his parachute had developed he then started doing somersaults in his rigging.

'Bloody hell!' I said. 'That man's an absolute nutcase.'

Jack Marlborough paused for a second. 'Aye,' he said, nodding his head. 'I suppose he is.'

Please don't try that at home, boys and girls, whatever you do!

The only difference between the first barrage balloon jump and the second was that, as opposed to jumping out of the side of the cage, we jumped out through a hole in the floor, which is what one or two of the aircraft in service had. As somebody who ended up doing all of his jumping out of a Dakota, which has a side exit, the experience was academic. It did offer me a slightly different perspective, however, especially prior to the jump. On this occasion I was last to go, with the first jumper being nearest the hole. As daunting as jumping first had been, as I watched the other four drop through that small hole I suddenly began to appreciate its advantages, both in terms of the tension that was building watching them drop, and the view. On the first jump, all I could really see was the horizon, which, because it was at eye-level, or thereabouts, made me feel like I could almost step on to it. It might have been an illusion, but it was still quite comforting. This time, all I could see was the ground. In terms of distance, it was actually closer than the horizon, but without that illusion of it being at eye-level, it was quite terrifying. Many of the world's tallest buildings have glass floors at the top these days and I dare say that some of you will have stood on one or two. Scary, aren't they? Well, just imagine standing over a small one without the glass! There's your feet, there's the ground, and there's nothing in between except a few birds and an awful lot of air. It's a very different perspective, believe me.

The first lad to jump that day was a pal of mine called Haddert, and I saw his face as he looked down. At this point, I could only see a crescent of the ground, whereas this lad was standing directly over the hole and had just taken in his first glance of it in all its glory. I swear to God that his face went white at the same speed at which his feet hit the air. It was bloody frightening. Looking back I can almost laugh about this but at the time I was trying to remember some prayers from my days as an altar boy. I couldn't think of one. My mind was blank. The second man to jump did exactly the same as the first: as soon as he jumped, he went white.

By the time it was my turn I was shaking like a proverbial leaf. The difference between how I felt on the first jump and how I felt now was ridiculous. I couldn't understand it. As I shuffled up to the side of the hole – slowly – I said to Jack Marlborough something along the lines of, 'I'm not sure I can do this.' Old Jack had a smile as wide as the horizon I'd tried to step onto the last time I'd jumped, and that's exactly what he did, he smiled at me. Then, just as I was expecting a hand on my shoulder and a few words of comfort, he shouted, 'Go!' at which point my sense of duty and my respect for Jack took command of my actions and I jumped through the hole. I can't say exactly what colour I was when I jumped, but I bet it was as pallid as my predecessor's. Isn't it funny that when you think there's a chance of you becoming a ghost, you start looking like one.

Once I was through the hole and my parachute had opened I felt myself relax a little. It takes a while before you can be sure it's developed correctly. The landing for this jump was a carbon copy of the first one and it couldn't really have gone better: feet and knees together, land, roll-up and run. Sorted. I was definitely a bit quiet afterwards. I was a bit more reflective. 'It's a Dakota next, lads,' enthused Jack Marlborough when he was brought back to earth. Nobody said a word.

The following day we had what's called a flight experience (my first ever flight in an aeroplane), where you get all your gear on, go up in an aeroplane, but you don't actually jump. As we were coming back in to land Jack Marlborough called me over.

'Would you like to see the wheels, Private Cribbins?' he asked me.

'What do you mean?' I replied.

'You know, the wheels as they hit the tarmac. Would you like to see them?'

Although I didn't know my instructor very well I trusted him implicitly and so without even thinking about it I said yes. About a minute later I was hanging out of the cargo door on the side of a Dakota with my head in the slipstream and my instructor sitting on my feet. Health and safety? Erm, not today thanks. I must say, the sight of those wheels touching the runway was amazing, and the moment they made contact with the concrete a great plume of smoke went up.

'Good, isn't it?' said Corporal Marlborough as he pulled me in.

'Not 'arf,' I said gleefully.

That was real *Boy's Own* stuff. Great fun!

The following day ten of us went up again and this time we all jumped. It went like clockwork. I was first out and once the lad behind me had checked my static line (you always check the static line of the man in front), I was ready.

'Red on,' said Corporal Marlborough, which was my cue to stand in the door. 'Green on, go!'

No problems at all.

Unfortunately, jump number four didn't go quite as well for me: just as I came in to land a gust of wind took hold of the chute, whipped me around and I was dumped on my back. I can't say for sure that this was responsible, but ever since then I've always suffered from back problems and I have a feeling that this was the catalyst. No matter. It's just one of those things. I certainly didn't get up and run, though. Not that time.

When you jumped out of a Dakota, the slipstream turned you around very smartly, you'd lift up your legs, and away you'd go. Once again, your weight would open the parachute and the moment that had happened, you knew you were OK. The only time I ever saw this go awry was when a lad from Aberdeen called Private Coburn got stuck under the plane. I kid you not. After jumping out as normal his parachute failed to detach from the plane, which left him dangling underneath and banging against the underside. What they used to do in that situation was throw out a block and tackle. Whoever was dangling underneath had to try and attach it to their webbing. Not easy when you're about seven hundred feet in the air and travelling at 150 miles an hour. Once you'd managed to do that, they would then wind you back in. As soon as Private Coburn was safely through the door they landed the plane, got him a new parachute, went back up, and he was first out the door.

Incidentally, the reason they used to fly so low to the ground was so that those who were jumping would spend as little time as possible in the air. Why? Because in wartime the longer you spent in the air the more chance we had of getting picked off! It was that simple. The faster you got to the ground the better.

We did our penultimate jump with a 60-pound kit bag strapped to our right leg. It sounds quite bizarre, doesn't it? You see, once our parachute was open, we then had to take a couple of pins out of this bag and lower it down on a 20-foot line. It certainly gave us a soft landing, that's for sure.

The last of our eight jumps during parachute training was a night jump. That was just silly really, as all you could see as you jumped were exhaust sparks flying out of the engines. Talk about a leap into the unknown. A pal of mine called Jock Graham very nearly landed on top of me after this jump but before I could even remonstrate with the daft bugger he got up and started running around in circles shouting, ''Ave got me wings, 'ave got me wings!' While he was doing that a voice suddenly came out of the darkness.

'Private Graham!' it boomed. 'Pack up your parachute and shut your big bloody mouth this instant.'

'Yes, sir! Sorry, sir!'

Jock was right, though. We had got our wings. I felt great after that. A real sense of achievement. We were just young lads, remember. Eighteen-year-olds who'd left school at fourteen and who prior to this hadn't really achieved anything very much. We hadn't been wasters, but because of the state the country was in after the war our options had been restricted. Becoming paratroopers and then getting our wings had been a dream come true, and regardless of what happened thereafter, nobody could ever take that away from us. I remember telling Mum and Dad the news and they were absolutely over the moon. Contributing to the family pot had been a big thing for me but making my parents proud had been something else!

Shortly after receiving our wings we were moved to the Training and Holding Battalion where we waited to be stationed. Before that happened, we were each given a report on how we'd fared during training. According to my pal in the know, who has visited a website called Para Data, the report for Private Bernard Cribbins stated that I was a good performer, well-disciplined and a likely NCO, which means a non-commissioned officer! Not bad, eh? To be honest, I don't remember reading any of that at the time, but I'm taking it.

Both the highlight and the lowlight of my time in the Training and Holding Battalion happened when I took part in a guard of honour for the legendary Field Marshal Bernard Law Montgomery, 1st Viscount Montgomery of Alamein. To save you young ones from reaching for your tablets, Field Marshal Montgomery, or Monty as he was affectionately known, was one of the most important military figures to emerge from the Second World War and he was involved in literally dozens of battles and campaigns, including the Battle of the Bulge, Operation Overlord, the Siegfried Line Campaign and the invasion of Germany. In those days, only Sir Winston Churchill was more associated with the military campaign than Monty and so, with the war still fresh in everyone's minds, this was a huge honour.

Because our uniforms were a bit tatty, we were all issued with a brand new one as well as a new rifle. The rifles were what's called a Jungle Carbine rifle, which was a derivative of the standard issue Lee Enfield rifle. We used to call them Burma rifles, on account of them being used in the jungle. They were a bit shorter than the Lee Enfield and they had a bayonet that was about nine inches in length.

A few days later, there we were standing on parade waiting for the field marshal's car to arrive. We were in close order – three ranks – and I was in the rear rank. As the car finally pulled up, the sergeant major shouted, 'SQUAD, FIX BAYONETS!' I have to do it in capitals as he was rather loud.

Just so you can picture it in your head, here's what's supposed to happen while the man with the loud voice is shouting, 'FIX BAYONETS.' As we're standing there, the bayonets are on our left-hand side and, as the sergeant major shouts 'FIX', we then take the bayonets by the handle and turn them upside down with the blade up. Then, when the sergeant major shouts, 'BAYONETS,' we bring them around and attach them to the end of the rifle – click.

Unfortunately for me, the soldier standing directly to my right during this inspection decided to bring his bayonet up in a kind of circular motion and so instead of it going up above his rifle it went straight into the side of my right hand, about a centimetre away from an artery.

The soldier standing next to me who'd inflicted the wound knew what had happened and, after removing the bayonet from my hand and muttering sorry, he'd carried on fixing it to the end of his rifle. I was looking forward like a good boy, but I had a very good idea of what had happened and I was starting to feel the effects quite keenly. I didn't say or do anything. I simply carried on fixing my bayonet, the same as the other lad. After that we came back to attention, sloped arms, made the salute to the field marshal, came back to attention, and then waited to be inspected. By now I was in a wee bit of pain and although I wasn't aware of it there was a steady stream of claret pouring out of my hand and down the side of my trousers. Some of the blood had made it onto the parade ground, and by the time Monty had made it to the rear rank there was a nice little pool of it by my right foot. Or, at least I assumed there was. It was Monty, who was now standing behind me, who noticed it.

'I say,' he said. 'This man appears to have stabbed himself

with his bayonet. Had a little accident, have we? I think he'd better fall out, Sergeant Major, don't you?'

While my reputation was quickly being destroyed my inner voice was saying – no, it was actually screaming – *'That wasn't me, Monty, it was the twerp standing next to me!'*

Obviously, I had to remain schtum, and after being ordered to fall out, that's exactly what I did. I just did a right turn and marched off in the direction of the Medical Inspection room. I didn't salute. That wasn't because I was angry or anything. I just panicked. After the boys in the medical room had put a tack in my hand I found my commanding officer and told him exactly what had happened. And I got the lad who'd injured me to verify it, which he did. Bloody typical though, isn't it? I jump out of God knows how many aeroplanes – nothing – yet a few days before I finish my training, one of the most decorated soldiers in the entire British Army turns up and I get stabbed by a member of my own platoon! The only bonus, I suppose, is that Field Marshal Montgomery actually addressed me directly (although from behind), and he didn't address any of the others. They all got a nod or nothing at all, whereas I got, 'Had a little accident, have we?'

Me and Monty? Like that, we are.

Shortly after my Monty incident some heath fires started around the Cobham area, which was about 20 miles away. We spent three or four days and nights up there with beaters trying to put these fires out. Because we'd been sent there in an emergency we didn't have any equipment with us, apart from the beaters, and we ended up sleeping on the floor in people's sheds and greenhouses.

Anyway, it's time for Private Cribbins to be stationed overseas. Are you coming? I warn you, though, you might need a tin hat.

On 30 November 1947, the Palestine War officially began. Prior to then, the British Army's 6th Airborne Division had been serving as peacekeepers in Palestine since the Second World War. We were sent out to take over from them and were transported to Palestine on what has now become one of the most infamous troopships ever: the HMT *Empire Windrush*, which sank after a fire in 1954.

The *Empire Windrush*, or the MV *Monte Rosa* as she was christened at launch, had been built by the Germans in the late 1920s and she had originally been used as what was known as a 'Strength Through Joy' vessel. Strength Through Joy, or *Kraft durch Freude*, was a large state-operated leisure organisation in Nazi Germany and was supposed to bridge the class divide by making middle-class leisure activities available to the masses. Some of these activities had obviously taken place on the ship but, after spending time as a hospital ship, she had been captured by the British and renamed the HMT *Empire Windrush*.

We arrived in Malta, which was our first port of call, on 19 November. The reason I know it was 19 November is because, on the day after that, Princess Elizabeth and Philip Mountbatten, as they were known then, got married, and we spent two days in Malta's Grand Harbour. To celebrate the wedding, all the ships in the harbour were decked out in bunting, but because of the weather the mood inside most of the ships was at odds with their joyful exteriors. All we did for two whole days was rock back and forth, back and forth, and almost everybody on board our ship was sick, including me. Blurgh! That was 'orrid!

After that, as we set sail again down to the Suez Canal, I began to get my sea legs. This meant that I felt able to explore the ship a bit and late one evening while were sailing through the Mediterranean me and a fellow paratrooper from Manchester called Downe (his nickname was Ben, as in Ben Downe) crept right up to the prow of the ship. We only did this because we weren't really supposed to but when we arrived there we were treated to something quite special. For a start, the water was phosphorescent, like the Northern Lights at sea, and there, swimming through these amazing colours alongside the ship was a school of dolphins. I'd never seen a dolphin before and there they were about 40 feet below us, just coming up in the bow wave. Amazing! After about five minutes we were called back by our sergeant and then given a bollocking for being up at the front end. It was worth it, though!

After a few days at sea we arrived in Port Tewfik, which is now called Suez Port. There was a transit camp nearby and we stayed there for about a week. Here, we had some Arab helpers who were all armed with pickaxe handles. I remember them well because they used to make these tiny little campfires and would squat in front of them, lift up their tunics and warm their parts! Well, it was bitter out.

After that we travelled across the Sinai Peninsula by train and then up to Azib, which then was in Northern Palestine. We stayed there under canvas for about four or five days before moving down to Peninsula Barracks in Haifa, which was where we were to be based. I think we arrived at Peninsula Barracks on about 8 December and I was on one of the first guards there. Lucky old me, eh?

On the morning of 11 December, after finishing a stag (which is a period of duty guard), the sergeant came up and told me to get the tea.

'Yes, Sergeant,' I said, before picking up the large metal bucket (yes, we transported our tea in a bucket) and walking down towards the nearby Mediterranean where the cookhouse was. As I walked I could see in front of me a lovely glow in the sky. It must have been about four o'clock in the morning and I assumed it was the sunrise – I smiled and it gave me a lovely warm feeling. Just then, I suddenly had a thought. If memory served me correctly I was pretty sure that the sun rose from the east, whereas at the time I was definitely facing west. Unless something pretty drastic had changed over the last twenty-four hours, such as the direction of the earth, I was not walking towards the beginning of a glorious sunrise. Also, when I said that it had given me a lovely warm feeling, I didn't just mean romantically. It was becoming ever so slightly warmer.

When I turned the next corner I got the shock of my bloody life as there in front of me was a huge hut that was on fire. This was part of a wooden encampment that encompassed the afore-mentioned cookhouse, the NAAFI stores and, the armoury. I'd got up to a trot by now and as the hut came more into view I could see a selection of squaddies, all in various states of undress, and all carrying boxes. By the time I was a few yards away it had dawned on me that the hut that was on fire was the NAAFI and that the one next door, which they were evacuating, was the battalion armoury! The first person I recognised was the regi-mental sergeant major, a man called Paddy Caughey, who was standing there with a 9-millimetre pistol supervising the evacuation of the armoury. I dropped my bucket and got involved. We were pulling out boxes of ammunition, hand grenades, mortar bombs, PIAT bombs; you name it, we were shifting it, and as fast as we bloody well could.

We'd been stacking this ammo about 40 yards away outside the cookhouse. Despite the advancing flames, RSM Caughey was still intent on us going in and carrying on with the evacuation but by this time it was getting beyond dangerous. In the end, he saw sense and everybody ran. Two minutes later, BOOM! I'd never seen anything like it. After a few seconds, another explosion went off and before too long the entire place had gone up, including the cookhouse and the ammo that we'd stacked up in front of it. Nobody had even had a cup of tea in that NAAFI! It was just carnage.

We were later told that two small children were killed as a result of the fire. A bomb had been blown about 200 yards away from the blaze, but it hadn't exploded. These two children had found this bomb and had started playing with it. Well, I don't need to tell you what happened. How tragic.

I later read the official report into the fire at Haifa and it came to the conclusion that it was an accident, something I'm afraid I do not believe. In fact, many years later I was working on a film in Israel and we had a first assistant on the film, who, after he knew my history with Haifa, claimed to have been there at the same time. 'I was in the Haganah,' he said. 'And I was sixteen years of age.' For those of you who don't know, the Haganah was a Jewish paramilitary organisation and, at the time, had we known each other, let's just say we probably wouldn't have been friends. He might just have been having a pop at me, but from the way he looked at me and the information he had, it's my theory that he was part of the team that set fire to the NAAFI, which then spread to the armoury. I obviously can't prove anything. That's just my theory. But you know when you get a feeling about something?

Shortly after this I was doing a patrol at the British Sailors' Society, which was just outside the main gates of the dock in Haifa. It was where the merchant navy boys used to stay and the main guard area was a little balcony on the front of the building that also had a Bren gun position. At about 4.30 a.m., I spotted somebody walking along the edge of a very tall building. I was still quite green at the time but even so I decided to get him in the sights of my gun, just in case. I didn't cock it, I just kept him in sight. I thought to myself, *If he makes a move I'm going to have to do something.* Several minutes later he started calling people to prayer. It was the muezzin! If I had been so foolish as to shoot the muezzin, I'd still be there, I should think.

A few weeks after the fire an opportunity came my way when a mate of mine – a Geordie lad called Harry Moffatt who used to work in the medical room – asked me if I knew anybody who might be interested in working with him. They had a lot on at the time, I can't think why, and because I'd done a bit of first aid with the Scouts and the St John Ambulance I offered up my services. Dr Cribbins, at your service. I said Cribbins, by the way, not Crippen! Well, it was better than walking around Haifa with a gun in your hand and I thought it might prevent me from being shot at.

Talking of which.

CHAPTER FOUR

Hang on, where's Charlie?

After being shown the ropes in the medical room I was let loose on the sick and injured and my first patient was a prisoner. I have no recollection about what he'd done wrong but what I do remember, worst luck, is that the reason he'd been brought in was because he had a carbuncle the size of half an orange on his backside. For those of you who never want to eat again, allow me to enlighten you as to what a carbuncle is. A carbuncle is a red, swollen and painful cluster of boils that are connected to each other under the skin. OK? Can you think of anything more vomit-inducing than that? I'm not sure I can. It gets worse, though. You see, my mate Harry Moffatt had very kindly nominated me to treat this posterior-dwelling prisoner carbuncle and clean it up. I very nearly grabbed a gun and just went back on patrol, but I eventually came to the difficult conclusion that even carbuncles were preferable to death.

After doing my duty and managing not to be sick, I stood up and told the military policeman who'd been escorting the prisoner that he could take him back to the guard room. 'OK then,' he said, collecting his felon. 'See you tomorrow.' After he'd left I asked Harry what he meant by 'See you tomorrow'.

'He has to have it seen to every day,' said Harry. 'It grows back in next to no time.'

'Please tell me you're joking,' I pleaded.

'Nope. You'll be on carbuncle duty for as long as you're here I'm afraid, Bernie. You may as well give it a name.'

'I'll give you a name!'

One day they brought somebody into the medical room who was covered in blood from head to toe, yet there wasn't a single mark on him. This poor fellow was in a state of complete shock and interspersed among the blood on his face were small pieces of tissue. The look on his face was heart-breaking, even without knowing what had happened, but at the same time it was slightly disturbing. He was petrified. Apparently, he and another chap had been carrying a box of ammo between them, and the other chap had had a Sten gun over his shoulder. As they were walking the box of ammo had started to slip and he'd tried to correct his position. The Sten gun had fallen off this lad's shoulder and, after hitting the floor, it had fired several rounds and had blown the back of the other chap's head off. I think that was the worst thing I ever saw in that medical room. How on earth do you get over something like that?

A few weeks into my tenure as medic extraordinaire at Peninsula Barracks in Haifa I was having a lie in one day in my dormitory. *Having a lie in,* I hear you say! *Paratroopers don't get lie ins, surely to goodness?* Well, I'm afraid this one did. I was slightly under the weather with sand-fly fever at the time, the symptoms of which are usually head, muscle and joint aches, flushing of the face and a fast heart rate. Sounds like a hangover, doesn't it? It must have been about ten o'clock in the morning when all of a sudden I was woken from my slumber by an almighty boom. A second or so later there was a noise on the wall behind my bed, as if it was being peppered by something on the outside. 'What the bloody hell's that?' I said, sitting up in bed. It felt like I was under attack.

In actual fact, that wasn't too far from what was happening. The only difference being that I wasn't under attack.

Allow me to explain.

It turned out that the Royal Engineers, bless 'em, had been picking up all the unexploded ordnances left over from the big fire, putting them in piles and then blowing them up. They obviously must have thought that the area where they were blowing up this particular pile was deserted at the time, but it wasn't! A few moments later there was another explosion and this time, in addition to the roof almost coming off – again – a couple of bits of shrapnel made it through the walls. Now I really was under fire! Quick as a flash (or as quick as I was able to) I leapt out of my nice comfy bed, ran to the door and made myself known to the Royal Engineers.

It was time for a shower!

Coincidentally, towards the end of my battalion's posting in Haifa we had to dispose of some ammo that was no longer deemed to be useful. As opposed to doing this next to a dormitory like my friends from the Royal Engineers, we decided to drag it down to the beach instead and dispose of it safely. Well, fairly safely.

I remember this beach as if it were yesterday. There were some rocks at one end and on those rocks was an old refugee ship that must have been beached there years ago. As we carried this ammunition onto the beach, just along from the rocks I could see two Arab gentlemen fishing in a small boat. Each was carrying a little jam jar full of explosives and every so often one of them would drop one of these explosives in the water in order to stun the fish, which they collected from the reef. We helped using some old grenades and there can't have been a single fish left on that reef. The two Arab boys were absolutely chuffed to bits, and because their catch had somewhat swelled in size I ended up swimming out to help them by throwing them some of the fish. I'm all heart, I am.

As you'd imagine, the old grenades tended to cause a ripple or two as they exploded and just as I was chucking a fish into the Arabs' boat, I felt one of these ripples. I looked back towards shore and the lads throwing the hand grenades had obviously forgotten I was there. Or had they? Either way, I was taking no chances and after bidding the fishermen adieu I started breast-stroking it back to the beach, all the time shouting, 'No more bloody hand grenades!'

The only time we ever came close to being done over in Palestine was when six of us went out to spend the night at an observation post. The observation post was partway down what are known as the Kishon Steps, which run all the way down from Mount Carmel, which sits just above Haifa. The steps are intercepted periodically by streets, which is how we were making our way to the observation point. There was rubble absolutely everywhere, and the observation point itself was a semi-derelict house.

The five lads with me that night were Corporal Hammond, Private Skeets Gallagher, Private Paddy Reilly, Private Charlie

Charlton and a signaller who'd been given to us for the night. As we picked our way over the rubble on the Kishon Steps down towards the observation point, we split into two groups. Corporal Hammond, Private Gallagher and Private Reilly marched on one side of the steps, and the rest of us marched on the other. Unfortunately for Team Cribbins a gentleman, who I assume was on a roof in front of us somewhere, decided to open fire. As you can imagine, chaos reigned for a few moments and I knew from the cries that at least one of us had been hit. Not me, though. Fortunately I was fine.

Quick as a flash we all took cover in our old house and Corporal Hammond did a head count.

'One, two, three, four . . . Hang on, where's Charlie?' he said. 'Charlie, where are you?'

'I've been hit,' he said. 'I'm out here.'

We looked out and there was Charlie lying in the rubble, clutching his foot. The bullets must have passed me at chest height and about ten inches to my right. Charlie had been marching a few feet behind me and because the street was sloped one of them had hit him in the foot. The signaller, who'd been marching behind Charlie, had also been hit in the foot, but fortunately for him the heel of his boot had taken the bullet. The one thing I gleaned when I realised that Charlie had been shot in the foot was that the bloke firing at us must have been a rubbish shot.

With Skeets Gallagher covering us with a Bren gun, Paddy Reilly and I crept out onto the street again and managed to pull Charlie to safety. We put a field-dressing on the wound and made him comfortable.

After that, Paddy and I, while being covered by Skeets again, ran back to our little HQ, which was about a quarter of a mile away, to ask them to radio for an ambulance. The signaller who was with us had been carrying a radio but unfortunately he'd dropped it when the valves had smashed. After doing that we ran back to the others and hoped to hell that Skeets would still be covering us. He was, fortunately.

A little while later, a Palestinian policeman arrived. As peace-keepers, we weren't allowed to arrest anybody in Palestine. That was their job. Once we'd been informed that the ambulance had arrived, the policeman went to help Charlie to his feet, but, just as he did that, the gentleman on the roof, who must have had something wrong with his eyesight, took another shot, which this time hit the wall directly between Charlie and the policeman's head. After that Skeets had sight of this fellow and, as far as I'm aware, he blew him away. It was kill or be killed, I'm afraid.

It was a very noisy place, Haifa. There were a lot of explosions and the sniper fire was incessant. I couldn't live under those conditions. Not long term.

There is one other story about me coming under fire in Palestine, except this one's quite amusing. Can coming under fire be amusing? Well, I think so. So long as you don't die!

Right then, get a load of this.

I was at a Bren gun post at about two or three in the morning and it's safe to say that I was in a rather precarious position. We were in a long valley close to Haifa and at one end of this valley there were Arabs, at the other end there were Jews and, in the middle, there were peacekeepers. So there I was, standing there behind this gun surrounded by sandbags, when suddenly my sergeant came up. His nickname was Rocky, on account of his surname being Mountain, and he'd fought at the Battle of Arnhem. Hard as nails, he was. He had a fag on the go and, as he sloped into my post, he said, 'I've just had word from the top. You're not to return fire unless you're hit, OK?'

At that very moment a shot was fired from the Jewish end and the bullet landed in the parapet right between us. SMACK! Instinctively, we both dropped to the floor, but without batting an eyelid Sergeant Rocky took a drag of his fag, looked at me and said, 'Remember, Cribbins, not unless you're hit,' and then crawled away. You couldn't make that up, could you? I still laugh about it.

On 16 April 1948 our time in Haifa came to an end and, much to the relief of the inmates at Peninsula Barracks – or, at least the ones who were poorly – we were shipped back to England on an old but slightly less notorious vessel called the RMS *Empress of Australia*. After docking at Liverpool we were sent to barracks near Cirencester in Gloucestershire, but before that happened I received an unexpected but very welcome visitor. We were still on board at the time and somebody started asking if there was a person named Barney Cribbins on the ship.

'That's me,' I said, waving an arm. 'There's somebody on the quayside wants to talk to you,' said the messenger. After making it on deck I looked over the side and there, about 40 feet away on the quayside, was my best mate Jim Cassidy. I should have known as he always called me Barney. He'd been waiting to catch a ferry over to Ireland and when he saw the *Empress of*

Australia coming into dock he'd asked somebody where it was coming from. When they said Palestine he put two and two together and got Cribbins! It was a lovely surprise and we managed to squeeze in a quick chat before his ferry left.

I have to say it was damn good to be back. Those bombs and all that sniper fire had started to lose their lustre a bit. What I needed was some rain and some nice warm beer.

Shortly after we arrived in Cirencester, the medical officer, who was a captain, and his sergeant decided to take a weekend off, and, because we were no longer working in a warzone, we weren't expecting anything big to happen. This meant that for an entire forty-eight hours, I, Dr Cribbins, would be responsible for the medical wellbeing of the 3rd Battalion Parachute Regiment. Talk about lunatics taking over the asylum.

On Sunday at about half past one in the morning somebody started banging on my door. 'Quick, you've got to come quickly. Darky's cut his head.'

'Who's cut his head?'

'Darky, the cook sergeant.'

'Oh bloody hell. All right, where is he?'

'He's in his quarters. You'd better come quick.'

After grabbing a kidney bowl and some bandages I made my way to the sergeant's quarters expecting him to have a cut above the eye or something. I figured he was probably just drunk and had banged into something. Well, I certainly got the first bit right. Except I appeared to have underplayed the situation somewhat. Darky wasn't drunk. He was as pissed as a fart. He was also covered in an attractive mixture of vomit and blood, and instead of sporting a small cut on his forehead like I'd been expecting, there was a large wound on the top of his head that, if you moved the flap of skin, revealed his skull. It was almost a semi-circle in shape and must have been a good five inches long.

Realising that this was slightly out of my league I asked for the duty ambulance driver to be sent for immediately. 'We have to get Darky to hospital,' I said.

'But that's twenty miles away,' said the guy who'd fetched me.

'I don't care. There's nothing I can do for this. It needs stitching. We have to take him to Gloucester.'

After waiting about ten minutes the private who'd gone to look for the duty ambulance driver returned. 'I can't find him or the ambulance anywhere,' he said, puffing and panting.

Blooming marvellous!

'What about a different driver?' I pleaded. 'Look, just find me a duty driver or anybody who can take Darky to Gloucester. And quick!'

Do you know what he came back with? An open 15-hundred-weight truck. 'OK,' I said. 'We've got no choice.'

After making a turban out of bandages I patched the cook sergeant up the best I could, wrapped him in about fifteen blankets, and then some of the lads and I got him onto the back of this open truck. As soon as the driver started this thing we immediately started rattling around and I thought, *There's no way we can stand twenty miles of this. It'll be like a human pinball machine.* Luckily, just as the driver was letting out the handbrake of this truck the ambulance arrived and, after offering a few carefully chosen words of welcome to the driver, we transferred Darky into the back.

As we set off I looked at Darky and realised that he was still very much under the influence and he was coming out with all kinds of rubbish. One minute he loved me, the next he loved the driver, and so on. You know the kind of thing. After about 5 miles or so Darky got his second wind and decided he was going to take off his turban. 'Please don't do that!' I said, as he reached up. But it was too late. He'd uncovered the wound and exposed his skull again.

'Have I hurt my head or something,' he slurred.

'Yes, yes,' I said irritably, while trying to restrain the inebriated sergeant and at the same time replace his headpiece. It was impossible. Every time I held one of his hands in place and then tried to reattach his turban the other hand would fly up and start playing with his wound.

God knows how but eventually I managed to quieten the sergeant down and get him patched up again. 'Right then, Sarge,' I said. 'We've still got a while to go so I want you to promise me that you're going to behave. OK?

'Behave?' he said indignantly. 'BEHAVE? Of course I'm going to behave.'

With that, he started dropping off to sleep. Perfect, I thought.

Darky must have been asleep for about fifteen seconds when suddenly he woke up. 'What the 'eck's going on here? Where am I? What are you doing with me, Cribbins? And why have I got this thing on my head?'

'Not the bandage!'

The whole thing started again.

'If you do that once more,' I said, 'I'm going to chin you and knock you out.' I meant it too.

He behaved from then on in and we must have reached Gloucester casualty department at about four o'clock in the morning. After checking in with a nurse we were shown into a cubicle and a few minutes later the matron appeared. I have to make a *Carry On* reference here as this woman was exactly like Hattie Jacques. She was large, quite nonchalant and *very* much in charge. 'Oh, I see we've been hit by a bottle or a brick,' she said casually as she removed the sergeant's turban. With that, she then picked the sergeant up – literally – plonked him on a trolley and started wheeling him away. 'You fellows can go now,' she said as they disappeared to God knows where. 'You won't be needed again.'

I never did find out what happened to the sergeant that evening. I think Hattie Jacques was right, though: it was definitely either a brick or a bottle. Unbelievable!

After spending a month or two in Cirencester I got some leave and so went up to see the family in Oldham. It was wonderful seeing Mum and Dad and, for obvious reasons, I decided not to tell Mum about getting shot at. If I had, she'd never have let me out of her sight again.

Shortly after returning to Cirencester I was sent to a barracks in Schleswig-Holstein, Germany, where I remained until I was demobbed in 1949. I really fell on my feet there, both in terms of job and accommodation. The camp we were in had been a German seaplane base during the war and it was very swish. They may not have come out the winner, but the Germans certainly knew how to build a camp. It was rather splendid.

As opposed to having barracks sleeping thirty, like we had in England, they had rooms sleeping about six – and they even had a shower room attached. En-suite facilities? In wartime? Well, fancy that.

The role that the powers that be had bestowed on me in Germany, and I mean bestowed, was as a batman to officers who were coming through to do refresher courses in jumping. There were six of us altogether – batmen, that is – and we had our own dorm and so had our own little community.

But it wasn't *what* we had to do that made me feel like I'd fallen on my feet, it was what we *didn't* have to do. Because the Berlin airlift was still in operation (it had started in June 1948 to supply food and fuel to West Berlin, which was being blockaded by the Soviets, and it didn't finish until after I'd been demobbed in May 1949) there were no planes available, which meant there was no jumping! What's not to like about that? In the end, I got myself some fishing tackle and every day I went down to the Schlei, a large body of water, connected to the Kiel Canal, which was a five-minute walk away. Over the course of a day I'd fill a great big fire bucket up with roach, perch and bream, and then I'd take the fish back for the German cleaners. They were all delighted because they were a bit short of grub and so everyone won. Except the fish, of course. What a life, though. All I ever did, day in, day out, was sit on this little jetty and fish all day. I didn't even do guard duty.

It didn't last the full term, unfortunately. But it wasn't far off. One day the commanding officers were looking for some guards and as they were sitting there scratching their heads one of them had a eureka moment. 'What about the batmen? They're doing absolutely bugger all.' Blast! We were rumbled. To be fair, things weren't that much different for us after that. We were put on a rota and that was that. It was like having a part-time job.

After returning from Germany I was then sent up to York where I was demobbed. Actually, that's not true. I was asked if I wanted to stay on, first of all, but I politely declined. It had been an eventful couple of years but as much as I'd enjoyed restraining drunken sergeants with dodgy nicknames, fishing and being shot at occasionally, I was desperate to get back to the theatre. The question being, was the theatre desperate for me to go back?

Before we move on, I just want to tell you a very quick story about something that happened to me many years later. Actually, it was almost forty years later.

Right, listen to this for a coincidence.

I was touring in a farce in Australia and New Zealand some-time in the late 1980s. I forget the name of the farce. Could it have been *The Love Game?* Possibly. Anyway, we were in Christchurch in New Zealand at the time and I was standing in my room one afternoon eating rock oysters and chips. It was a Saturday, and whenever we had two shows in a day I'd always treat myself to rock oysters and chips. Do you know, I'm actu-ally starting to drool thinking about rock oysters? Beautiful!

As I was happily munching away, the stage-door keeper knocked on my door and told me there was someone to see me.

'He's waiting at the stage door,' he said. 'Used to be in the Army with you, apparently. His name's Essex.'

'Not Fred Essex?' I asked immediately.

'That's the one. Do you want me to tell him you're here?'

'Yes, I do! Tell him I'll be there in a second.'

After devouring what was left of my late lunch I whizzed up to the stage door. Fred Essex had been in the same platoon for training and jumping, and when I saw him at the stage door he was wearing a New Zealand Air Force uniform.

'Private Essex!' I shouted as I came down the stairs. 'What on earth are you doing here?'

'It's actually Staff Sergeant Essex,' said Fred, holding out his hand. 'Good to see you, Bernie!'

Good old Fred had simply been passing the theatre and, after seeing my name, he'd inspected the stills outside. Well, forty years or not, there's no mistaking my ugly mug, is there? Only I'm allowed to say that, by the way.

It turned out Fred had stayed in the Paras after the rest of us had gone, and after emigrating to New Zealand he'd become a staff sergeant in the Royal New Zealand Air Force and he'd specialised in weapons training. It was wonderful seeing him again and the ten or fifteen minutes we had together that afternoon evoked a plethora of marvellous memories. I love coincidences like that.

About a year later, I was at home one evening watching a television programme about an SAS team operating in Malaya. Things like that are right up my street and the only thing that was missing on an otherwise perfect evening was rock oysters and chips. The team they were reporting on was made up of four men and about five minutes in I had the feeling that one of the men seemed quite familiar.

'See that one on the end,' I said to my wife, Gill. 'I'm sure I've seen him before.'

We hadn't really had a proper look at this chap yet but when we did I was left in no doubt.

'My God! That's Fred Essex,' I shouted. 'I only saw him a few months ago.'

The programme was a few years old, so he'd obviously served with the SAS as well as the Paras prior to moving to New Zealand. 'He didn't say anything when I saw him in Christchurch,' I said to Gill. She just shot me a glance, as if to say *It's hardly surprising, given he was sworn to secrecy*!

Actually, while we're in Australia, which we were a minute ago, I must just tell you a quick story about a tree. Why now, I hear you ask? Because I can't think of anywhere else to put it, that's why! It's to accompany one of the photos in the book and in a second you'll know which one. Gillian and I were in Kings Park in Perth and, as we were walking through the park, we saw a trunk of an enormous kauri pine – or *Agathis robusta*, if you want to get all botanical – lying on its side. Because it was so huge – it must have been at least five metres in diameter – I went to the end of it, got my hands underneath and pretended to lift. While Gill was taking a photo of me, which is in here somewhere, a park warden rode by on his bike and without stopping he said, 'Put it back when you've finished.'

I love that!

Anyway, back to coincidences.

Believe it or not, that very same thing happened to me on another occasion when I was appearing in a show, except this time it was in England. And I wasn't eating rock oysters, more's the pity. I was appearing with the late Donald Sinden in a show that I'll come on to later called *Not Now Darling*. You can tell by the name what kind of show it was, can't you? That's right. It was a farce. Like my old mate Richard Briers, Donald Sinden was a consummate farceur and was regarded as one of the best in the business, if not *the* best. Even so, Donald could be a consummate pain in the backside sometimes and one day I had to take him to task over it. Anyway, that's for later.

One afternoon I arrived at the Strand Theatre for a matinee of this show. You could actually park in the street in those days and after finding a spot I made my way around the front of the theatre towards the stage door. Just as I was walking past some of the framed stills of me and the rest of the cast, I noticed a chap looking at them and smiling.

''Ere, I know you,' I said to him.

'And I know you,' said the man. 'Hello, Bernie. How are you?'

It was John Conway, my old sparring partner from Aldershot who had also been in the same platoon as me in Palestine. This was the late 1960s and was only the second time I'd seen anyone from the Parachute Regiment since leaving in 1949; the other being a lad called Nobby Clarke whom I'd met on Brighton seafront a few years earlier.

You remember I told you about Harry Moffatt, the man who turned me into a carbuncle squeezer? Well, he used to work for a very large booze distributor and when I was working at the Criterion Theatre in London on another farce I'll come on to later, called *Run for Your Wife*, he used to pop in for a chat and give me a couple of bottles of Scotch. Those were the days. It was shortly after appearing in *Run for Your Wife* that I gave up booze altogether. It didn't agree with me any more, so I knocked it on the head.

Funnily enough, just a couple of years ago in 2016 I was

invited to Merville Barracks in Colchester where the 3rd Battalion are now based to present the regiment's official charity, Support Our Paras, with a cheque for £17,000 that we'd raised via a fishing day. I was one of many people who'd helped to raise the money for this worthwhile cause. While I was at the barracks they did some demonstrations for me and after giving me a tour I even got to have a look round an old Dakota. One of the demonstrations they did was how to land after a jump, and from memory that hadn't changed too much. After they'd done it some bright spark suggested that I have a go myself, but at eighty-seven years old and with two titanium knees I had to decline. One thing that had changed quite a bit was the weaponry and I had to admit that I wouldn't have known where to start with the stuff they use these days. Everything was so big and bulky, and they made our weapons look like bows and arrows. Same effect though, I suppose.

Anyway, let's get back to the theatre.

CHAPTER FIVE

The one-legged darts player

When I arrived back in Oldham after being demobbed all I did for the first couple of weeks was relax and play catch up. Two years is a long time to be away from home and if my friends and family didn't have much to tell me, I certainly had a lot to tell them. As well as my own stories, I'd learned more about the world in those two years than I had in my previous eighteen. And about myself, if I'm being honest. It was good to be back, though. Have I said that already? I think I probably have.

Nothing much had changed in Oldham. Mum, Dad and the girls were fine, and the Pennine Rangers were still eating sooty beans in a hut.

But how were things at the theatre?

After a couple of weeks I decided to pop down there, just to say hello. I obviously had no idea who was working there. Perhaps that's why I left it for a while, but faint heart never won fair whatsit, so one afternoon I popped down there; partly to say hello and introduce myself if needs be, but also to make them aware of my availability.

The new producer, so I'd learned, was a chap I already knew called Harry Lomax and when I into Fairbottom Street the first thing I saw was Harry standing outside the theatre talking to a tall, dark-haired gentleman with a bit of a cheeky grin, who he quickly introduced to me as Mr Eric Sykes.

'Very pleased to meet you,' I said, shaking his hand, as I hadn't managed to meet him before I left to do my National Service.

'And you,' said Eric, as only he could.

Although he was still appearing as an actor with the Oldham Repertory Company, Eric had continued to write and, as well as providing scripts and gags for Bill Fraser, Eric and his writing partner, a chap called Sid Colin, had also been writing for radio. They were even providing scripts for this new-fangled box-shaped thing that I was sure would never catch on called television. We didn't know it then, but in less than a year's time Eric and Sid would make the bigtime by writing for a new radio show that would attract more than 15 million listeners – *Educating Archie*.

Anyway, enough about Eric. This is about me, remember?

After chatting to Harry and Eric for a while, the subject of what I was going to do suddenly arose. To be honest, I'd been thinking about giving variety a go and the moment I voiced my intentions Mr Sykes slapped me on the chest with the back of his hand and said, ''Ere, I've got an act for you.'

Before I could even ask him what it was he started hopping on one leg. I looked at Harry, as if to say, *What's going on*, but he was too busy laughing. When I looked back, Eric was now pretending to throw things with his right hand.

'It's a one-legged darts player,' he said, and, after pretending to throw a dart, exclaimed, 'Double top. Look at that, amazing. How do I do it?'

I thought, *You're just a lunatic!*

I'm pleased to say that Eric Sykes became a very dear friend of mine and I miss him even today. He was unique was our Eric and a decent golfer too!

Funnily enough, not long after impersonating a one-legged darts player on Fairbottom Street, Eric was sacked by Oldham Rep for demanding a pay rise and so he supplemented his writing career by touring the variety halls. I wonder if he ever did the one-legged darts player?

Answers on a postcard please . . .

The following day I had another chat with Harry Lomax and he eventually asked me to come back to Oldham Rep as the assistant stage manager. Now, I know what you're thinking: *Isn't that what he was doing when he left to do National Service?* Absolutely right. You see, I told you nothing much changed in Oldham. It wasn't long before I was elevated to the heady heights of stage manager, however, so it was worth me going back.

I had some unusual experiences working in stage management, even during my first, youthful stint with Oldham Rep. In 1945, we were lucky enough to have the great Robert Newton perform at Oldham Rep in a new play called *So Brief the Spring* by Walter Greenwood, who famously wrote *Love on the Dole*. Robert Newton was one of the biggest actors in the world in the 1940s and when he arrived with us he'd just had a huge hit playing the lead in the David Lean film, *This Happy Breed*. In addition to being adept at delivering lines, Mr Newton was also quite handy in the drinking department and was undoubtedly one of the original hellraisers of the British film world.

After the opening night of this play we had a party to celebrate, where I talked to Walter Greenwood while nursing a small beer. I was only seventeen, remember, and hadn't yet discovered my drinking shoes. As we were chatting away Robert Newton sidled up to me, looked at my glass and said, 'What's that?'

Ever so slightly star struck, I paused for a second and when I finally found my voice I said, 'Erm, it's a small beer, Mr Newton.'

'A small beer?' he said disappointedly. 'I'll tell you what, let's liven it up a bit. How about a drop of gin?'

Before I could say, 'No thanks, I'm fine,' he'd whipped out his hip flask, which was a good size, and had put a huge – and I mean huge – glug of gin into my small beer. 'There you go, lad,' he said, giving me a wink. 'That'll put hairs on your chest.'

I think he meant hairs on my palms.

After downing whatever it was I was now drinking, and feeling great, I might add, I got myself another small beer, propped myself up against a wall, and started grinning to myself. Halfway through that, I was paid another visit by the generous Mr Newton. 'What's the verdict then. Enjoy it?' I can't say for sure if I answered him or not, but I have a feeling I just smiled at him. After saying something like, 'Good lad,' Mr Newton whipped out his hip flask again and before I could say 'Yes, please,' he'd filled up my glass with more gin. Or 'Cribbins' ruin', as it was about to be renamed.

After taking a deep swig I slurred my appreciation of the great man and then carried on grinning, 'Sank you very much, Mizter Nooton. Zat's velly kind of woo.'

'No problem, sonny,' he said, giving me another wink.

By the time I'd downed my second beer and gin cocktail I'd missed the last bus and so I had to walk home. I have to admit that I was three sheets to the wind by this point and when I got as far as Mumps Bridge I decided I needed a pee. Not only was this the first time I'd ever been properly under the influence, but it was the first time I'd ever had gin with my beer and the effect it had on me was to make me feel tearful. I don't know if they were happy or sad tears, but by the time I'd found a public convenience at Mumps Bridge I was definitely having a gin-induced blub about something. When I finally emerged from the Gents there was a copper standing outside and, after giving me a knowing look, he said, 'Are you all right, lad? What's up?' By now my tears had definitely become sad ones and I very drunkenly, and tearfully, tried to convey to him that I wasn't OK.

'Am zorry, ossifer, but av bin at the feater and av bin drunk-ing jun with oburt nooton – you no, the vilm staaa. I dun't feel velly well, ossifer. Wot am I guing to do?'

I don't know whether it was the prospect of having to get me home that put the officer off helping me but after hearing my plea he just shook his head and said, 'On yer way, lad,' and then walked off! Mind you, if I'd come across me in my state in the middle of the night I think I'd have done exactly the same. Thanks to Mizter Nooton I was in a right state.

I also used to get asked to do some bizarre things, sometimes with animals, in my roles in stage management. Just before I had left to do my National Service, we did a show called *Theatre Royal* and the leading actor had to have a dog. The actor was called Harald Norway (not Harald *of* Norway, as in the King) and, after much deliberation, it was decided that I would have to find this dog for Harald. Believe it or not, there weren't that many dogs around in those days. Not like there are now. In fact, the only dog I could think of that might be suitable for the role was a big mastiff that belonged to the landlord of a local pub. It was a bit of a sloppy old thing (that's the dog, not the landlord) but wasn't too excitable. That was the only require-ment, really. Apart from being a dog.

After paying the landlord a visit he very kindly acquiesced to allow us to borrow his unflustered mastiff for the week and on the Monday afternoon I popped down to the pub, got him on his lead and walked him up to Fairbottom Street. So far, so good.

The dog's part was a non-speaking role, by the way, and entailed him being led on by Harald, sitting still for a few minutes, and then being led off by someone else. Actually, we haven't given this dog a name yet. I can't remember it so for the sake of this book, let's call him Tomsk, OK?

Well, at the dress rehearsal Tomsk took to his part very well indeed and was regarded by all as being not only a consummate actor, but also a fine addition to the company. If and when we needed any dogs, that is. Come the evening we were obviously expecting the same kind of dedication and professionalism he'd shown during the rehearsal, but when people started arriving, old Tomsk started getting a bit twitchy. At first, I put it down to first-night nerves. After all, we've all had 'em. In hindsight, I think it was all the people running around backstage that put the wind up him and I should probably have given him his own dressing room. That would have gone down well with the cast.

By the time curtain-up was upon us Tomsk was all of a quiver and when Harald tried to lead him onto the stage at his cue he point blank refused to budge. For thirty seconds or so Harald tried pulling Tomsk onto the stage but in truth he'd have had more chance of pulling the stage onto Tomsk. Mastiffs are big old dogs and if they don't want to do something, that's the end of it. Harald ended up getting into a tug-of-war with Tomsk and with one final pull Harald yanked the collar off Tomsk and went flying onto the stage. Not surprisingly, this raised a titter or two among our audience and he ended up getting a round of applause. Apart from going a bit red, Harald took it all in his stride and finished the scene with a pretend dog. After he handed the collar and lead to me, I then ran off to find poor Tomsk. God only knows where he was. On a bus back to the pub, most likely! In the end, I found him cowering behind some old scenery that was resting against a wall. He was actually shaking, bless him.

As soon as the show was over I took Tomsk back to the landlord of the pub and explained what had happened. 'I'm afraid he got stage fright,' I told him. 'He was great in rehearsal, though. If he can get over his nerves, he's definitely got a future.'

The following day I went to the butcher's, bought a huge bone, and took it down to the pub. Apparently Tomsk was back to his old lethargic self, no thanks to me, so I left the bone with the landlord, just in case he recognised me!

Despite making enquiries I have no idea what happened to Harald Norway, although if he were still alive he'd be at least 110. He, like many actors I've known over the years, liked the odd drink, and every night he used to give me a bag which had four empty quart bottles in it, which is the equivalent to about eight pints. After he had also given me some money, I'd then go across to the local pub and have them filled up with mild beer. I don't think he ever drank before a show, but he'd certainly have a quart in the interval and then after the show had ended it would be back to his dressing room and glug, glug, glug, glug. He could certainly put it away could old Harald.

Another animal reared its head when we were doing a play called *Lot's Wife*. When I was handed my prop list, right at the bottom it said, 'One Goat'.

I found the stage manager and said, 'It says here I've got to find "one goat". You don't mean a live one, do you?'

'Have you ever seen a stuffed goat?' replied the stage manager.

He had me there. 'No, I don't think I have,' I said.

'Well, you'd best find a live one then.'

Fortunately, he had already cast a goat and all I had to do was go and collect it. He'd borrowed it from a farmer who was based about 7 or 8 miles away and so I had to get a bus up there. I had to do this trip every day, by the way. There and back. When I arrived at the farm on the first occasion I suddenly wondered how on earth I was going to get the goat back to the theatre.

'You can take her by bus,' said the farmer. 'She's tame enough. Don't worry, lad. She won't cause you any bother.'

I knew you were allowed to take dogs onto a bus, but I had no idea goats were allowed too. The things you learn. I did get some very strange looks as we boarded and when the conductor clocked us he almost lost his cap.

Me and my sister Veronica. I'm the pretty one on the chair with the page-boy bob. I'd have been about two at the time.

Tudor Wench. Not me, of course. That's the name of the play. I was paid a guinea and a Dinky toy for standing like that.

Me in my first long trousers with Oldham Repertory Company a very long time ago. I think it was the Christmas party. I'm on the right, obviously, and the man standing next to me is the wonderful Douglas Emery. Happy days!

Me in my first collar and tie. I must have been about fifteen here.

Playing a young Welsh boy in *The Druid's Rest*. Look at that hair! I had to learn one or two Welsh words for this.

Me (back row, second left) and some fellow Paras. Fred Essex is bottom left and right there in the middle is the genial Jack Marlborough. Look at that smile! Next to him is Jock Graham, who almost flattened me, and right at the end is Private Haddert, who was almost clubbed to death with a Swan Vesta.

I knew I'd find it! Here I am collecting my shooting certificate from the Mayor of Altrincham.

If you see me cock my leg, run for it! Here I am playing Boris the St Bernard in *Antarctica* at the Players' Theatre. I can't believe it was 1957. *(Michael Boys)*

One of my all-time favourite co-stars. With Sid James in *Tommy the Toreador*.

With Tommy Steele and Sid James in *Tommy the Toreador*. I spent several weeks in Seville with these two and, if you believe Mr James, I ended up winning a boxing match.

As Paco in the very enjoyable *Tommy the Toreador*.

With Ron Moody and David Kossoff in Richard Lester's film *The Mouse on the Moon*.

Me on a wire filming *The Mouse on the Moon*. The poor devil at the bottom is my old friend Gerry Crampton.

Oldham's very own Errol Flynn. *(Harry Gillard)*

With Juliet Mills and Kenny Williams in *Carry On Jack*, my favourite of the three I made.

Wearing a nightie and clutching a toy rat with Percy Herbert and Charles Hawtrey during *Carry On Jack*.

As midshipman Albert Poop-Decker in *Carry On Jack*. I had a lot of fun filming this but still managed to get into Kenny Williams's bad books.

Put her down, Cribbins! Taking Barbara's measurements – and nothing else – during a scene in *Carry On Spying*.

With Ronnie Fraser and Barbara Windsor in *Crooks in Cloisters* in 1964. *(Associated British Picture Corp. Ltd)*

Bella *(above left)* and Megan *(above right)*. Adopted enemies who ultimately became the best of friends.

(left) With Gill and Bessie, sitting on the banks of the River Thames at a friend's house.

As Albert Perks in *The Railway Children*. This was Lionel's film. No doubt about it.

With James Mason, taking direction from the genial Mr Jeffries.

With Alfred Hitchcock and Barry Foster in Covent Garden during a break in the filming of *Frenzy*. *(Popperfoto/Getty Images)*

'Upstairs with that,' he said, pointing at my friend.

When he eventually came to collect the fares I got to utter the immortal line, 'One and a goat, please.' I thought I was being quite humorous, but the conductor didn't think so. He just took my money and shook his head at us both. It was tuppence for me, by the way, and a penny for the goat.

For two weeks every year we'd have to vacate the Oldham Coliseum and make way for a visiting company – something like the Old Vic or a company funded by the Arts Council. You know the kind of thing. Although I still had to work as normal it gave the actors a break, which was nice, and it also gave the rest of us the chance to work with some big names and on some West End productions. I saw my first Shakespeare due to one of these visiting companies. The play was *Twelfth Night* and the star was Wendy Hiller, who played Viola. They came up for an entire week and every show was packed to the rafters.

But it wasn't all animals, film stars and gin at Oldham Rep. Oh, my word no. I once played the role of Stanley in a production of *A Streetcar Named Desire*. You're confused now, aren't you? You're thinking, didn't Marlon Brando play Stanley? Well, yes, he did. In the film. We did ask if he'd like to come over to Oldham to reprise his portrayal, but he was otherwise engaged. They're a temperamental lot these Hollywood types. Anyway, picture this, if you would.

I hadn't long been demobbed when this took place, so I was in fairly good shape. I made my entrance wearing a pair of jeans and a tight-fitting T-shirt and the first thing I had to do after making my entrance was to take off the T-shirt, wipe it under my armpits and then throw it away. I did this on the first night and a gentleman on the front row actually threw up! Talk about a showstopper. I stood there looking at him for a second and, once the shock had worn off, I carried on.

Without a word of a lie, I could dedicate this entire book to my time with the Rep, but we've only got space for a couple more tales.

One of the most memorable plays we had in my second spell at Oldham Rep was called *The Fourposter*. Written by a Dutchman called Jan de Hartog, it tells the story of a thirty-five-year marriage via what goes on in the bedroom and features two people – the man and wife, obviously – and a fourposter bed. That's about it. It was made into a film in 1952 starring Rex Harrison and Lilli Palmer and although I haven't seen it since the 1950s, I thought it was good at the time. The play starts with them arriving in the bedroom on their wedding night and the entire first scene concentrates on them getting ready for bed. The first thing the husband does as they enter the bedroom is throw his new bride playfully onto the bed and on the first night in Oldham the damn thing collapsed! Isn't that supposed to happen towards the end of the wedding night? Anyway, the assistant stage manager and I, a delightful chap called Brian Carlton, obviously had to act quickly as, despite the prop malfunction, the show had to go on.

'What the heck are we going to do?' asked Brian.

'Hang on a second,' I said. 'Let me think.'

As prop malfunctions go this was quite a big one as the bed was the entire focus of the play and we had to somehow fix it without stopping the first act. What we had going for us was the fact that the foot of the bed was facing the audience, and that there was a drape covering the underneath bit.

After exercising my enormous brain for a few seconds I came up with an idea.

'Got a penknife?' I asked Brian.

'I think so,' he said, rifling through his pockets.

'Good. Well, follow me.'

The back wall of the set, in front of which the broken bed stood, was made out of canvas and when Brian and I arrived behind the bed I asked him for the knife.

'What are you going to do?' asked Brian.

'First, I'm going to cut the canvas,' I said confidently. 'Then, you and I are going to creep in under the bed, turn onto our backs, and prop up the bed with our knees.' I probably said the second part of the plan slightly less confidently than the first, but it was all I had with regards to any bright ideas, so we had to run with it.

Fortunately for Brian and me, there was an awful lot of dialogue in the first scene, which meant I was able to cut a hole without the audience noticing. OK, so the walls might have flapped around a bit, but that was standard practice in repertory theatre. Everything wobbled!

After creeping through the canvas and then under the bed we got into position. 'Ready,' I whispered to my fellow ninja.

'Ready,' confirmed Brian.

'OK then, one, two, three, lift!'

I have no idea what this must have looked like to the audience but unless they were aware that Brian and I had cut a hole in the canvas they must have thought it was magic. One minute, the man and wife are lying on a broken bed chatting away about their wedding or whatever, and the next minute they're slowly rising skywards. Brian and I stayed there for the whole of act one, which was about an hour. That bed weighed an absolute ton and it was touch and go at one point as to whether we'd make it to the interval. We did, fortunately, and once the curtain came down we were able to support the bed with some boxes ready for act two. I've already told you that my knees are made out of titanium these days, haven't I? I wish I'd had titanium knees then.

Not too long after *The Fourposter* had finished, which would have been sometime in 1952, my penknife-wielding assistant Brian Carlton left Oldham Rep for pastures new. This obviously left a vacancy in the stage-management department and after not very long at all a replacement was found. Gillian McBarnet was her name and she was medium height, slim, very attractive and she had dark brown hair. Little did I know, but her arrival would have a dramatic effect on my life. I say, *little did I know*, because the lovely Miss McBarnet couldn't stand the sight of me for the first few weeks and if somebody had suggested to either of us that we might end up getting married – not to mention staying married for over six decades – I think we'd have laughed in their faces. I know Gillian certainly would. She'd probably have bashed them over the head, too! Apparently, I was bossy. Me, bossy? That's an outrageous suggestion. Cuts like a knife, it does.

It's fair to say that Gillian and I were very different. For a start, she came from quite a posh family, unlike me, and while I probably sounded a bit like George Formby, she sounded like

Vivien Leigh. Gillian's father had been a major in the Scots Guards and unfortunately he'd been killed at the Battle of Anzio in 1944. Her mother, Barbara, lived in Chelsea and, as I'd find out later, Gillian had lots and lots of disapproving aunts!

She may well have thought I was a bossy old so-and-so, but I rather liked Miss McBarnet. She was fiery, just like me, and she didn't suffer fools. She was also very, very pretty, so once we'd come to an understanding professionally – i.e. I'd stopped being quite so bossy (all right, I might have been a little bit) – we started stepping out together. Now there's an old-fashioned idiom for you. I haven't heard that one in years. It pre-dates courting, that one.

In 1954, after spending almost ten years at Oldham Rep, if you discounted my two years of National Service, I finally managed to pluck up the courage to break away. Some months prior to this, Gillian had moved back to London to live with her mother. I'd already been considering giving London a go but with my beloved now residing there in a big house in Chelsea my mind was made up. Professionally, it was almost a now-or-never situation. I was twenty-six years of age and, although I'd been in the business for a decade, I'd spent all of it with one company. Bearing in mind the life expectancy of an adult in the UK was probably about sixty at the time, I was approaching middle age! Family and friends had been willing me to give it a go for years and so, with Gillian waiting for me and the family cheering me on, I decided to pack my handkerchief, à la Dick Whittington, and go and seek my fortune. I didn't have a cat, though. There was just me.

Before arriving in London I'd managed to get some repertory work at Weston-super-Mare (birthplace of the genial John Cleese, don't you know) and, after wowing them with my talents for a few weeks, I finally arrived in the big city.

Despite having a few quid tucked away – at least enough to keep me in bedsits for a while – I didn't have an agent, so I really was starting from scratch. One of the first things I did was work for a company called Associated London Cleaning as a window cleaner, and luckily enough they were based out of Chelsea. I'd managed to find myself a little bedsit close by so when I wasn't working it was easy to see Gill. One of the best contracts Associated London Cleaning had was the Victoria and Albert Museum in nearby South Kensington, and one day I was sent off to work there. Whoopee! As somebody who's not averse to a little bit of art, history and design, this was right up my street and I literally used to run to work. The problem I had with this job was that I couldn't keep my eyes off the exhibits and so instead of cleaning the windows like I should have been, I just stood on my ladder gawping. That job didn't last long.

Gill, by the way, had needed to move back to London because Oldham Rep didn't have the money to keep her on. As with the vast majority of aspiring actors and actresses who became out of work, she'd ended up back at the family home and, just like me, she was looking for a way back in.

One of the other jobs I had prior to becoming a catwalk model and international superstar was at the Watney Stag Brewery in Pimlico. Now then, this'll take some of you back a bit. Back in the 1960s there used to be something called Watney's Red Barrel, which at the time was by far the most popular beer in the country. This was a few years before that but even then the company was producing about 40 million gallons a year. How do I know that? Never you mind. I just do.

I was basically a dogsbody in the cooperage at Watney's, which is where the barrels were made and managed, and all I really did was shift and carry the empty ones about the place and then stack them. There's a bit of a knack to rolling and stacking beer barrels, let me tell you. And believe me, you've got to be fit. As you might imagine, not all of the empty barrels were empty, if you see what I mean, and there were always one or two that mysteriously had some beer in them. Some of the blokes I worked with had been at the brewery for a good thirty or forty years and they'd got it off to a fine art. They weren't exactly stumbling around, but there was always a pint on the go if you fancied one.

''Ere, where's the ale, Frank?'

'It's over there on that stack by the door. Bottom barrel.'

'Lovely!'

I used to start my shift at 7 a.m. and there'd always be at least four or five blokes walking around with one on the go. Because I was the youngest and fittest, I was the one who did the majority of work. 'Get Bernie to do it,' was the usual refrain when anything strenuous needed doing.

You're going to want to know if I imbibed, I suppose. Well, what do you think? I did have the occasional libation, just to be sociable. Gill used to complain that when I came home after a shift I always used to stink of beer. Funny that. I'll tell you what, though, it was a very happy place to work was Watney Stag Brewery. Lots of lopsided smiles!

Now, what else did I do while I was waiting for stardom to sweep me away? That's it, I spent time labouring on a building site. This was quite prophetic in a way because, in just a few years' time, not only would I be singing a song about being a labourer, but I'd also be appearing as one in a short film along-side Ronnie Barker. That's for later, though.

Because the money was OK, one thing this particular job enabled me to do was to get married to Gill, so although it wasn't as sociable as the job at Watney's, it was better for our future.

Believe it or not, one of the first things I had to shell money out for with regards to our wedding was a shirt for my best man. I'm not joking. You remember Jim Cassidy, my fellow Pennine Ranger? Well, he'd moved back to Ireland by this time and when I asked him if he'd like to be my best man he agreed immediately. 'Of course I will, Barney,' he promised. 'Just you say where and when.' Jim was true to his word and he arrived the day before the wedding, with no luggage, wearing a short-sleeved sports shirt with just two buttons on it.

'Jim,' I said. 'You do realise there's a wedding taking place tomorrow? My wedding?'

'Yes, of course I remember,' he said indignantly. 'Why on earth do you think I'm here?'

'Yes, but what are you going to wear to my wedding, Jim?' I asked patiently. 'You're the best man.'

After looking himself up and down Jim shrugged his shoulders. 'Well. This, I suppose.'

After depositing a fiver in his hand I sent Jim down to Barkers department store on Kensington High Street to buy a new shirt.

Fortunately, he came back with one that had more than two buttons on the front of it and, with his best man's speech already written and memorised, he was ready for the big day.

Next thing I had to do was to get the family down from Oldham. They all loved Gill to bits and when I told them about the wedding they were over the moon. I don't think I'm speaking out of turn by saying that I also got on very well with Gill's mum, and so despite the obvious social differences between our two families we seemed to have a lot more going for us than against us. The only people who didn't approve of the union were the aforementioned aunts. Actually, disapproving is probably too strong a word. For some of them. They were just worried about Gill marrying an actor, which is understandable. And I was acting, by the way. Of course, I've forgotten to tell you this. While I was working on the building site I'd managed to get some work in Hornchurch doing, yep, you guessed it, rep. Well, it was paid work, and at least it stopped me from going rusty.

I'd appeared in an initial show at the Queen's Theatre Hornchurch, a pantomime, at the end of 1954, and had been invited back there while I was labouring. That initial production was *Aladdin*, by the way, and I was appearing alongside an actress called Joan Plowright. I played a member of the Peking constabulary (there were two of us, Wobbli and Bobbli), and Joan – the future Tony Award and Golden Globe winner and Mrs Laurence Olivier – played Itti Sing.

Apparently, while questioning Gill about the man she was going to marry, one of her aunts said to her, 'But Gillian, you don't know where he's been,' to which she replied, 'Actually, I know exactly where he's been. I've been going out with him for three years!' My wife is, and always has been, a very strong woman and so the aunts didn't stand a chance.

About a week before the wedding the producer at Hornchurch, a chap called Stuart Burge, came to see me just before a show – *Witness for the Prosecution* by Agatha Christie.

'I've been thinking, Bernie,' he said. 'You know you're getting married next Saturday afternoon?'

'Yes,' I replied. 'That's right.'

'Well, you do realise you've got two shows that day.'

Stone me, he was right! I hadn't thought about work.

When I arrived home that evening the first thing I did was go straight round and see Gill. 'Erm, we've got a slight problem about Saturday,' I said.

'What do you mean, a problem?' she replied nervously. Heaven only knows what she was thinking.

'I've got two shows,' I said. 'One at three p.m., and one at seven-thirty p.m.'

Instead of giving me a right hook, which is what I thought was coming, Gill just looked at me, smiled, and said, 'Well, we'll just have to change the time of the wedding then.'

She's a wonderfully resourceful woman, my wife. Nothing fazes her.

The following morning we asked the priest if we could have the wedding in the morning as opposed to the afternoon.

'How does eleven-thirty a.m. sound?' he said.

'Perfect,' we replied. 'Thanks!'

Next, we had to tell the congregation. That wasn't much of

a problem, fortunately, and so, with a couple of days to spare, we were all systems go.

Gill and I were married on 27 August 1955 (that's right, over sixty-three years ago!), at the Church of Our Most Holy Redeemer and St Thomas More on Cheyne Row in Chelsea. Back then I was a practising Catholic and Gill, who isn't and never has been, very kindly indulged me. It's an absolutely stunning little church. Beautiful. Our priest was a man called Canon Alfonso de Zulueta and, because Gill's father wasn't around, he'd also acted as her chaperone prior to the wedding. We liked to do things proper in those days.

Once the service was over it was back to Gill's mum's house for the reception. Bearing in mind that rationing had only just finished, she'd done a marvellous job catering for what were about thirty people and had been helped out by some of the aunts. They fell into two categories, by the way: the ones who were more curious than disapproving came along, and the ones who were more disapproving than curious stayed at home. They all sent us whacking great presents, though, so we didn't really care either way.

At first, I think my family were totally over-impressed by everything. Apart from our holidays to Blackpool, they didn't have reason to travel very much and everyone was on their best behaviour. Mum saw to that. She was a very proud woman, was my mother, and despite feeling like a fish out of water she was still on duty. At the reception, when the wine began to flow she just sat there with a straight back and kept a close eye on everyone. Nobody was going to overdo it. Not on her watch! When Gill and I left for Hornchurch at about 1 p.m. she cried her eyes out, bless her. I think I might have shed a tear too.

One of my abiding memories of that reception is seeing my best mate and best man, Jim Cassidy, who was looking resplendent in his Barkers attire, leaning against the mantelpiece in the living room (after having had a few) with a glass of champagne in his hand saying, ''Ere, it's better than Guinness!'

That evening, Gill's mum, Barbara, had the unenviable task of entertaining the Oldham contingent and so she took them all up west to see a show. There were people from both families, I think – a great gang of them – and they all went to see a comedy. Mum needed cheering up so it was just what the doctor ordered. Poor Barbara, though. Having to entertain members of your own family's bad enough (especially when you've just catered for your daughter's wedding!) but also being responsible for a coachload of emotional Lancastrians?

CHAPTER SIX

From the sublime to the ridiculous

We're a fair way in now and as well as appearing in nothing but repertory theatre I haven't even got an agent. You must be wondering what's happening. Well, we're not far from my big break now and before you know it you'll be knee deep in *Wombles*, *Railway Children* and portly film directors answering to the name of Alfred. Can you guess who that is?

Here we go then.

After acquitting myself rather well at the Queen's Theatre Hornchurch I was offered a season there, which I duly accepted. At the time Gill and I were living in a lovely ground-floor flat in a place called Redcliffe Square, which is in Earl's Court. The thing is, before I was offered a season at Hornchurch I'd been commuting and it was taking me well over an hour each way on the tube. 'Sod this for a lark,' I cooed to my young wife. 'Let's move to Hornchurch,' and that's what we did. Well, at least for the duration of the season.

Fortunately, as well as me getting paid for acting the fool at the Queen's Theatre, Gill managed to get a job in the pub across the road, which was handy. Although it was frequented by theatrical types and theatregoers, the majority of its clientele seemed to come from the Ford factory in Dagenham. Just like the old boys at Watney's, the blokes who worked in this place could drink a bit and Gill said that the foundry workers would come in after a shift and drink twelve or thirteen pints. What she found most difficult to believe was that they'd always leave the pub walking in a straight line, but after sweating so much in the foundry all they were doing was replacing what they'd lost.

The season at Hornchurch was quite pleasurable, as instead of doing weekly rep we'd do a show every two weeks. We did a lot of comedies, which enabled me to hone my skills as a comedy actor. Not that I wanted to be a comedy actor. I just wanted to act. I did seem to have a gift for it, though, not to mention a face! One of the first plays we did during that season was a farce about civil dignitaries called *The Mayor's Nest*. It was written by Pauline and John Phillips and starred *moi*, Anna Wing, who went on to play Lou Beale in *EastEnders* (she was already in her forties then), Patsy Byrne, who played Nursie in *Blackadder*, and a tall, distinguished-looking actor named Graham Crowden. Remember him? He appeared in hundreds of things over the years but is probably best remembered for playing Tom Ballard alongside Stephanie Cole in the marvellous sitcom, *Waiting for God*. Not a bad little cast.

Because these shows ran for a couple of weeks rather than a few days we were able to do them justice. And ourselves. This was reflected in the reaction we got from the press, not to mention the public. The *Stage* was one of the first papers to come and see *The Mayor's Nest,* and the review was amazing. How about this for an opening paragraph: 'It cannot be postulated that the patrons of the Queen's are endowed with greater risible faculties than theatregoers elsewhere, and as they filled their theatre with almost continuous laughter last Monday night it can be deduced there was a lot about which to laugh.'

To be honest, I only understand about half of it. It sounds good, though!

Another play we did was *The Recruiting Officer* by George Farquhar, which follows the social and sexual exploits of two officers, Captain Plume and Captain Brazen. Yet again, the *Stage* was one of the first newspapers to review the play, swapping verbose flattery for damning with faint praise: 'The acting is very good, even by this theatre's standards. Bernard Cribbins, playing the ingenious Sergeant Kite, gives a comedy performance that will long be remembered here.'

'Even by this theatre's standards'? Despite what they said about my performance I wanted blood after that.

After a succession of comedies we ended up doing a production of *Saint Joan* by George Bernard Shaw, which is when I was spotted. I was playing Bluebeard, but I also doubled as the English soldier in the epilogue. So, after all that talk about comedy, I end up getting spotted in a drama! The English soldier has a little song to sing. *Rum tee tum tee tum*, or whatever. So I suppose, between that and Bluebeard, it showcased my talents quite well.

In our company at the time there was a lovely chap named David Dodimead. He was quite a popular actor in his day – he did loads of TV and films – and he and I got on very well together. One day, a friend of David's called James Cairncross came to see the play. He came backstage afterwards to congratulate everyone, so he'd obviously enjoyed it. James was also an actor, by the way (he was in *Doctor Who* quite a bit in the 1960s), and a few days later he heard on the grapevine that a man called Lionel Harris was setting up a musical version of Shakespeare's *The Comedy of Errors*. The music was being written by Julian Slade, who'd had a big hit with *Salad Days*, and it was being staged at the Arts Theatre, which is on Great Newport Street just off Charing Cross Road. Apparently, the only roles Lionel Harris hadn't cast yet were the twin clowns, Dromio of Syracuse and Dromio of Ephesus, and when he got word of this James Cairncross very kindly got in touch with Lionel and recommended me for both parts. 'Go to Hornchurch and have a look at Cribbins,' he said. 'As well as playing Bluebeard he sings in the epilogue, so you'll see him doing a bit of everything.'

To cut a long story short, Lionel came to see me in *Saint Joan* and straight afterwards he offered me both roles. I don't know if this had ever been done before, one actor playing both, but it was a nice idea and was certainly doable.

We started rehearsing at the start of 1956 and once again I was surrounded by a lot of very talented people. Patricia Routledge (you don't need me to tell you who she is) played Adriana and Jane Wenham was Luciana. The Duke was played by James Maxwell, one of my colleagues at Hornchurch, and David Dodimead got a role too, playing Aegeon. I'll tell you who else was in this production of *The Comedy of Errors*: an actor called Roy Skelton, who played Shift. Although he's not a household name, a lot of people reading this will know exactly who Roy Skelton is. In the 1960s Roy began providing the voices for *Doctor Who* villains such as the Cybermen, the Krotons and my very good friends, the Daleks. I've got a wonderful story to tell you about them later. I can't wait to tell it. Roy also provided the voices for both Zippy and George in *Rainbow*, so even if you don't know his name, you'll definitely know his voice.

Some of you might be wondering how it was possible for one person to play twins, especially live and on stage. To be honest, the twins only really had one scene together and we achieved that by me walking around a huge pillar. I'd made them very different, by the way, so they were totally distinguishable. One was a bit of a Jack the Lad, and the other was soft and a bit dopey. That was important, especially for the pillar scene. I'd go around talking as one twin, and then the next time I appeared I'd be the other one. It sounds a bit strange, but I promise you it worked. Very well, as a matter of fact. The critic at *The Times* said, 'Mr. Bernard Cribbins plays both Dromios and makes a decided success with the double part, neatly distinguishing the lugubrious one with the happy-go-lucky counterpart who gets his master into the more serious trouble.' That was one of my first reviews in a national newspaper. If only they'd all been that good!

After *The Comedy of Errors* had finished some of us were invited to take part in a short tour of *Salad Days* to Ireland, which, given my heritage – or at least some of it – I was more than happy to accept. I say a short tour. It was really a week in Dublin, but it was great fun. One of the highlights of my time there, or, at least, the thing that makes me laugh the most, happened during the show although not on stage. As with *Saint Joan* and *The Comedy of Errors*, I had to play more than one role in *Salad Days*. I also had one or two quick changes and so given all the activity I was given a dresser. Whenever I think about dressers I'm always reminded of Ronald Harwood's play called *The Dresser*. Harwood had once been a dresser to the great Shakespearean actor Donald Wolfit (who was soon to be a co-star of mine) and so he'd written a play about it. In the play, the dresser is devoted, attentive and he continually fusses around the actor, much to the old boy's annoyance. The reason I mention this is because in Dublin I had the antithesis of Ronald Harwood's creation. In fact, there is but one word to describe my Gaelic helper – apathetic. Whenever I had to do a quick change I'd run off stage, rip off my costume and start scrambling around for what I needed to change into. All the time my 'dresser' would be standing there watching me with a look of mild interest. Then, once I'd finished dressing myself, he'd say in a broad Dublin accent, 'Are you all right?' That was his contribution to the evening's entertainment. 'Are you all right?' He should have been helping me!

On returning we then had a two-week stint in the West End and so, after centuries doing rep, I'd appeared in two West End theatres and had done a tour overseas, albeit in Ireland, in the space of a few months. Most bizarrely of all, both shows had been musicals. Tipped to play comedy, discovered in a drama, and then ends up in two musicals. I ask you! You couldn't have guessed that one. Or two.

Not long after arriving back in England from Dublin I was offered my first television role. I'd been approached by an agent during the run of *The Comedy of Errors* and he'd put me up for a television series called *The Black Tulip*, in which I played a Prince's Guard in an episode called 'Danger' (I think that had something to do with pirates), and *David Copperfield*, in which I played Thomas Traddles. I did six episodes of that and I appeared alongside dear old Robert Hardy, who played David. Funnily enough, that was directed by Stuart Burge who was the director at Hornchurch when I went there.

The only thing I really remember about those early television appearances is being absolutely bloody terrified. I gave an interview in the early 1960s and I'd literally just finished doing a live television play. It had gone OK but on several occasions I'd come close to drying up and I told the journalist all about it. You see, if you're doing theatre and you make a mistake, you can usually recover. Not always, but usually. Make a mistake in live television, however, and there really is no hiding place. Everything is timed to the nearest second and if you balls it up the camera doesn't wait for you to try and make amends, it just moves on. Also, if the cameraman or the director make a mistake, it looks like it's your fault, so you can't win. The very thought of live television used to make my stomach turn somersaults.

Something that's worth a quick mention here is that soon after leaving Hornchurch I was invited back there. Not as a company member, but as a visiting actor. Now I was getting a name for myself I was becoming slightly newsworthy, I suppose, and from the company's point of view I was able to slip back in no problem. I did have to think twice about this as I feared it might be a step backwards, but I was wrong. A lot of actors and actresses who'd started in rep kept going back for a variety of reasons. Some of the roles they offered me at Hornchurch after I was no longer part of the company were marvellous and one of the most memorable was Estragon in Samuel Beckett's *Waiting for Godot*. Richard Dare, who was about to appear on television as Harrison, the Private Secretary, in *Quatermass and the Pit*, played Vladimir and Dinsdale Landen and Tom Chatto played Pozzo and Lucky. That really was a great experience but, as much as I enjoyed playing straight theatre, that wasn't where I was destined to go.

By the end of 1956, the only thing that I hadn't done that was on my immediate 'to do' list, apart from going sea fishing, winning millions of pounds and travelling the world, was get the chance to appear in a few films. This had started to change once I'd got myself an agent, and the first film I was put up for was *Yangtse Incident: The Story of HMS Amethyst*. Richard Todd, William Hartnell and Akim Tamiroff played the leading roles and it was all about a British warship getting caught up in the Chinese Civil War. To be honest, I had to look up the synopsis as I couldn't remember what the film was about. All right, clever dick! I know it was about HMS *Amethyst*; I just couldn't remember what happened. You see, in those days, if you had a small role in a film you'd literally turn up having learned your lines, play your scene or your scenes, and then go off and do your next job. If you were lucky enough to have one, of course. Some actors, people such as Sam Kydd, Cyril Chamberlain or my old pal David Lodge, used to make hundreds of films and would sometimes make two or three in a week, depending on where they were being filmed. It was a conveyor belt.

Yangtse Incident was being produced by Herbert Wilcox, who was married to Anna Neagle, and it was being directed by Michael Anderson, whose previous film, *Around the World in 80 Days*, had just won the Oscar for Best Picture. The part I went up for was Able Seaman James Bryson, who was a sonar operator, and when my agent called me and told me I'd got the part I was really rather pleased. The money wasn't much good, but it was being filmed at the famous Elstree Studios and on HMS *Amethyst*. She was about to be scrapped, apparently, but the producers managed to get her a stay of execution. It's not often you get to make a film about something and use the real thing as a set. One other bonus, for me at least, was that I was going to have a short scene with William Hartnell. He hadn't yet appeared as Doctor Who, but William Hartnell was a big name in the 1950s and he was a considerable actor. To have a scene with him in my first film was a big deal.

I can't remember how many days I did now – three or four, maybe – but the majority of scenes I appeared in were quite tense. There was one in which we were supposed to be sailing through some shallow waters down the Yangtse River and I had to call out the depth of the water underneath us. 'Three fathoms. Two fathoms.' As the water became shallower the camera had to zoom in on my face in order to build up the suspense and by the time we got to two fathoms all you could see on the screen were my eyes and part of my perspiring face. Shortly before we shot this scene, the lighting cameraman, a chap called Gil Taylor, took me to one side and said, 'Now look, Bernard, we're going to be right in your face for this shot, so whatever you do, don't blink. If you do, it'll look like two condors mating.'

Because I was trying to be professional, and because I'd never seen two condors mating before, I just nodded, but in hindsight it was a great line and it still makes me chuckle to this day. I knew exactly what he meant, though, and being put on the spot like that was great experience. I think I managed to pull it off.

There's an ever so slightly sad footnote to this story. One day when we were filming on the HMS *Amethyst*, the chap Richard Todd was playing, Commander John Kerans, came on board as a guest of the producer. Commander Kerans had taken command of the ship in 1949 after it had come under fire on the Yangtse River during the final stages of the Chinese Civil War. This was the premise of the film, of course, and in hindsight I think Commander Kerans wished he'd refused the invitation and stayed at home. The *Amethyst* was just weeks away from being scrapped and it had also been turned into a film set. He looked quite upset, bless him. Sometimes it's best not to go back.

Now, if you're ever looking for an example for that old saying, 'From the sublime to the ridiculous', I've got one for you. You see, straight after making my film debut at Elstree Studios, where literally dozens of Oscar-winning movies had been made (that's pretty sublime in my mind), I started appearing in a musical fantasy at the Players' Theatre, which was famous for producing Victorian-style music hall; the show was called *Antarctica*, in which I played – wait for it – a St Bernard dog! Bernard playing a St Bernard. I bet you weren't expecting that! I think it's reasonably ridiculous, don't you? This is worth a mention as the Players' Theatre, which used to be based in the arches underneath London's Charing Cross Station, is where they got the idea for the music hall programme, *The Good Old Days*, which I appeared in back in the 1970s – sometimes, with a friend of mine called Barry Cryer. They've been repeating that on BBC4 recently and it's brought back some wonderful memories. More on that later.

The reason I accepted this role, apart from having nothing else on, was that it was a musical and I love a good sing-song. The St Bernard could talk, by the way, so I wasn't having to woof my way through the proceedings. Nor did I have to cock my leg! It was also quite a big role, for a dog, and I had one or two good tunes to sing. One of these was a duet with the actor Gordon Rollings, who played Glob, the Abominable Snowman. Because it was such a bizarre little show (it was only an hour long) I've decided to do some digging and my pal in the know has managed to find two quotes from the press: one good, and one not so good. I can take the rough with the smooth, you know.

The good one is from the *Birmingham Daily Post*, whose drama critic said, 'Bernard Cribbins enjoys the part and his duet, *Dumb Friends*, with Gordon Rollings as the Abominable Snowman. The piece is very well presented, as everything is on this stage underneath the arches.'

The other quote is from a reviewer from the *Stage*, who thought there was too much Cribbins and not enough everything else. 'Bernard Cribbins takes every chance with Boris, the talking St. Bernard, which unfortunately is allowed such a big share in the story that it inevitably steals the show. Boris is amusing in himself, but should not be allowed to overshadow romance, character, and story, except, of course, if the idea was merely to please the kiddies.'

I actually find that quite a compliment. Also, if you bear in mind which direction my career went in, it was quite prophetic.

My next film role after *Antarctica* was in a Harry Secombe picture called *Davy*, in which Harry plays an entertainer who has to decide between taking a stab at stardom as a solo performer or staying with his family's music hall act. It was the last ever comedy made by Ealing Studios and the part I played was a stage manager in a music hall. How ironic! It was Collins Music Hall, to be exact, which was in Islington and is now a bookshop or something. There used to be an actor called Clarkson Rose who was very famous for playing pantomime dames and I had to get him on stage. That was really all I had to do, and I don't remember much about it. I remember Harry Secombe, though. Boy, do I remember him! He was my first Goon, was Harry, as I hadn't met Peter Sellers or Spike Milligan yet. And what a lovely chap he was. All that laughter was genuine, you know. None of it was fake. Harry was like a counterbalance in *The Goons* – a gifted rose between two mad but supremely talented thorns – and it's no wonder Spike and Sellers adored him.

Spike was a funny old thing. The last time I saw him was a bittersweet experience. Sweet because he came out with a great line, and bitter because he was obviously suffering with the black dog at the time, which is how Churchill used to refer to his depression. Poor Spike used to suffer with this and that last time I saw him he looked like he was in the depths of it. We were at an awards ceremony and Spike and I were on the same table, although at opposite sides. At some point during the proceedings there was only him and me at the table and suddenly I saw him staring at me. Something told me that Spike Milligan wasn't thinking happy thoughts at the time, and as I sat there feeling increasingly awkward he spoke.

'You're not funny,' he said with a sneer.

'Thank you, Spike,' I replied, trying to force a smile. It was a very uncomfortable moment really. Fortunately, some guests then came back to the table and Spike went back into his shell. I could be wrong about the black dog, of course. He might simply have thought I was rubbish!

About thirty or forty years ago Harry asked me to appear in a television special he was making, and naturally I agreed. One day, during filming, I was walking down a corridor at the studios when I bumped into Harry, who was walking the other way. As often happens in these situations, both Harry and I tried moving aside to let the other past, but we ended up going the same way. This went on for about ten seconds until Harry took matters into his own hands. Literally! First, he grabbed me by the neck with his left hand, then, he grabbed me by the crotch with his right. Before I could protest he then raised me up above his head, turned around, put me down, gave me a quick slap on the cheek, said, 'All right Jim,' (Harry called everybody Jim for some reason) and then went on his way. This was all done in one move, by the way. It was seamless. I must have weighed about twelve stone at the time and Harry was well into his sixties. Twelve stone! He was built like a bull was Harry, and he had the strength of one too.

One of the strangest roles I've ever played – even stranger than a talking St Bernard dog, in my opinion – was a moustachioed Brazilian racing driver called Fernando Fernandez. The reason it's even more bizarre than the St Bernard is partly because I'm from Oldham – which is about as far removed from Rio de Janeiro as it's possible to get – but also because I had absolutely no idea how to drive a car, let alone race one. It was called *Lady at the Wheel* and it was yet another musical comedy. As far as I know the show had started life as an undergraduate production at Cambridge University and was being choreographed and directed by a woman called Wendy Toye. Prior to this, Miss Toye had directed many of the most famous musicals and operas in London, and she'd also directed several hit films. Working with her could only do my career good and when the show opened at the Lyric Hammersmith in January 1958 I was riding on a bit of a wave.

The reason I remember this show sixty years on is because I had a showstopping number towards the end of it called 'Siesta'. The song was written by Leslie Bricusse and Robin Beaumont, as were the other numbers in the show, and it was a tango. A few months later it was covered by the Beverley Sisters and released as a single.

I even remember some of the lyrics, God help me. Before you read them, imagine me in overalls with a moustache pretending to be a Brazilian racing river. It's not an easy image to depict but give it a go.

> In Rio de Janeiro in the middle of the day,
> when some of them are working,
> and others are at play,
> in the middle of a wedding or fiesta,
> everything stops – siesta.

It wasn't until November 1958 that I got my first starring role in a big West End play. The Lyric Hammersmith isn't in the West End, by the way, although it's a nice little theatre. I'd certainly had plenty of supporting roles, such as in *The Comedy of Errors*, but nothing in the first division as of yet. The closest I'd come in one of the larger theatres (the Arts only holds 350) was in a play called *The Big Tickle* at the Duke of York's. This comedy by Ronald Millar had started off in April 1958 with the title *A Ticklish Business*, and had premiered in Bournemouth. By the time it had reached London the name had been changed but its chances of a long West End run hadn't. To be honest, it just wasn't very good, and even with the likes of Yvonne Arnaud, Jack Hulbert, Moyra Fraser and Peter Bayliss in the cast, it couldn't be saved. In the end *The Big Tickle* ran for just twenty-seven performances, and, as privileged as I was acting alongside the likes of Yvonne Arnaud and Jack Hulbert, who were both a delight, I was pleased to get out of it. Incidentally, the chap who wrote *The Big Tickle*, Ronald Millar, went on to become a speech writer for Margaret Thatcher and ended up writing her famous phrase, 'the lady's not for turning'. Neither was the play, unfortunately. I think he should have bypassed plays and gone straight into writing speeches.

The premise was that there were three of us, Peter Bayliss, Rex Garner and myself, and we were all burglars. One day, we decide to burgle a house belonging to a famous concert pianist (played by Yvonne, who was a concert pianist in real life), but she collars us and threatens to call the police. In a kind of plea bargain, we agree to help her pull off an insurance scam, and it goes on from there. Quite profound, don't you think?

The most significant thing I remember about this show is Yvonne Arnaud breaking wind, which perhaps tells you all you need to know. It was during a scene when the three burglars had to throw cushions around the room while Yvonne stands centre stage and directs the mayhem. One day, she moved and walked slowly downstage left and as she did we heard a series of farting sounds that seemed to be in time with her steps. *Squeak, parp, phut, blurp.* It was a litany of little trumps. She then turned around and said in her gorgeous French accent, 'Gud evans. Did you 'ere zat squeaky chair?' Peter, Rex and I were done for, I'm afraid, and it took us several minutes to recover. That was a rare highlight.

The only good thing, apart from Yvonne's wind, to come out of *The Big Tickle* was that a producer named Robin Fox came to see it. He was about to stage a new comedy called *Hook, Line and Sinker*, which had been adapted from a French play by André Roussin. The person who'd done the adapting was none other than Robert Morley, who was also the star, and the people playing his wife and his brother-in-law were Joan Plowright and myself. Want to know the plot? Well, I, the brother-in-law, tell my sister that while I was there I overheard Robert's character, Sebastian Le Boeuf, telling another chap that he's been to see the doctor and the chances are he hasn't got long to live. He's got pots of money and so, after relaying this news to my sister, Arlette, we cook up a plan for her to marry Sebastian and then pocket his fortune when he pegs it. Following so far? Not difficult, is it? Unfortunately for Arlette and Kiki, which is my character, Sebastian makes a full recovery and so Arlette and I then proceed to cook up another plan and bump him off. It wasn't what you'd called highbrow, but the audiences absolutely loved it.

There is a part during this play where Kiki has to meet Sebastian after he's sussed what's going on and, because he's in the know, he starts to play Kiki like a fool. This is when the fun really started with this play and I always looked forward to the scene. After a few months Robert started getting bored and, unbeknownst to me, when Robert Morley became bored Robert Morley tended to ad-lib a bit. Even then, ad-libbing was a trait I could not abide and so we were in for trouble. So, in the red corner you had Robert Morley: mischievous and a bit bored, and in the blue corner you had me: contented, unsuspecting and against any kind of improvisation what-so-blooming-ever. What could possibly go wrong? Or indeed right. I bet you're intrigued now.

The day it started was a Saturday during the matinee performance. At the beginning of the aforementioned scene, Robert's supposed to look at me and say, 'Your sister says you've been away in the colonies.' You know, the way that only Robert Morley could? Nobody, but nobody did pompous quite like Robert Morley. After a bit of a pause, I have some dialogue and the scene continues except, during this matinee, instead of saying, 'Your sister says you've been away in the colonies' and then waiting, he then said, 'So what were you doing in the colonies?' I immediately thought, *You bastard!* He was looking at the audience now, as if to say, *You watch him get out of this.* With the audience now au fait as to what was occurring – and they were loving every moment, by the way – I knew I had a fight on my hands. I was on form, though. In fact, I was bouncing.

'I used to work in the jungle,' I said.

'Oh, in the jungle,' said Robert, loving every second. 'How very interesting. Tell me, what did you do in the jungle?'

I knew that whatever I said, he was going say, what or why, so I had to deliver a killer blow.

'Well, I was in charge of the trees,' I said.

'In charge of the trees? What did you do with them?'

'I used to count them.'

No reply. I had him!

After going back to our corners – or our dressing rooms – we reconvened for round two, which was the evening performance. We made it as far as the same scene without any incident but the moment he said, 'Your sister says you've been away in the colonies' a smile came on Robert's face and I knew exactly what was going to happen.

'So,' he said. 'What did you have to eat in the colonies?'

Robert was obviously very happy with this line as after delivering it he turned to the audience and almost bowed. I was ready for him, though. I'd had my Weetabix!

'Oh, all sorts of things really. There's a lot of choice on the jungle.'

I think he thought he had the better of me here.

'Well, what did you have for breakfast?' he said casually.

Quick as a flash, I said, 'As a matter of fact, I used to have an ostrich egg.'

'How fascinating,' said Robert. 'And what did you have for lunch?'

It was time for the killer blow.

'Well, if you have an ostrich egg for breakfast, you don't need any lunch.'

Big laugh!

He wasn't just on the ropes. He was flat on his back doing the death rattle. I have no idea where that came from, by the way. It just appeared in my head.

Robert and I had a bit of fun with this for a while, much to the annoyance of our co-stars. They obviously wanted to finish the play and get off home and while Robert and I were ad-libbing they'd be in the wings pointing at their watches.

After a few days Robert got bored again and took it to another level. This time it didn't work, though, and we ended up having an almighty row.

Later on in that scene I had to walk away from Robert and after turning around again he was supposed to have pulled a gun on me. One day when I turned around he was just standing there with his hands in his pockets laughing. There's nowhere to go in that situation so, as opposed to him opening up the door for us to have a bit of fun, it was just embarrassing. After the show I went to remonstrate with Mr Morley, telling him what I thought, but all I got was, 'I'm the star, darling, I'm the star!' The following night we were back to the script, so it was all forgotten about. Eventually, though, it all started to creep in again, except he always made sure I could reply. He was a mischievous old bugger, but a great actor and an amazing human being.

CHAPTER SEVEN

Checking each other for bogeys

One of the first films in which I had a supporting role, as opposed to just a bit part in a couple of scenes, was *Tommy the Toreador*, which came out in 1959; it was a lovely and lively little musical comedy starring Tommy Steele, Janet Munro and Sid James. I also had my first song and dance number in this one – in a film, at least – called 'Where's the Birdie?'. Me, Sid and Tommy did that number and luckily for the audience it was Tommy who did most of the singing.

Shortly before I was asked to appear in *Tommy the Toreador*, I had a week or so on a film with Arthur Askey entitled *Make Mine a Million*. It was about a soap-powder salesman who manages to get some free TV advertising. One thing about this film sticks out in my memory. As with *Tommy the Toreador*, the majority of my scenes in *Make Mine a Million* were alongside the amiable Mr Sidney James, which was lucky, and this would have been the first time I'd met him.

After a few days the director, Lance Comfort, came up to me and said, 'Right then, Bernard. This is where you drive the ambulance.' He didn't wait for an answer. He just walked off. After catching him up, I tapped him on the shoulder.

'Excuse me, Mr Comfort,' I said.

'Yes, what is it, Bernard?'

'Erm. Well it's like this, see. I can't drive.'

'You can't what?'

'I can't drive.'

'But everybody can drive these days, can't they?'

'I can't.'

'Oh my God!'

He looked around at his crew, as if to say, *Why didn't somebody tell me that this man couldn't drive?* But they all quickly turned their backs on him.

To cut a long story short, they decided just to film me pulling up in this ambulance, which meant I had to steer it, out of gear and with the engine turned off, for about ten yards. There must have been fifteen people pushing this big ambulance and I'd been told exactly when to put my foot on the brake. Sid was sitting next to me, so why they couldn't just let him drive it I don't know. After the first take something wasn't right and so Lance Comfort asked us to do it again. 'Push them back,' he said. The response to his request was, as you can imagine, not exactly enthusiastic and for the next few hours I was about as popular as a skunk at a garden party.

Tommy the Toreador was directed by a chap called John Paddy Carstairs, who was one of those annoying people who could turn their hand to just about anything. As a director, he'd enjoyed all kinds of success and one of his biggest films to date had been that wonderful Norman Wisdom film, *Trouble in Store*. You remember the one where he's working in a department store? That was Norman's first hit film. But as well as directing, John Paddy Carstairs also wrote the screenplays for many of his films and, when he wasn't working in the film industry, he'd either be painting pictures in preparation for an exhibition of his work or writing a successful novel. Doesn't that make you sick? On top of all this, Paddy was a lovely bloke and when he cast me as Sid James's sidekick, Pedro, I may even have done a little dance. This was the first time I ever saw my face on a film poster, by the way. It was done as a cartoon and I'm standing next to Sid wearing a trilby hat and a pinstripe suit.

Tommy the Toreador was filmed at Elstree Studios and on location in Seville, and it's there that most of my surviving memories of this film originate. And they're all good, by the way. Occasionally you get a job where everything just works – socially and professionally – and this was one of them.

I spent most of my time in Seville with Sid James and Tommy Steele, and if you can't have a good time with those two when there's a bit of sun and a few glasses of sangria knocking around then there's something seriously wrong with you.

The funniest thing that happened out there involved a horse-drawn carriage, a case of mistaken identity and very nearly a punch-up. Tommy, Sid and I had just finished filming one day in the centre of town, and Tommy and I hitched a ride back to the hotel in a horse-drawn carriage that had been used in the film that afternoon. As well as being in costume we had make-up on and, as our carriage passed down the main avenue, we started attracting quite a lot of attention. At first I thought they must have recognised Tommy, but after paying more attention it appeared they were shouting something.

'What are they shouting?' asked Tommy.

'It sounds like "marica" to me,' I said.

'They must think we're American,' he said. 'We're British,' shouted Tommy. 'BRITISH!'

'Hang on,' I said. '*Marica* means poofter in Spanish. That's it, Tommy. They think you're a poofter!'

Tommy was wearing a rather colourful toreador's outfit. With the make-up and the hat he did look rather theatrical and the people of Seville had made their decision.

'You what?' said Tommy. He was all for getting out and having a punch-up but fortunately I managed to stop him. We did our best not to laugh (or at least I did), but it wasn't easy.

The day after we'd finished filming in Seville I went out for dinner with Sid and his wife, Val. After the meal – we had prawns covered in garlic followed by crayfish, he said, drooling – and a lot of wine, we wobbled off back to our hotel. On the way Sid spotted a sign saying 'Boxeo', which is Spanish for boxing. After a quick enquiry we found out that it was nearby and outdoors. ''Ere, Bernie,' he said. 'How do you fancy watching a boxing match? It starts in ten minutes.' Val took a taxi back to the hotel and Sid and I headed off. After handing over some pesetas to a fat bloke in the box office we got ourselves a couple of Fundadors, which is a make of Spanish grape brandy, and took our ringside seats. Sid and I were both big fight fans, and as the boxing started and the Fundadors carried on flowing we got more and more excited. We were really quite refreshed! Always one for a good story, when he got back to England Sid told Tony Hancock that I'd become so incensed by what was going on in the ring that I'd taken my jacket off, jumped in under the ropes and had finished off the reigning champion! I didn't, by the way. I was absolutely sloshed!

No sooner had I finished making *Tommy the Toreador* than I was invited to audition for a role in a new film called *Two-Way Stretch*. Directed by Robert Day, who'd been at the helm of an absolutely marvellous movie called *The Green Man* starring Alastair Sim, it had a cast that, even today, has to be one of the best ever assembled for a British comedy. We're talking Lionel Jeffries, David Lodge, Irene Handl, Liz Fraser, Wilfrid Hyde-White, Maurice Denham, Thorley Walters, Beryl Reid, and in my opinion one of the most talented people ever to appear on a cinema screen, Peter Sellers.

The premise, as if you didn't know, involves three cellmates; Dodger Lane (Peter), Jelly Knight (David) and Lennie the Dip (Cribbins), who, with the help of an old crook named Soapy Stevens (Wilfrid Hyde-White) who's pretending to be a priest, break out of jail to commit a robbery before breaking back in again, thus giving themselves a perfect alibi. The script, which was written by John Warren and Len Heath, had me in stitches the first time I read it and I don't think I'd ever been as excited about a job before. Let's be clear, though. As amusing as the script was and as gifted as the supporting cast were, the trump card for *Two-Way Stretch* was Peter Sellers. The previous year he'd made a film called *I'm All Right Jack*, which, as well as going down a storm at the box office, had earned him the BAFTA for Best British Actor. Everybody knew how talented he was, and I think everybody knew that it was only a matter of time before he flew the nest to Hollywood. And we were right. We had him for a couple more years, though, and my word did we make the most of it.

Prior to filming, I hadn't ever met Peter Sellers and I was a bit nervous. I wasn't quaking in my boots exactly and it was nothing to do with Sellers's reputation as a difficult man, as I don't think he had one then. It was just a bit of first-day jitters.

What was different about this film, at least the first part, was that we filmed it chronologically. This might not seem strange to some people, but the fact is that the scenes that make up a film are very rarely shot in chronological order. In fact, sometimes they're shot completely back to front. Some of you will be aware of that, but a lot won't. This can be down to a variety of reasons – logistics, availability, etc. – but because it's so random it can be hard to develop your character sometimes. With *Two-Way Stretch* I had no such issues as the first ten days were spent in a specially built prison cell at Shepperton Studios with Peter Sellers, David Lodge and George Woodbridge, who played the avuncular prison officer, Mr Jenkins. This also allowed me to get to know some of my co-stars and, because we got on well together, that set the scene for the rest of the shoot. Peter Sellers and David Lodge had already been pals for years, but fortunately they weren't at all cliquey and they welcomed me with open arms.

Although he hadn't been poached by Hollywood yet, Peter was obviously earning very good money and at the start of the shoot he was in the process of buying a new car. Because of who he was, different vehicles were being delivered to the studio and luckily for me he took me for a ride in one or two. This was obviously a completely different world to the one I'd been used to, and I was very impressed. I don't think I'd ever really worked with an actual film star before – not for more than a few days – and at the time Peter was very kind, very generous and very accommodating.

One day, a ginormous American Chrysler arrived for him at the studios and, after running out to have a look at it, Peter jumped into the driving seat. 'Do you fancy a ride?' he said to Lodgey and me. Before he'd even finished the sentence we were on the back seat playing with the buttons and telling him to put his foot down. He drove all over Shepperton Studios for about twenty minutes and when we arrived back in the car park he jumped out, threw the keys to the salesman and said, 'Nope. Don't like it.' I just stood there with my mouth open and my eyes on stalks. *What does he mean, he doesn't like it?* I thought. *It's a dream car!* That was Sellers, though. You could never second guess him.

There was a sequence later on in the shoot where Peter, David and I all had to break stones in a quarry. It was filmed near Aldershot, and the day before the shoot was due to take place, Peter asked me how I was getting down there.

'I'm not sure,' I said. 'I'll probably go by train.'

'You don't want to go by train,' said Mr Sellers. 'With all the hoi polloi? I'll tell you what. I can pick you up if you like.'

'Really? That would be great.'

'I'll pick you up outside Waterloo Station at seven a.m.'

The following morning I got up at about 5 a.m., cycled to Weybridge Station, and then got a train to Waterloo. After alighting I waited outside Waterloo and about five minutes later this huge Rolls-Royce pulled up. Lodgey was in the front seat and Sellers was driving.

'Get in quick,' shouted Peter, 'before we get a crowd.'

Naturally I did as I was told and the moment I'd closed my door I said, 'Aldershot please, driver. As fast as you can.'

'Certainly, madam,' said Sellers obediently. 'Hold on tight.'

After the day's shoot Peter gave me a lift back to Waterloo and while dropping me off he got mobbed by a dozen or so people and so signed a few autographs. He and Lodgey sped off in the direction of Waterloo Bridge and I caught my train. I remember thinking, *How the other half live!*

In addition to me, Lodgey and Sellers becoming a bit of a trio, I also became very friendly with Irene Handl, who played my mum, Mrs Price. Irene was an absolutely fascinating lady and was as delightfully eccentric as anyone I'd ever worked with, or have done since. Her mother was Austrian and her father German, and she hadn't started acting until she was almost forty. The only thing you had to be wary of with Irene were her Pomeranian dogs. Yappy little sods, they were. She always had at least two in her handbag, and everyone apart from Irene seemed to be fair game. One morning, she'd just arrived on set and after waving hello I went over to her.

'Good morning, my dear,' I said. 'And how are you today?' Just as I went to kiss Irene on the cheek one of these deadly balls of fluff leapt out of her handbag and went for me. 'Jesus Christ!' I cried, flying backwards. How the hell I managed to avoid the little swine I'll never know.

'Now, now, Foxy,' said Irene pretending to scold her little friend. 'Bernie's a friend of ours. You know Bernie? Come and say hello to Foxy, Bernie. Come and make friends.'

I'd have done anything for Irene and so once I'd made sure I hadn't wet myself, I put a smile on my face, walked forward and went to wring the little bugger's neck. Sorry! I meant, I went to make friends with Foxy.

'That's better,' said Irene. 'See, Foxy. Bernie's not a scary man, is he?'

I did actually contribute a gag in *Two-Way Stretch*. I can't remember it verbatim, I'm afraid, but you remember the scene where Irene comes to see me in prison on visiting day? I'm wrongly assuming you've seen the film, but if you haven't, that's what happens. I get all excited about seeing Irene, 'Oh Mum, it's wonderful to see you,' and then end up pressing my face against the grille. 'Don't do that,' she says. 'You'll mark yer face.' That was my idea, that was. On paper it's not much of a gag really, but when it's delivered by somebody as skilled as Irene Handl in that disapproving cockney brogue of hers, it's just marvellous. Nobody could tell people off quite like Irene Handl. She was an extraordinary actress.

Another great part in *Two-Way Stretch* is Lionel Jeffries's unforgettable prison officer, Sidney Crout, or *Sour Crout*, as everyone called him. The voice that Lionel created for this character was on the button; a kind of bark with a squeak at the end. The performance itself was quite extraordinary, as he managed to amalgamate consummate comic timing and delivery with nervousness *and* authority. I don't think I'd ever seen that before. Nor have I seen anybody steal as many scenes in a film, which is ironic, bearing in mind he was playing a prison officer. Like Peter Sellers, I'd never met Lionel prior to us making *Two-Way Stretch* and I'm both pleased and proud to say that we became very good pals. We remained friends for over fifty years, until his death, God bless him. That happens rather a lot when you get to my age, but there's no point getting hung up about it. It's what happens.

As well as providing me with friendship, not to mention the odd libation, Lionel also offered me a number of roles, one of which became one of the biggest of my career. I wonder which that could be? Every few weeks he used to ring me up, usually in the evening, and when I answered the phone he'd say, 'Hello Bernie. It's Li.'

As soon as I knew it was him I'd attract Gill's attention and say, 'It's Li.' She knew I'd be engaged for at least an hour and would go off and do some washing up or something.

'What have you been up to then, darlin'?' he'd say, in that deep, deep voice of his. He'd usually have a glass on the go, and after sitting down and making myself comfortable we'd talk about this, that and the other.

I went to a party at Lionel's house once in the late 1960s when he must have been making *Chitty Chitty Bang Bang* as one of the first people I saw was Dick Van Dyke. He was sitting in the corner with a glass of something and feeling no pain. Funnily enough, despite playing his father, Lionel was about six months younger than Mr Van Dyke. He must have had a difficult paper round. Somebody else I met at that party was Roald Dahl who wrote the screenplay for *Chitty Chitty Bang Bang*. Not a lot of people know that. Or that it is based on a book by Ian Fleming. What a team, though, Roald Dahl and Ian Fleming.

At the time, I had literally just finished reading *Charlie and the Chocolate Factory* for *Jackanory* and later on that year I did *James and the Giant Peach*. I'd never met Roald before, who was also a neighbour of Lionel's, so it was great timing. I've met a lot of famous people in my life, but I've only met one or two people whom I consider to be a genius, and he was certainly one of them. He was very quiet and also incredibly modest. It was very difficult to flatter Roald Dahl. He just wasn't interested.

Something quite hilarious happened at that party and, if I'm being honest, it was a result of one or two people having one or two too many. Me included! This must have been at about midnight and I was trying to teach Lionel how to throw a stunt punch.

'What you have to do, Li,' I said, 'is bring the punch up like this and then just at the last second you pull it, just like that. You see?'

'Show me once more, would you, Bernie?' said Li, looking through one eye. 'Then I'm going to try it out myself. I reckon I can do it. I reckon I can, Bernie.'

'OK, are you watching closely, Li?'

If it's familiar to you, try and bring Lionel's voice to mind.

'Oh, I'm watching, my old darling. Don't you worry, I'm watching very closely. Very closely indeed. Off you go, Bernie.'

'Bring the punch up and round, like that, and then pull it. Got that?'

'I got that. I most certainly got that. I'm ready, darling. I'm ready to give it a go. Now just you watch this. You're going to be well impressed.'

Unfortunately, instead of trying it out on me like he should have, Lionel decided to make it a family affair and so tried it out on his son. After forgetting to pull the punch – which was predictable, given what time it was and how much we'd had to drink – he ended up smacking his lad right in the mush. BANG!

What do you think followed? That's right. Absolute chaos.

'Oh my God!' screamed Li as he went to pick up his son. 'Are you all right, my boy? Speak to me. SPEAK TO ME!'

Fortunately no noses had been broken or eyes blackened, but I think that was down to luck and a bad aim rather than judgement. What a night that was.

A few years later I was making a film and Lionel was on the set next to us, starring in a different production. Li came onto our set one day just for a quick nose around and after five minutes or so he said, ''Ere, Bernie. Why haven't you got a chair with your name on the back of it? You're making a film, aren't you?'

'I don't know, Li,' said I. 'I just haven't got one.'

'You haven't got one? YOU HAVEN'T GOT ONE?'

Feigning outrage, Li then started looking around and attracting the attention of members of the crew. 'Did you hear that?' he said pointing at me. 'He hasn't got a chair. He's a star, and he hasn't got a chair! I'll tell you, Bernie, that's a disgrace, that is, because you're a star, my boy, and stars on films should have chairs. Big chairs! I've always said that. Oh yes. It's something I've always said.'

The following day, while everybody was on set, Li came in and presented me with a very old armchair that wouldn't have looked out of place on a tip, and on the back of it he'd written CRIBBINS in chalk. 'There you are, darlin',' he said, patting me on the back. 'That's a chair fit for a star, that is. Fit for a star.'

There is one other story about *Two-Way Stretch*, which I simply must tell you. Towards the end of the film, Dodger, Jelly and I get released from prison and, because he thinks we've had something to do with this robbery, Chief Prison Officer Crout decides to follow us. This part was filmed at Windsor & Eton Central Station, which is on Windsor High Street, and after having lunch one day Lionel and I decided to have a bit of fun. Because I'd supposedly been released from prison I was wearing civvies whereas Lionel was still in prison officer uniform. As we left the café where we'd had lunch Lionel put on his prison cap, grabbed me by the arm, put it up my back and proceeded to escort me up Windsor High Street.

'Right then, you little bastard,' he said. 'Just you wait till we get you back to the nick. We're going to give you a right good kicking.'

Obviously the film had not come out yet and so the members of the public who witnessed this were completely and utterly flummoxed. Some of the older people had no idea who Lionel and I were so they thought it was genuine.

'What's he done, officer?' one old lady said as we passed her. 'He looks like a wrong 'un to me. Lock him up and throw away the key!'

'He's the worst kind of human being, madam,' said Li. 'That's what he is. Don't you worry, though. We know exactly how to deal with his sort.'

I honestly thought this old dear was going to whack me with her umbrella but before that could happen Lionel put my arm behind my back and started pushing me up Windsor High Street again. As all this was going on I was protesting my innocence. I do a very good line in protesting innocence!

'Come on, Mr Crout,' I cried. 'I haven't done anything wrong. I was only looking at that car. I wasn't going to steal it. You ask my mum. She'll tell yer.'

'Ask your mum? She's as bent as you are, Price.'

The people who recognised us were obviously quite bemused at first, but once they realised that it was just a lark they started following us. As we went further up the High Street people started moving out of the way, so it was like Moses parting the Red Sea. Once he'd had enough, Lionel turned a corner and let me go.

I have always wondered whether *Two-Way Stretch* was the inspiration behind the classic Dick Clement and Ian La Frenais sitcom, *Porridge*, with the three main characters, Fletch, Godber and Mackay being based on Dodger, Lennie and Prison Officer Crout. If that's the case, it's a huge compliment. Not for me, Peter or Lionel, but for the film. It's still one of my favourites.

By the end of 1962, not only had I been lucky enough to have a starring role in a couple of West End plays, but I'd also started seeing my name on posters outside cinemas. It was only in small writing, but it was enough to give me a bit of a thrill. It doesn't take much! Despite this progression, I certainly wasn't averse to falling down the billing occasionally, providing it was for the right role and for the right fee. If it provided me with a new experience or two, all the better.

To be fair, I wasn't really that famous then. Not like Peter Sellers. He was a household name at the start of the 1960s, whereas I was more of a recognisable face. Does that make sense? This meant that I could still get away with appearing as an ensemble cast member in a film. At the end of the day, I was a jobbing actor. Actually, I still am. I'll consider any offer that comes along (even a book!) and unless I think it's going to damage my career or ruin my hair, I'll usually give it a go. Game and intrepid. That's me. Incidentally, one of the strangest things I've ever been asked to do was a series called *We Want to Sing* back in the early 1970s. I think I was offered the job because of *Jackanory*, and the idea was that people such as me, Anita Harris, Ken Dodd, Sandie Shaw and one or two others would take it in turns to, as the producers put it, 'have a rousing uninhibited sing-song with 300 children'. What's that saying, never work with children or animals? I didn't know what to make of it at first, but I thought I'd give it a try. I'm pretty sure it was made in Manchester, this series, and each week we were accompanied by the BBC Dance Orchestra and a guest band. We had the Spinners one week, who I'd heard of, and then lots and lots of pop bands, who I hadn't. One week they decided to increase the kiddie-count to 1000 and uncle Bernard here was on duty. Have you ever tried controlling 1000 children in good voice? It's not easy.

Sometime towards the end of 1960 I got a call from my agent, who asked me if I'd be interested in appearing in a film with David Niven. I forget what I said now, but it must have been something like, 'Do bears pooh in the woods?' As well as being a fine actor, David Niven had a reputation for being one of the nicest people in the business and I was really looking forward to meeting him.

The film in question was an Anglo-Italian production called *The Best of Enemies* – or, *I Due Nemici*, as they say in Rome. It was produced by Dino De Laurentiis, who was as mad as a hatter, and it was co-directed by Guy Hamilton and Alessandro Blasetti. Guy Hamilton had recently directed Kirk Douglas, Burt Lancaster and Laurence Olivier in *The Devil's Disciple*, and

Mr Blasetti was considered the father of Italian cinema. The cast, too, represented both countries. On the British side, in addition to David Niven and myself, there was Ronnie Fraser, Duncan Macrae, Harry Andrews, Noel Harrison and Michael Wilding, among others, and on the Italian side, a load of actors who you'll never have heard of. Unless you're Italian.

The film is set during the East African Campaign of the Second World War and tells the story of an Italian captain who wants to release his British prisoners of war so that the British Army will leave the divisions that are under his command alone. With me so far? Before he's able to do this, some Ethiopian tribal warriors sabotage the captain's plans by pinching everyone's shoes and so, in order to survive a long trek through the desert, the Italians and the British have to become friends. ★SPOILER ALERT★ The film concludes with the Ethiopians allowing both the Italians and the British safe passage through the desert, providing that they take their horrible war away with them. It's all a bit silly really, but it was supposed to be a comedy, so why not?

Incidentally, there's a funny little story regarding the dubbing on this film. You see, the English contingent – me, David and Ronnie, etc. – obviously had to be dubbed for the Italian cinemas, and vice versa. The chap playing the Italian captain, Alberto Sordi, was one of the most respected actors in the Italian film industry and before becoming famous he'd dubbed Oliver Hardy's voice for all of the Laurel and Hardy films. When it came to dubbing Alberto in English, the producers decided to use somebody with the most exaggerated, cod Italian accent you have ever heard in your life. Remember the bloke out of *'Allo 'Allo*? The Italian captain with the feathers? Well, it was worse than that. A lot worse! Subsequently, when it came to dubbing the English actors, they all sounded like Italian David Nivens! 'Oh-a hello-a old-a chap.' Terrible! I hope Alberto never got to hear it. He'd have gone absolutely bananas.

Before I go on, there is a connection between me and David Niven. Or, to be a bit more precise, a connection between Gill and David Niven. Niven's older brother, Henry, had been at Sandhurst with Gill's father and he used to stay at their house from time to time, as did David.

Actually, there is another small connection. Although this one's slightly more tenuous, it involves both of us. Just as Gill and I were about to get married in Chelsea we were accosted by somebody from a film crew. It turned out they were shooting a scene for a new film called *Around the World in 80 Days* starring who else but Mr David Niven. Filming had only just begun, and apparently this was one of the very first scenes they shot. After a quick chat they agreed to take a break while the wedding service took place so a disaster was quickly averted. After suffering one or two flops, this ended up being David's comeback film and it bagged no fewer than four Oscars, including Best Picture.

Incidentally, this scene they were shooting involved several horses and just before entering the church I realised that I recognised one of them. 'You see that horse at the end,' I said to my friend Jim. 'The one with the moustache? I'm sure he used to be at Watney's Brewery.'

The horse in question was also called Jim and after closer inspection I realised that it was the very same nag. I used to give Jim a biscuit every morning when I started work and, because he had hair above his top lip, he reminded me of the actor

Jimmy Edwards. I did go and say hello to him but he wasn't interested. No biscuits, you see, and I was wearing a suit. What an amazing coincidence, though.

Right, let's bring in the great man.

The scenes in *The Best of Enemies* that were supposed to be in Ethiopia were actually filmed in the Negev Desert, in the south of Israel. The rest of the location filming took place in Italy, south of Rome. While we were filming in the Negev I invited David out on a fossil hunt one day and while we were walking and talking I mentioned the connection with Gill's family. When I asked him about the McBarnets he seemed to clam up, so I just left it.

I don't know whether you're aware of this, but David's first wife, Primmie, had died in a tragic accident in 1946 after falling down some stone stairs. It happened at Tyrone Powers's place shortly after she and David had moved to America, and I'd heard from quite a few people that he didn't like talking about anything that had happened in his life up to her death.

A few days after that we were filming halfway up a wadi (that's Arabic for a ravine) and it must have been about 120°F. There was me, David, Ronnie Fraser, Harry Andrews and Noel Harrison, as well as the crew. Instead of a trailer, David had this little tent thing that he used to sit in to keep the sun off and the rest of us had umbrellas. When it got to lunchtime David called over to me and said, 'I say. Do you fancy going swimming, old bean? It's rather hot, don't you think?'

Too right I did. I was melting!

'Call the others.' said David. 'We'll take my car.'

Within a few minutes the five of us were heading down this

wadi in David's car towards the Red Sea. Because of the heat we always took our shorts and our snorkels with us, just in case we got the opportunity for a dip, and so we were all set to go.

'We'll have a twenty-minute dip,' said David. 'And then we'll head back and try and eat some of that muck they give us for lunch. We must try and keep our strength up.'

David was right when he said muck. I appreciate that the Negev Desert probably isn't known for its cuisine, but some of the grub they gave us was just inedible. It was all yesterday's stuff warmed up, although where it was the day before I have no idea. Certainly not with us. Fortunately, the heat seemed to act as an appetite suppressant so unless they'd found some fruit from somewhere you just left it.

The moment we reached the Red Sea we put on our shorts, held in our bellies, and went for a swim. The water may have been quite warm, but it was still sub-zero compared to the open air. As we submerged ourselves all you could hear was a collective sigh of relief. Then, once we'd become acclimatised, it was on with the goggles and snorkels, and we were off having a splosh. After about ten minutes Ronnie, Harry, Noel and I were treading water chatting away when all of a sudden David emerged from the deep.

'I say, you chaps,' he said. 'Make sure you keep checking each other for bogeys!'

I think one of us must have had something dangling from our nostrils but instead of pointing out the guilty culprit David took the diplomatic route, which was very him.

Later on in the shoot, while we were filming in Italy, we'd been on location about 200 miles from Rome and the studios.

After the shoot, I was expecting to go back with Noel Harrison, for some reason, but he only had a Mini and couldn't fit me in. Gill was with me, which was nice, and while we were wondering how on earth we were going to get back to our apartment we were approached by Mr Niven. 'I hear you two have been left high and dry,' he said. 'Fancy a lift?'

We didn't need asking twice.

Naturally, Mr Niven had a nice limousine and a driver at his disposal, but instead of him getting in the back with us, he sat in the front passenger seat, leaned over his seat, and told story, after story, after story. Have you ever read *The Moon's a Balloon*, David's autobiography? If you haven't, you really should. It's one of the biggest selling showbusiness memoirs ever written and has sold millions of copies. Gill and I got the majority of that book, verbatim and in person, sitting in the back of his limo. What a charming man he was. He simply loved having an audience.

For the duration of our stay in Italy we were sharing a small apartment with Noel Harrison and his family. It was a bit of a slum, but it was cheap, right on the Mediterranean, and Gill and I rather liked it. Instead of dropping us off there, David, who was staying nearby, asked if he could join us all for supper and, after decamping to a local restaurant on the quayside, he carried on with his 'An Audience with . . .' We had fish soup, white wine and David Niven in full flow. What a combination! Gill still maintains that it's one of the best nights of her entire life, and do you know what, it's probably one of mine, too. There may only have been six of us at the table, but as you'd expect the entire restaurant knew it was him and so really he had an audience of about a hundred and fifty. Days like that don't happen very often.

We finished *The Best of Enemies* in Rome and the last thing I did on the film was a night shoot. Alessandro Blasetti was directing, and the usual crowd were with me: Ronnie Fraser, Harry Andrews and Noel Harrison. I think Mr Niven was there too, but my scenes were with the other three.

For one shot the camera had to be put on a stretch of railway line. It was also attached to a crane, and so as it went back and started filming it was elevated by the crane. These days a shot like that would probably be a doddle but back then it was like raising the *Titanic*. He had a bit of a temper on him did Mr Blasetti, and although it was quite dark he would run alongside the camera as it was going back, shouting, 'VIA VIA VIA VIA VIA!' He may not have been attached to a crane, but I promise you he very nearly took off!

A few days later at the wrap party Gill and I were sitting having a meal in the Villa de Alberto Sordi which, according to a member of staff, had once belonged to the leader of the Fascist Party. It was absolutely massive and outside there was a swimming pool the size of Lake Windermere. Underneath was a room with windows onto the pool so if you weren't in the mood for a dip yourself you could pop down there and watch everyone else splashing about. I have absolutely no idea why, but during the wrap party there was a ginormous rubber duck bobbing about on this pool – it was the size of a cow – and Dino De Laurentiis had paid somebody to push the duck from one end of the pool to the other. That's all they did all evening!

Talking of young Dino, Gill and I were sitting with the great man for dinner that evening. His brother was also with us, as well as a couple of associates. There was an awful lot of Italian flying around and so Gill and I were just onlookers for most of it. Italians seem to talk very quickly, so even if we had understood the language I'm not sure we'd have been able to keep up with them. You need to be fit to speak it. Every now and then we managed to grasp a few words, and I think we even managed the odd reply. At the end of the meal Dino stood up and said, 'Bernard, Gill. How very nice to meet you both,' and then he walked off. The bugger could speak perfect English! It was a great experience, though.

You see what I mean about jobs that might offer one or two new experiences? Everybody wants to work, and everybody wants to do well, but sometimes you have to look beyond the billing and pay packet. We had a couple of weeks in the Negev Desert and then a couple of weeks in Rome. And we got to know David Niven. It's not a bad life.

The next time I bumped into David was in 1966 during the making of the Bond spoof, *Casino Royale*, which took several years to make and had six different directors at the helm. That's right, six: John Huston, Robert Parrish, Joseph McGrath, Richard Talmadge, Ken Hughes, Val Guest and a partridge in a pear tree.

I played a British Foreign Office official called Carlton Towers who drives a female agent pretending to be James Bond from London to Berlin in a taxi. Funnily enough, I hadn't passed my driving test then and while we were filming the taxi driver had to lie down in the cab next to me.

Although filming took place at Pinewood, Twickenham and Shepperton Studios, I'm pretty sure my bit was filmed at Shepperton and my director was the legendary Val Guest, who would later, in about 1980, direct me in a TV movie called

Dangerous Davies: The Last Detective, in which I played the title role, and *Shillingbury Tales*, a rather quaint television series set in a fictional village starring Robin Nedwell and Diane Keen. I played a tinker in that one, called Cuffy, and the character became so popular that I ended up getting my own spin-off series.

I must mention him as he only recently passed, but the wonderful Bill Maynard played my oppo in *Dangerous Davies*. We used to share a caravan while we were on location and one day, after finishing a scene, I ran in to get changed for the next one. Bill, who obviously wasn't required at the time, was sitting there reading his paper, and while I was reaching for my clothes and trying to sort myself out, I started grumbling. 'I'm absolutely knackered, Bill,' I said. 'It's non-stop, this is. It's going to be the death of me.'

Before I could go on, Bill looked up from his newspaper and said, 'Now, now, you said you could do it when you wrote in.' What a killer line! After that I shut up, got changed and went to film the scene.

Peter Sellers played one of the lead characters in *Casino Royale* and by now both David and I knew him of old. I'd appeared with him in *Two-Way Stretch* and *The Wrong Arm of the Law*, which we'll come on to, and David had been in *The Pink Panther*, which had been made shortly after my two. By this time, Peter had started behaving like a prick, for want of a better word, and quite a few of the problems the film had encountered during its production – and there were many, believe me – were down to him. He could be a bit of a pillock, could Peter. But we still loved him.

The genial Mr Niven must have spotted me at Shepperton and as I was sitting there waiting to be called on set (there's an awful lot of waiting around in our business), I suddenly heard a very familiar voice.

'Bernard! How the devil are you, old chap? How lovely to see you. How's Gill? What have you been up to? Are you on this picture too? Oh dear, poor you.'

David had one of those voices you never, ever, tired of hearing, and he could have carried on greeting me all blooming day if he'd cared to. I only had ten or fifteen minutes with him, but it was a complete joy. David didn't just talk, by the way. He was also a very, very good listener, and despite the passing of time he'd remembered everything we'd talked about over in Italy and Israel, and appeared to have seen everything I'd been in. 'That film you did with Sellers. What was it, *The Wrong Arm of the Law*? Absolutely marvellous. I loved your Dublin accent.'

Some people just have it, don't they?

Speaking of Peter Sellers – again – the last time I ever saw David Niven was at Peter's memorial service, which was held at St Martin-in-the-Fields church in London on 8 September 1980. Harry Secombe sang 'Bread of Heaven' – beautifully – and David delivered a very eloquent eulogy. Thanks to a mutual friend of mine and Peter's, a stuntman named Gerry Crampton who was acting as one of the ushers, I'd been seated right at the front and when David got up to read the eulogy, he got to the pulpit, had a look around, spotted me and gave me the biggest wink.

When David died, the porters at Heathrow Airport sent a huge wreath and a card that read: 'To the finest gentleman who ever walked through these halls. He made a porter feel like a king.'

The mark of the man. And what a man he was.

God bless you, sir.

CHAPTER EIGHT

Right Said George

Now then. Do any of you know what a revue is? I expect some of you might. Those of a certain vintage, so to speak. Well, for those of you who aren't yet crumbling away, the revue is a theatrical genre that originated in France. It usually consists of a series of short sketches, songs and dances, dealing mainly with topical issues. It was at its pomp, in this country at least, in the 1920s and was massive in America for decades. By the 1950s the steam was beginning to run out for the revue and some of the last successful ones before it died a death were *Share my Lettuce*, which starred Kenneth Williams and Maggie Smith, and *Pieces of Eight*, which starred Kenny and Fenella Fielding. Because it was basically a form of variety, you used to get all kinds of people both writing for and appearing in revues. Peter Cook wrote his famous 'One Leg Too Few' sketch for *Pieces of Eight*, and later used it himself with Dudley Moore. To great effect, it has to be said. Strangely enough, one of the things that killed off the revue, in its original form, was *Beyond the Fringe*, which really revolutionised comedy. The revue had always been a kind of satirical form of variety, I suppose, and *Beyond the Fringe* took that to a completely different level. It did it properly.

One of the last traditional revues to do well in the West End was called *And Another Thing*, in which yours truly appeared alongside Joyce Blair, her brother Lionel, Sandra Caron (Alma Cogan's sister), Donald Hewlett, Anna Quayle and Anton Rodgers. Everybody in that show went on to do well, including the writers. Most of the songs were written by two chaps called Myles Rudge and Ted Dicks, who you'll hear about in a minute, and the additional songs and material were down to Alan Melville, who had BAFTA coming out of his ears, Charles Zwar, who had been the king of the revue scene in the 1950s, Lionel Bart, who could knock out a tune if he had to, and a gag writer called Barrington Cryer from a rough part of Leeds. *What? Not him again?* I hear you cry. That man would get where water couldn't go. It's not a bad line-up, though, don't you think?

One of the sketches that Barry wrote for *And Another Thing* was an absolute cracker (it was one of many, if memory serves) and if you don't mind I'm going to try and bring it to life here. It featured me, Anton and Sandra, and we're all sitting next to each other at what's supposed to be a tennis match. Anton and Sandra are supposed to be posh, by the way, and I'm the idiot in the middle wearing a flat cap.

As we're sitting there a rally starts and as they follow the ball one way, I go the other. This immediately gets a titter from the audience and then we settle into the sketch. After a while Anton Rodgers's character starts getting annoyed at this and by the end of the rally he's apoplectic. Afterwards he just has to say something (although politely, as he's terribly English) so he leans over and says, 'Do you mind me asking

148

why, when we were looking to the right, you were looking to the left?'

Pause.

'I came in late.'

As soon as I said the line there was an immediate blackout and it always took the audience a second or two to get the joke. When they did though – BOOM! It always got a big laugh.

Incidentally, *And Another Thing* was staged at the Fortune Theatre which is alongside the Theatre Royal Drury Lane and the show that followed us at the Fortune was the aforementioned *Beyond the Fringe*. After that, it was goodnight Vienna for the traditional revue, so we got in just in time.

One evening, after the show, I was visited in my dressing room by a very tall and very well-spoken gentleman named Mr George Martin. As well as being a producer for the record label Parlophone, he was also their A&R man which stands for Artists and Repertoire. One of George's jobs as an A&R man was to visit all the musicals and revues in London to see if there was anything worth recording and, having seen our show, there were a couple of tunes he was interested in. Although I didn't know it at the time, George had a reputation that was second to none in this department and since 1952 he'd produced dozens of hit records. Most of these were what are called novelty records, which are usually nonsensical or humorous little ditties with a bit of a folky feel. They defined British culture pre-Beatlemania and the charts were absolutely full of them. George's first big success had been with a song called 'Mock Mozart' which he'd made with Peter Ustinov and a young Anthony Hopkins. Since then he'd had collaborated with Peter Sellers and Spike Milligan on their Goon-associated LP, *The Bridge on the River Wye*, and about a dozen comedians, actors and actresses, including Terry Scott ('My Brother'), Flanders & Swann ('A Transport of Delight'), Joy Nichols, Jimmy Edwards and Dick Bentley ('Little Red Monkey'), Peter Sellers and Sophia Loren ('Goodness Gracious Me') and Charlie Drake ('My Boomerang Won't Come Back'). He even went on to produce a live recording of *Beyond the Fringe*, which did rather well. That was a bit later, though.

The two songs that George was interested in recording from *And Another Thing* were 'My Kind of Someone', a love song that I sang with Joyce Blair, and something called 'Folk Song', which I sang on my own. For that one I'm a yokel who's supposed to be getting married and it's all about the last seven days. The opening lines are as follows:

> Upon the Monday morning-o, the rain it was a-raining.
> My love she came to me and said,
> 'When will you and I be wed,
> I have bought a double bed,
> and mother is complaining.'
> (I can't abide 'er mother!)
> And all the while the rain it was a-raining.

When I did 'Folk Song' on stage at the Fortune I had to pull a petal off this enormous daisy for each day of the week, but by the end of the week I get fed up and decide to go fishing.

> I caught four, I did.
> One of them was a great big fat feller.

It's actually quite a catchy tune, and after a chat and a cup of tea George suggested that we release it as a single. Joyce and I would record 'My Kind of Someone' for the B-side, and 'Folk Song' would be the A-side.

'Why not?' I said. 'Everyone else is doing it.'

Both songs had been written by Myles Rudge and Ted Dicks, and with their permission we went ahead. 'It's all sorted,' said George after speaking to them. 'I'll see you on Monday morning at 10 a.m. Studio Three. Abbey Road Studios.'

We recorded them both in a day and, to be honest, I didn't really think anything of it. It was a job, I got paid, and that was that. The world and his wife had been recording these songs for years and I was just one in a very long line. Bernard Bresslaw had done a couple, and they'd been massive. 'You Need Feet' was one, and 'Mad Passionate Love' was the other. He'd also done one called 'I Only Arsked', which was his catchphrase from *The Army Game*. I was in that, you know. Oh yes I was. I did one episode called 'Don't Send My Boy to Prison' and I played 'Peanuts' Perry. For anything more than that, I'm afraid you'll have to send me for regression therapy as I don't remember a thing.

What's my name again?

About a fortnight after making my recording debut at Abbey Road Studios I started hearing 'Folk Song' being played on the radio. Not all the time, but enough to make me notice. This was a strange experience, I can tell you. I kept on thinking, *That's me, that is! I'm actually singing on the radio!* The arrangement George commissioned for 'Folk Song' was quite different from the one we used on stage. It was very fluty and folksy, and I love the flute!

Talking of the wireless, it was about this time that I was offered my first radio play. A producer called Alfred Bradley had also come to see *And Another Thing* and, after coming back and introducing himself afterwards, asked me if he could contact me about any roles that he thought I might be interested in. 'You most certainly can,' was my reply.

It took a while but when Alfred and I finally got together we ended up doing a lot of plays together. He was an exceptional radio producer and, just like George Martin, he had an acute ear. He taught me how to act on radio, I suppose. He's dead now, unfortunately, but whenever we worked together I'd always stay at his house in a town called Boston Spa near Leeds. He had a wife called Judith and six children. Six! One of them, Jonathan, is my godson. It was always noisy in that house, and never dull. I loved it.

Because it was radio, and because it was the BBC, the money was always dismal, but the work itself more than made up for that, as did the friendship.

The first thing I did for Alfred was Alan Plater's *The Mating Season*, just a year after this in 1963. It's about a man who becomes lonely after his best friend gets married and so he decides to find himself a wife. I'm pretty sure I played the man, who was called Stan, and the actor who played the barman in the pub where I tried to pull a wife was Colin Welland. Had I known what I do now, I'd have told Mr Welland to go back to teaching. Anyway, that's for later. Remember him, though.

A few weeks after that first single was released I received a telephone call from George. He told me that 'Folk Song' had sold over 25,000 copies and although it hadn't made the top twenty, or whatever you under-sixties call it, it had made enough noise to make the bigwigs at Parlophone sit up and say, "Ello, 'ello, 'ello, there's money in that there Cribbins.'

'Do you fancy recording something else?' George asked.

'Sure. What do you have in mind?'

'Let me speak to Myles and Ted,' said George. 'I think we should ask them to write something for you.'

'Sounds good to me.'

The result of George's chat with Messrs Rudge and Dicks was a funny, simple tune called 'The Hole in the Ground', which they wrote in just a few days. It's all about a cockney workman who, while trying to dig a hole, keeps getting bothered by a posh know-it-all in a bowler hat. ★SPOILER ALERT★ The cockney workman ends up burying the know-it-all in the hole, and, to quote the last two words of the song, 'That's that.'

We recorded that song in less than a day and as clever and as attentive as George undoubtedly was, nobody could have guessed that, with the help of four lads from Liverpool, he was just months away from changing popular music for ever. He was just a kind and amenable gentleman, who, at the time, specialised in making novelty records.

'The Hole in the Ground' was released in January 1962 and after just a month it had crept into the top twenty. Two weeks after that it was at number nine and it remained in the charts for thirteen weeks. 'Congratulations, Bernie,' said George. 'You've had a top-ten hit!' I have no idea how many copies 'The Hole in the Ground' sold but in the early 1960s you had to sell a lot of records to make it into the top ten. Over a hundred thousand.

People often ask me if I ever sang the song on television but

I'm afraid I didn't. There was no such thing as *Top of the Pops* or *Ready Steady Go!* until a year or two later and, besides, I was getting on with being an actor. People also want to know if it made me rich and, again, I'm afraid the answer's no. I earned a few quid, but the vast majority of the spoils went to the record company and the writers, which is fair enough. The best thing to come from me recording 'The Hole in the Ground' is beyond price, and it happened almost exactly a year after it was released on 23 January 1963. The genius that was Noël Coward was appearing as a guest on *Desert Island Discs* and one of the songs he chose, in between music by the likes of Sergei Rachmaninov and Giuseppe Verdi and Dame Edith Evans reciting a sonnet by William Shakespeare, was 'The Hole in the Ground', which in itself was a huge accolade.

Right at the very end of the show, when the presenter Roy Plomley asked Mr Coward which record he'd most like to keep, he said, 'I think the only one I would never get sick of is "The Hole in the Ground" by Mr Cribbins.' When asked why by Roy Plomley, Coward said, 'Because I could translate it into French as I walked up and down on the beach.' Now that, my old darling, is what you call a compliment. It's worth more than any royalty cheque. Well, almost.

Unfortunately, I never got to meet Noël Coward, which is a pity as I'd have loved to have a little chat about the song. A friend of mine accompanied him on the piano a few times at the Savoy, and one day he said to me, 'I'm fed up with you. The Master keeps playing that blasted record of yours!'

'Does he really?' I replied, trying – and failing – to sound nonchalant.

I did once come perilously close to meeting Coward. This would have been in the very late 1960s or early 1970s, so not that long before the great man passed away. I was driving through Parliament Square one day. Actually, that's not quite true. I was sitting in traffic in Parliament Square moving at about 2 miles an hour, when all of a sudden a limousine started crawling up alongside me. Because I had nothing better to do I tried to see who was in the back of this limousine (I love a bit of star spotting) and, yes, you've guessed it, it was the man himself. He would have been around seventy by then and because he was a bit weathered and quite tanned he looked a little like a Chinese Mandarin. Because the traffic was moving, albeit very slowly, I was a bit limited as to what action I could take but if it had been at a standstill I'd have got out of my car and knocked on his window. 'It's me, Mr Coward, Cribbins! I sang "The Hole in the Ground".'

'Yes, of course you did. Go away! Drive on, driver.'

As it was I had to try and wave at him from behind my wheel, but it was no good. He started moving on before I did, and, to quote the last two words of that blasted song again, 'That's that!'

It really was a shame, though, as I always had the greatest regard for Coward as a writer. I still do. I've got a recording of *In Which We Serve* at home, the patriotic and extremely moving war film that he wrote himself and directed with David Lean. It's a beautifully written film. A real tearjerker. I did appear in one of his plays in rep many years ago. Which one was it now? That's it, we did a production of *This Happy Breed* at Oldham. That's another one of my favourites and the film is very powerful. If you're not familiar with the works of Noël Coward, I urge you to have a delve. He wasn't called the Master for nothing, you know, and his taste in music was just impeccable!

About a minute after 'The Hole in the Ground' had entered the charts, the venerable Mr Martin had been knocking on the doors of Messrs Rudge and Dicks asking for another song. 'We want another one, please,' he said. And so, a week or so later, the two talented songwriters came back to George and me with a song called 'Right Said Fred'. Sticking with the labourer theme, this one was about three manual workers who are trying to move a large object, which, although it isn't specified in the song, is probably a piano. As well as taking endless teabreaks they start dismantling the house they're moving this thing from, just so they can shift it, and, just like 'The Hole in the Ground', it finishes with somebody pegging it. Fred, in this case. What a theme, though: labourers and death. Well, if it isn't broken, why mend it? Actually, having just played it back in my head, 'Folk Song' also finishes with a corpse as on the Saturday my love gets struck by lightning. That's the hat-trick then. Three songs and three deaths. What were Messrs Rudge and Dicks thinking?

'Right Said Fred' got to number ten in the charts, which wasn't too shabby, and the actor Jack Warner – aka Dixon of Dock Green – chose it as one of his favourite tracks when he was interrogated by Plomley. Many, many, many years later two bald gentlemen named their band after the song and they went on to have a couple of number one hits, the most famous of which being (I had to be told this, by the way) 'I'm Too Sexy'.

Perhaps I should do a cover version?

Perhaps not!

With two top-ten singles to my rather unique name it was suggested that I might like to make an album and, partly because I enjoyed working with George Martin so much, I said I'd do it. Lots of actors and comedians had made singles, but very few had gone on to make an album. I suppose that made me a bit different. Most importantly of all, it was work, and as well as being grateful, I was looking forward to it. That's the thing about recording songs. Each one is unique and so each one brings you different experiences. The album, by the way, was called *A Combination of Cribbins* and the cover features a photo of me sitting on a low chair with a high back wearing a pair of long johns with a carnation pinned to the front and some black hobnail boots. I look quite lovely.

The first song we recorded for the album was called 'Gossip Calypso' and it's basically about three women, Mrs Brown, Mrs Booze and Mrs Ware, who swap gossip about their husbands.

'Gossip Calypso' was written by an actor called Trevor Peacock who went on to play Jim Trott in *The Vicar of Dibley*. No, no, no, no, no, no, yes he did. He's a clever chap is our Trevor. His biggest hit as a songwriter is one that many of you will have heard of. Remember Herman's Hermits? Of course you do. Well, in 1965 they released a song called 'Mrs Brown, You've Got a Lovely Daughter', and that was written by Mr P. It didn't do that well over here, but it got to number one in America.

Because 'Right Said Fred' was still doing well in the charts the powers that be decided to release 'Gossip Calypso' as a single as soon as we'd finished recording it. Due to the fact that it didn't have a death in it (this is my theory, and I'm sticking to it), 'Gossip Calypso' stalled at number twenty-five in the charts and it never got going again. It was still a hit, but after that I think the writing was on the wall for my singing career.

For some strange reason 'Folk Song', 'The Hole in the Ground' and 'Right Said Fred' didn't appear on *A Combination of Cribbins*, but there's still some interesting stuff on there, if occasionally a little risqué! One of the songs, called 'Verily', is a madrigal featuring a harpsichord and some double entendres. Shall I give you one? A verse, that is.

> Verily, the fairest rose,
> thou hast these and thou hast those,
> and Verily, very verily,
> all of it where it shows.

Not very subtle, is it? Myles Rudge wrote the lyrics and we did have a chuckle when we recorded it.

When George and I first started talking about the album he asked me if there were any songs I'd like to do, and I suggested one called 'I've Grown Accustomed to Her Face' from the musical, *My Fair Lady*. I've always been a big, big fan of musicals, and Gill and I had been to see the original London production of *My Fair Lady* at the Theatre Royal Drury Lane in 1958. It ran for over five years and the cast that we saw included Rex Harrison, Julie Andrews, Robert Coote and the great Stanley Holloway. Rex Harrison, who by his own admission was not a natural singer, used to half-sing and half-speak the song, and although that worked for him I thought it was too beautiful a refrain to be said and not sung. Nat King Cole, Johnny Mathis and Dean Martin (I was a fan of all three) had all done cover versions of the song and so I thought, *Why not give that a go?* George agreed, and he went off and asked a chap called Bernard Whibley to prepare an arrangement. He did an absolutely marvellous job and the arrangement featured a jazz quartet – piano, double bass, guitar and drums – and a string section.

While we were recording 'I've Grown Accustomed to Her Face' I learned an incredibly valuable lesson from George about how to use a microphone. I think we were about halfway through the first take and suddenly he brought the proceedings to a halt and asked the musicians to take a break. I was standing in my booth at the microphone at the time and once the musicians had scarpered he came in to see me. Over the next five minutes George Martin basically taught me microphone technique. Everything I'd sung for him thus far had been at my normal pitch, whereas this required something much softer. To be honest, I wasn't used to singing quietly – I'm not really a quiet person, unless I'm fishing – and after giving me the confidence to do so George then told me where to stand in relation to the microphone. He had me down to almost a whisper for this song, but that was all that was needed. I'm not one to blow my own trumpet, but I'm very proud of that particular number. Very proud indeed.

Looking back, I can now appreciate how incredibly lucky I was. I had as my mentor a man who is now regarded as being one of the most talented record producers who ever lived, some first-class musicians, and a recording studio that, thanks to George and those four young pretenders who came after me, is now music's answer to Mecca.

'What do you fancy recording, Bernard?'

'Well George, how about "I've Grown Accustomed to Her Face"?'

'Fine. Shall we record it at Abbey Road Studios with some professional musicians and then release it through Parlophone on an album bearing your name?'

'Yes, let's.'

That was my life for about a year.

Me, smug?

Absolutely!

Something I only recently found out about that track is that in 2011 it was chosen by the wonderful DJ and music aficionado Danny Baker as his favourite track on *Desert Island Discs*, which means I'm the favourite of two men of distinction. Mr Baker called the arrangement of the song sumptuous, apparently, and I'd have to agree with him. That's all down to George and the arranger, Bernard Whibley, though. They were the brains of the outfit. Danny's a lovely fellow and I must remember to thank him when I see him.

I'm often asked why I didn't carry on making records and really it was because I couldn't commercialise it. I was an actor, first and foremost, and the only way I could have made it work long-term was if I'd given up being an actor and started singing full-time. The truth is, I made novelty records generally, and novelties tend to wear off after a while. I always refer to that period of my life as a delightful little interlude, and that's exactly what it was.

Literally a few weeks after we'd finished recording the album at Abbey Road, George started working with the Beatles and the rest is musical history. But it wasn't just a record producer and a recording studio that the Fab Four nabbed from me. They also half-inched a film director, too.

Allow me to elucidate.

In 1963 I made a film called *The Mouse on the Moon* starring Ron Moody, Margaret Rutherford, Terry-Thomas and David Kossoff. It was a follow-up to an earlier film starring Peter Sellers called *The Mouse that Roared* and was about a small fictional European country called the Duchy of Grand Fenwick that joins the race to reach the moon. The Americans hadn't got there yet, by the way. It was a satire, first and foremost, and as well as taking the rise out of the 1960s space race it also lampooned the Cold War and politics in general. I played the son of the Prime Minister of Grand Fenwick, played by Ron Moody, but the majority of my scenes were with the marvellous David Kossoff who I end up going to the moon with in a second-hand Russian rocket travelling at about 15 mph. Oh yes I do. It's not a bad little film and because of the space connection the American premiere was held at Cape Canaveral with lots of astronauts in the audience. I didn't get to go, unfortunately.

When the producer, Walter Shenson, was looking for a director for *The Mouse on the Moon* he contacted Peter Sellers and Sellers had recommended Richard Lester. Lester had co-directed a short film with Sellers in 1959 entitled *The Running Jumping & Standing Still Film* and Sellers had apparently taken to Lester. I've never seen that particular film, so I can't comment, but Walter Shenson took Peter Sellers's advice and hired Richard Lester.

To cut a long story short, the next film Richard Lester made after *The Mouse on the Moon* was *A Hard Day's Night* starring those four pesky musicians from Liverpool. Once again, they'd been clinging on to the coattails of my greatness. In fact, the only time I ever followed the Fab Four at anything was in 1966 when I was invited back to Abbey Road. My pal George had recently finished producing the Beatles' long-forgotten long player, *Sgt. Pepper's Lonely Hearts Club Band*, and he asked me if I'd like to come back to Abbey Road and record a version of one of the tracks. Whether he thought I might improve on what they'd done, I'm not sure, but for the love of George, I readily agreed.

In 2013, when BBC Radio made a retrospective of my career entitled *Bernard Who?*, they contacted George and he very kindly agreed to do an interview. As well as saying that I was always easy to work with, he also called me a natural. Me! You must allow me a little gloat for that one. Best of all, though, he said that he'd loved making my records and suggested that whenever you heard one, you always felt better for it.

Thank you, George – very much!

The song we ended up recording together was 'When I'm Sixty-Four', and the reason George had suggested the song was because it had a kind of novelty feel to it. I thought it was a great idea. Before you could say Bernard in the sky with diamonds, I was 'getting older' and 'losing my hair' in a sound booth in Studio Three at Abbey Road. You see what I did there?

My new and improved version of the Beatles' 'When I'm

Sixty-Four' was released by Parlophone in May 1967, about a month after the original, and one of them became a huge world-wide hit.

Sometime after George passed away in January 2016 his widow, Lady Judy, got in touch and asked me if I'd like to perform at his memorial service which was planned for that spring. I told Lady Judy that I would be honoured to perform at George's memorial service and asked her what she'd like me to sing. 'We'd like you to sing "The Hole in the Ground", if that's ok.' The irony of the family's request obviously wasn't lost on me and I thought it was marvellous. 'Consider it done,' I said.

With the help of George's son, Giles, I rehearsed the song with a small orchestra at AIR Studios and on the morning of 11 May I made my way, with Gill, to Trafalgar Square which is where St Martin-in-the-Fields is situated. As you'd expect, the place was absolutely packed to the rafters. Paul McCartney delivered a marvellous eulogy about the effect George had had on his life and after that I don't think there was a dry eye in the house. I was obviously a little bit nervous when I got up to perform 'The Hole in the Ground' but the sense of love and admiration I had for the man I was singing it for more than got me through. It was such a great honour. Afterwards, as I was walking back to my seat, Paul McCartney gave me a big wink. That took me right back to Peter Sellers's memorial service when David Niven did just the same. Do you remember? As we were leaving the church Elton John came up and gave me a big squeeze. 'Why didn't you sing "Right Said Fred"?' he asked.

What a great occasion. And for a great man.

Anyway. Shall I tell you about the rest of my criminal records? Well, in addition to releasing one or two compilation albums since my time as a pop star, I've also released three singles and an EP. The EP (that stands for extended play, by the way, and they usually feature four or five songs) was released in 1975 and on it I'm pretending to be Paddington Bear. I know what you're thinking. You're thinking, *Michael Hordern narrated* Paddington *Bear, not you, Cribbins. You're a* Womble *man, not a bear man!* Not strictly true, I'm afraid. You see, shortly before recording the EP, I narrated all of the Paddington Bear books for a company called Pinnacle Storyteller and they released them all on cassette and LP. The reason I didn't narrate the television series, which started in 1976, was because, on television, at least, I was very much associated with the aforementioned *Wombles* and so the baton was passed to Mr Hordern. I certainly couldn't have done a better job than him, but the fact is I was Paddington Bear's first voice. I recorded three songs for the EP: a title track, which is called 'Paddington Bear', a song called 'Marmalade', which is basically a homage to Paddington's favourite food, and, to complete the set, a song called 'Cocoa Samba', which extols the chocolatey virtues of Paddington's favourite drink.

Shortly after the 'Paddington Bear' EP was released I was asked to record a version of the song 'I'm Hans Christian Andersen', which Danny Kaye had made famous in a film in which he played the Danish writer. That one was recorded with a full orchestra, which was fun, and because it was aimed at small children they included a picture of Hans Christian Andersen on the back of the single that you could colour in at home. It's a wonder it didn't get to number one.

My penultimate attempt at resurrecting my career as an international recording artist (if you don't include a flexi-disc I made for Hornby Model Railways in the 1980s, which was given away with each new trainset) was, again, done in character. This time I was pretending to be Buzby, the talking yellow cartoon bird that had been around since the mid-1970s and had been used by British Telecom, and their predecessors, to make us talk more on the phone. Remember the 'Make someone happy with a phone call' slogan? Some of you will. Well, I was the voice of Buzby so the person who was actually doing the persuading was me.

The song was called 'Make Someone Happy Every Day' and it was released in 1979. As far as I can remember, it was a tie-in with yet another advertising campaign and it might also have been given away through Buzby's fan club. That's right, Buzby, a fictional cartoon bird who appeared on adverts actually had a fan club! I never did.

Are you ready for some serious excitement here? You might not be able to take it. Well, when you joined the Buzby Fan Club, you got a free knitting pattern that, if you followed it correctly, would result in a lovely blue jumper with Buzby on the front. I never saw anybody wearing one!

My last effort before I finally gave up the ghost – and believe me, it was definitely a ghost by this point – was a novelty song that was released in 1980 called 'Giggling Gertie the Laughing Traffic Warden'. This was actually just 'The Laughing Policeman' with different lyrics and it also featured the actress Miriam Margolyes. She provided the laughs, bless her, and it was arranged and conducted by Kenny Clayton who'd worked with everyone from Shirley Bassey to Matt Monro. I wonder if either he or Miriam have 'Giggling Gertie the Laughing Traffic Warden' on their CVs?

A fiver says they don't.

While we're in the 1970s the very last thing I remember about that decade is seeing Douglas Emery, my first boss and mentor. I was walking from Soho onto Shaftesbury Avenue and just as I was passing the Globe Theatre, which is now the Gielgud, I saw an elderly gentleman picking some fruit from a barrow. *Christ*, I thought, *it's Douglas*. I hadn't seen him for the best part of twenty years and I couldn't have been more surprised. He'd long since retired from producing and acting and must have been in his late seventies.

'Hello, Douglas,' I said. 'Do you remember me?'

He looked at me and smiled, although he was totally unfazed.

'Hello, dear,' he said. 'How are you?'

'I'm OK. I'm working, at least. What are you doing here?'

'I'm tearing tickets here at the Globe.'

'Anything to stay in the theatre, eh?'

As we chatted, all these memories started coming back. It was because of Douglas that I became an actor rather than a carpenter or something, and he'd taught me so much. One afternoon when I was about fifteen, I was watching a Tarzan film at the local cinema when I suddenly realised I was meant to be at the theatre for a matinee. Douglas gave me the biggest telling-off ever, but rather than sacking me and telling me to get out – which he would have been well within his rights to do – he said, 'If you're in this job you must be disciplined.' That had a profound effect on me and ever since then I've always tried to be as professional as possible. He also led by example, did

Douglas, and would sew curtains and put up pictures while playing leads and directing.

At the time that I saw him, I was engaged to do a Feydeau farce on TV and we needed someone for the very small part of the major-domo. After taking down his address I suggested Douglas to the director and he got the part. I never told him it was my idea, and afterwards he came up to me and said, 'It wasn't much of a part. I don't know why they asked me.' It was so typical of an actor's pride and I must admit that it broke my heart a little bit.

CHAPTER NINE

Put your head back in.
It looks like a cattle truck!

Although it didn't make me rich, being a pop star did give my profile quite a boost and when I wasn't fending off the groupies and being carried out of nightclubs at four in the morning I was being offered some fairly interesting jobs. One of these was a Sunday night play for the BBC entitled *The Canterville Ghost*. It was part of a series called Sunday Night Play, which ran for four years and spawned 138 episodes. Just about every actor, writer and director who was around then had worked on at least one of these plays and I was lucky enough to star in two. The first one had been *Charley's Aunt* in 1961 in which I'd played Lord Fancourt Babberley. That had been a real treat to do as not only was I being paid to dress up in women's clothing, but I was doing it alongside two giants of the theatre: Sir Donald Wolfit and Rosalie Crutchley. Back then *Charley's Aunt* was one of the most popular plays on earth, not just in the United Kingdom, and a journalist claimed that when our production went to air in April 1961 it was being performed in twenty-four languages and in more than thirty different countries. That's on top of the thirty or so British repertory theatres who were producing the play, not to mention hundreds of amateur companies.

How about a short synopsis?

Set at Oxford University in the 1890s, it tells the story of two undergraduates, Charley Wykeham and Jack Chesney, who pressure a fellow student, Lord Fancourt Babberley, to pose as Charley's Brazilian aunt, Donna Lucia. Their purpose for this is so they will have a chaperone when they visit two girls they're chasing called Amy and Kitty. The man who is responsible for these two ladies is a crusty old buffoon named Stephen Spettigue (Donald Wolfit) and complications begin when Sir Fancourt Babberley – in drag – becomes the object of, not only Spettigue's desires, but also Jack's father, Sir Francis Chesney. Somewhere along the way Charley's real aunt turns up and, as you can imagine, chaos ensues.

It's an absolutely cracking story and over the years the part of Fancourt Babberley has been played by the world and his wife. My pal Richard Briers played him twice, I think, and other actors who were obviously told they looked good in a dress include Jack Benny, José Ferrer, Ray Bolger, John Mills, Frankie Howerd, Tom Courtenay, Norman Wisdom and, perhaps less surprisingly, Danny La Rue. The most famous 'Charley's Aunt' on these shores is probably Arthur Askey. He played the role in a film called *Charley's Big Hearted Aunt* and did it dozens of times on the stage. The last person to play her in the West End was Griff Rhys Jones in the 1980s, so it's due a revival, I think. Any takers?

The most significant thing about this production for me – as in it's the only thing I can remember – is that Sir Donald and I made the cover of the *Radio Times*. This was a bit of an arrival for me, and my parents in particular were absolutely tickled pink. Their little Bernard, on the cover of the *Radio Times*, WITH SIR DONALD WOLFIT? Well I never. It was big news in certain parts of Oldham. You remember I said there was no finer feeling than contributing to the family coffers? This came a close second.

The Canterville Ghost, which was originally a novella by Oscar Wilde, tells of an American family who move into a British mansion called Canterville Chase, much to the annoyance of its resident ghost. That was my role, by the way. It was directed by my old friend Stuart Burge and it had been adapted for television by the famous Welsh writer, Elaine Morgan. Fay Compton was one of my co-stars, as was Ruth Dunning and a very young Samantha Eggar. We didn't make the cover of the *Radio Times*, unfortunately, but it was a lovely little role.

Towards the end of 1962, just when I was hanging up my microphone, I was asked if I'd like to make another film with Peter Sellers. Talk about a rhetorical question. Peter still hadn't been lured away to Hollywood full-time yet, although it wouldn't be long, and the part they wanted me to play was a leading role alongside Peter and Lionel Jeffries. Yes please! The film, incidentally, was *The Wrong Arm of the Law*.

Peter played Pearly Gates and I was Nervous O'Toole, two 'respectable' criminals whose crime syndicate loses its spoils to three Australian crooks impersonating police officers. The syndicate decides to cooperate with the police in an attempt to catch the frauds. The detective we have to work with, Inspector Fred 'Nosey' Parker, was played by Lionel, and Valerie, Pearly's intended, was played by Nanette Newman. Once again, the supporting cast was teeming with stalwarts and day after day I was working with the likes of John Le Mesurier, Bill Kerr, Davy Kaye and Graham Stark.

My character, Nervous O'Toole, is an Irish gangster who is a sort of friend/rival of Pearly and, as well as having a wife and several children, he also has quite a few anxiety issues, hence the name. It was a great part to play and it allowed me to practise my Dublin accent.

The shoot for *The Wrong Arm of the Law* was far more chaotic than *Two-Way Stretch*, in that hardly any of it was filmed chronologically. That was what I was used to, though, and it was tremendous fun. Lots of location work and car chases.

Pearly Gates's cover for his criminal activities is a fashion house with lots of ladies and so he's forever having to switch between being a camp coiffeur, who happens to be French, and a cockney criminal. Watching Peter shift from one to the other was just astonishing. Camp French to straight cockney in the blink of an eye. Seamless. There are very few actors I can think of – then or now – who could have done that. Or at least done it convincingly. He was at the height of his powers.

In my opinion, the work Peter Sellers did prior to becoming a global star is his best. I'm talking about anything between *The Goons* to *The Wrong Arm of the Law*. After that, superstardom struck and his ego started getting the better of him and, although he still gave some amazing performances, he was never quite the same. To me, at least. His life became a circus and his antics and reputation preceded, not just Peter Sellers the man, but the roles he played. Look at David Niven. One of the things that endeared David to the world was his unaffectedness. I'm not saying he didn't have his problems, but as well as being the perfect gentleman he always managed to maintain a quiet dignity. Nothing was clouded and you could always enjoy his performances for what they were. Despite being a good friend of David's, Peter became the polar opposite and his unique talent often played second fiddle to the aforementioned circus. Pity.

Anyway, we don't want to be getting all maudlin, do we? Let's concentrate on Peter's genius for a little bit longer.

One evening I had to do a scene with him in the back of a Rolls-Royce. The Rolls-Royce was mine, as in Nervous O'Toole's, and the scene starts with two of my heavies accosting Peter outside his salon and bringing him to the car. As they're doing this, I have to stick my head out of the window and tell them to hurry up, and when I did that during the first take Peter said, ''Ere. Put your head back in. It looks like a cattle truck.' Well, that was it. First of all the cameraman started to chuckle, then the two heavies, Barry Keegan and Arthur Mullard, started. Then I started, then Peter started, and pretty soon the entire set was at it. Alas, I'm afraid that set an audible precedent for the next hour and a half by which time we still hadn't finished the scene. We were on what was called an extended day and had been asked to stay on for an extra two hours specifically to shoot it. By this time the money men were twitching like a rabbit's nose so we pulled ourselves together and got on with it. Eventually we got around to filming the shots in the back of the Rolls and when the director, Cliff Owen, went to do a close-up with Peter, I sat by the camera to feed him my lines. For some reason, Peter seemed not to be trying and when they'd finished shooting it I was distinctly unimpressed.

When I saw the rushes the following day I realised that what I'd been witnessing wasn't Mr Sellers losing interest and putting in a bland performance. In fact, it was the opposite. He was playing *for* the close-up, and what I'd witnessed was simply a masterclass in technique. He was perfect. I remember thinking, *You clever sod, Sellers. I wish I could do that.*

The only shot we didn't have time to film that night in the Rolls-Royce was my close-up. Peter had to go as he had to be up at the crack of dawn and, because of the schedule, we ended up shooting it two and a half weeks later. I had to watch the scenes leading up to it beforehand, just to take in the atmosphere of the scene and get into character. That's the movie business, though. It's completely random.

Just a few months later I was sitting on a staircase at a party talking to Julie Andrews (or Big Julie, as I call her, as she's quite tall) and the subject of filming came up. We were at the house of her first husband's parents in Walton-on-Thames and she was about to fly off to make *Mary Poppins*. Julie had never made a feature film before and so I was passing on the benefit of my knowledge and experience. Or, should I say, Peter Seller's knowledge and experience. I just told her what I'd picked up working with him.

At the same party I ended up having a huge argument with the author T. H. White, who wrote *The Once and Future King*, which became *Camelot*. Our disagreement was about the noise puffins make when they're coming back to their nest with a beak full of sand eels. Drink had been taken, I might add, and because he lived on Alderney and knew about these things, I had to concede defeat. It's quite random, though, don't you think? Then again, I quite like random.

In March 1963, shortly after *The Wrong Arm of the Law* was released, Lionel and Eileen Jeffries and Gill and I were sitting in Leicester Square having a coffee. Just like *Two-Way Stretch*, the film had been premiered at the Warner West End Cinema, which was on Cranbourne Street at the bottom of Leicester Square. Although we hadn't engineered it, we ended up in a coffee house directly opposite this cinema and I don't mind saying that I was rather impressed by what I saw. Seeing your name on a poster in a frame outside a cinema is one thing, but seeing it in large neon lights on the front of a cinema about 30 feet in the air is quite another. If it makes me sound slightly egotistical, so be it. It's what keeps us actors and actresses going, really, a bit of recognition. The roar of the crowd, duckie!

The lights read,

PETER SELLERS, LIONEL JEFFRIES AND BERNARD CRIBBINS, IN

THE WRONG ARM OF THE LAW

'Look at that, Bernie,' said Lionel. 'Your name in lights. How does it feel, boy?' Just as I was about to answer him the neon lights went out. Every single one of them.

'Bleedin' 'ell, Bernie,' said Lionel. 'That didn't last long, did it?'

A minute or so later the lights came back on again, but I didn't dare look at them after that. I think it was God warning me not to become smug.

Another film I made in the early 1960s was *The Girl on the Boat*, which starred Richard Briers, Sheila Hancock, Millicent Martin and Norman Wisdom. My favourite memory from that film, or should I say only memory, is the effect that my rather interesting 'boat race', as a cockney would say, had on Norman Wisdom. For some reason, he found my features incredibly amusing and would start giggling the moment he saw me. 'I can't work with him,' he kept saying to the director, Henry Kaplan. 'Look at his bloody face!'

A few months after *The Wrong Arm of the Law* had been released, in the summer of 1963, I was asked if I'd like to appear in a new *Carry On* film and put said face to good use. To date there had been seven films made: *Sergeant*, *Nurse*, *Teacher*, *Constable*, *Regardless*, *Cruising* and *Cabby*, and I'm pretty sure I'd been to see one or two of them. Once again, I'm often asked if I had any hopes – or indeed fears – about becoming part of the *Carry On* ensemble when I started but it was just another job to me. It's not that I didn't want to become a *Carry On* actor, I just hadn't thought about it. In hindsight, I'm rather glad I didn't become a regular as I might have become typecast. That's one of the best things about being me, you see. I've been asked to do all kinds of things over the decades and the thought of being pigeonholed in one particular genre is not a nice one. I'm like a shorter Ian Botham. An all-rounder.

The *Carry On* film in question was *Carry On Jack* and it starred Kenny Williams, Charlie Hawtrey, my gorgeous self and the even more beautiful Juliet Mills, who we later found out was three months pregnant when we started filming. It tells the tale of Albert Poop-Decker (Cribbins), a newly commissioned but incompetent midshipman (it only took him eight and a half years) who joins the frigate *Venus* and ventures through the Spanish seas. While on board he discovers that a woman (Juliet Mills) has been impersonating him in order to go to sea and, while trying to prove his identity, he falls in love with her – obviously – and encounters pirates, mutiny and, worst of all, KENNETH WILLIAMS!

Although it's probably not among the nation's favourite *Carry On* films, it was certainly my favourite to make. For a start, there was lots of swinging about on ropes and things, which was fun, and I got to do all my own stunts. There wasn't anything especially dangerous. We had a mock-up ship at Pinewood that had originally been built for a film called *HMS Defiant* with Alec Guinness and Dirk Bogarde, and I had to swing from one end to the other a few times during some action scenes. I wasn't exactly Errol Flynn but I had a damn good bash at it.

This mock-up ship had been built about a quarter of a mile away from the main car park at Pinewood and one day when I was walking up to the set I noticed something strange. On closer inspection I realised that it was a model helicopter on a wire. It must have been about a quarter of the size of a real heli-copter, so pretty big, and it had something to do with a Bond film they were making there. It must have been *From Russia with Love* as that also came out in 1963. Because I rather liked the look of this helicopter, and because I knew some of the effects chaps who worked on the Bond films, I decided to take a diversion and see if I could purloin this model once they'd finished with it. Well, you know what they say, if you don't ask, you don't get. Am I right?

When I was about 50 feet away from the helicopter it suddenly exploded into a thousand pieces. BANG!

Did I scream?

I'm not sure. I'd been temporarily deafened.

It wasn't a closed set and because there was no security I thought approaching it would be OK. I didn't hang around to find out what they were up to. I just scarpered to the safety of our model ship and pretended to be Errol Flynn.

One thing we had on this film that I hadn't encountered before was an advisor who made sure we were being historically accurate. Surprised, eh? Commander Ian Fox was his name and according to a friend of mine called Robert Ross, who is a walking *Carry On* encyclopaedia, Commander Cox was paid £40 a week for his troubles. That sounds about right for a *Carry On*. Commander Cox made sure we got the uniforms right as well as all the different procedures, and when I first met him he very kindly lent me a book on the Royal Navy from the period we were portraying, which was the early nineteenth century. Or should I say the period we were lampooning!

Some of the things they used to dish out as punishments in those days were barbaric and were far too extreme for us to include in the film. One I read about involved prisoners being tied up on a crucifix attached to a longboat and then rowed about and whipped by the entire fleet. The Master at Arms would arrange six lashes from each vessel, and on one boat they'd be whipped by somebody who was right-handed, and on the next by somebody who was left-handed. That ensured they'd be cut both ways and would experience the maximum amount of pain. Most of the men would be dead after a few lashes but they'd complete the sentence anyway. Humans, eh? We're capable of the most remarkable achievements but when we get it wrong, boy, do we get it wrong.

I may already have mentioned this but when you're making movies there's often an awful lot of waiting around to be done, and so with boredom staring you in the face you have to try and amuse yourselves. On *Carry On Jack* we used to play cricket when we weren't working – or at least some of us did – and because we didn't have a cricket ball we used a rolled-up ball of camera tape instead. My arch rival on the film was the Australian actor Ed Devereaux who was playing one of the pirates. He'd played one of the thieves who were masquerading as policemen in *The Wrong Arm of the Law* and as well as doing a very good line in baddies he was also a fairly decent leg-break bowler. Decades later, while I was recording the audio commentary for the DVD release of *Carry On Jack* with Robert Ross, I brought this up and somehow he managed to find the score from one of our matches! It was included in one of the press releases for the film, apparently, and was billed as the Pinewood Test. I was caught and bowled for eleven after five overs and Ed was not out for five after two overs. We were called back on set after that and so it was declared a draw. You don't get much action from a ball of camera tape, do you?

One day we had to halt filming for a few minutes because some paratroopers were jumping a few miles away. It was towards Aldershot, I think, and do you know what, not one of them waved to me! Ex 3rd Battalion and not one shout of 'Hello Bernie.' I was mortified.

The only thing I found slightly unnerving on *Carry on Jack*, at least at first, was the fact that I had to wear a pigtail. The only person to comment on this in a derogatory fashion was my old colleague and sparring partner, Robert Morley – king of the one-liner. I was on my way to the restaurant at Pinewood one day when all of a sudden a big car pulled up and out stepped Robert. 'I see you're wearing a pigtail,' he said. 'Oh dear. Is that wise?' I hadn't seen him since 1958 and he didn't even say hello or wait for an answer. He just waddled off. Showbusiness is full of eccentrics and that's something I like about it.

Something I like about making films is that everybody on the set is there because they're good at what they do. Never was this truer than on a *Carry On* film because, in order to shoot a ninety-minute film in just a few weeks, you have to be right on the button and, believe me, there was nothing but gold on them there film sets. It's not always the same in our business and in certain areas off set you'll find lots of people who are only there because they're either friends with somebody or they're related to them. It's endemic within showbusiness, I'm afraid, and the best place to avoid it is on a film set.

I was thinking the other day that *Carry On Jack* doesn't really feel like a normal *Carry On* film and, after sitting on it for a while, I think there's something in that. Let's start with the shoot itself. With *Carry On Jack* we had eight weeks, which in *Carry On* terms is two weeks more than the usual. Most people don't believe me when I tell them that the majority of *Carry On* films were shot in six weeks but it's perfectly true. It was the proverbial well-oiled machine – a factory – and in my opinion the director, Gerald Thomas, and the director of photography,

Alan Hume, really made the most of the extra two weeks. The direction is slightly more considered than usual and some of the lighting in the early part of the film is superb. That said, when I suggested something to Gerald Thomas at the start of a scene it was dismissed outright because he was so used to editing on the go. The scene in question featured me being told off by the Admiral and what I'd suggested to Gerald during one of the rehearsals was that as I reached the door after being scolded I turn to the Admiral and give him one of my sickly grins. I'm rather good at sickly grins, he said modestly, and I thought it might tag the scene.

'I'm sorry, Bernie,' said Gerald, 'but as soon as you touch the door knob I've cut and I'm on the other side of the door.'

He had the whole thing planned out in his head. He was like a snooker player! The amount of scenes that were printed after just one take in that film was incredible so it's no wonder he used to come in under budget.

OK, now let's touch on the cast of *Carry On Jack*. The chap who played the aforementioned Admiral was an actor called Cecil Parker who, at the time, was probably one of the most respected stage and film actors in the country. I'm not saying the *Carry Ons* weren't worthy of an actor like Cecil. Anything but. It was just a bit strange, that's all. Like seeing Ian McKellen on *Coronation Street*. As if that would ever happen!

Because *Carry On Jack* is less ribald than many of the other films, Cecil's presence actually works. Also, it's a lack of slapstick that makes the film more like a historical comedy than a *Carry On*. What confirms my theory – and I'll shut up in a minute – is the fact that *Carry On Jack* only became a *Carry On* film at the very last minute and was originally to be called *Up the Armada*. True!

Anyway, would you like to hear a story about me painting Kenneth Williams's bum cheeks black? Of course you would.

Kenny was playing Captain Fearless and late on in the film he gets gangrene in one of his legs, which has to be sawn off – by me. In those days, every time you shot a film in colour you'd have to test the rolls of film and so every so often you'd hear somebody shout, 'Could we test for colour, please?' The Lord only knows why, but Kenny would use this as a cue to flash his bum. He didn't always need an excuse, but while we were making *Carry On Jack* that was all he needed.

'Could we test for colour, please?'

''Ere, have a look at this!'

'Kenny! For heaven's sake, put it away.'

'What's wrong with my bum? I've got a lovely bum, I have.'

You can imagine how it went down.

By the time we'd got to the scene where I had to cut off his gangrenous leg, I'd had an idea. During this scene Kenny had to wear a nightshirt and underneath it all he had on was a jockstrap.

'I'll tell you what, Kenny,' I said to him. 'If they want to test for colour at the end of the scene you can flash your bum. Go on, I dare you.'

'Oh, I don't like to,' he protested in that stupendously distinctive voice of his.

'Go on, you'll have us all in stitches.'

I'd already had a word with the person who called for the colour tests and so it was a certainty.

As soon as we'd finished filming the scene I helped Kenny to his feet and gave him a nudge on cue. 'Go on, Ken,' I whispered. 'Do it now.'

Without hesitation he turned around, whipped up his nightshirt and bared his little cheeks to all and sundry. The only difference with this full moon was that I'd just been handed a paint brush and a tin of black prop paint and the moment his bum was bared, I slapped two coats on each cheek.

As somebody who usually dislikes practical jokes I was acting like an idiot but at the time I thought it was a splendid idea. Doing the black bottom with Kenneth Williams? What's not to like? Had somebody sat me down beforehand and said, 'Look, Bernard, do you really think this is a good idea?' I'd probably have decided against it, but the damage was already done. It was quite a neat job, given the amount of time I'd had, but the owner of the posterior I'd just plastered with prop paint wasn't at all happy.

'What the bloody hell have you done to my bum, Cribbins?' cried Kenny, before removing himself from the set.

He didn't speak to me for a week after that. Every day I'd say, 'Morning, Kenny, how are you?' and he'd say, 'Fuck off, Cribbins.'

Fortunately we made friends again, but he certainly made me pay for it. Quite right too.

Some years later when I hadn't seen Kenny for a very long time I passed him in the corridor at the BBC. We were both there doing a programme about the *Carry Ons*, and when he saw me he stopped and said, 'You don't change, do you?' I *think* he meant it in a nice way but you could never quite tell with Kenny. He was a funny onion.

Just a month after I finished filming *Carry On Jack* I was asked if I'd like to appear in the next film, *Carry On Spying*, which was being filmed, at Pinewood, of course, between February and March 1964. You see what I mean about it being a factory? We'd only finished filming *Carry on Jack* on 23 October and it was released in the UK on 3 November. Just three months later, at the start of February, *Spying* started filming and that was released on 2 August.

I'm afraid I didn't enjoy making *Carry On Spying*, nor did I enjoy making *Carry On Columbus*, which appeared twenty-eight years later in 1992. That was my third and final appearance in the series and I think the majority of us who did it – at least with regards to the old guard, such as Leslie Phillips, Jim Dale and June Whitfield – did so as a favour to Gerry Thomas, whom we all loved. *Columbus* was a nice idea, but it was poorly executed and the script in particular was well below par. With their usual script-writer, the great Talbot Rothwell, having long since departed, the producer Peter Rogers and Gerald were forced to find some-body new but instead of approaching a current comedy writer – somebody like Ben Elton or Richard Curtis, perhaps? – they went to a chap called Dave Freeman who, while being top notch in his day, specialised in writing for television mainly and the last thing he'd done in this country had been a sitcom called *Keep It in the Family* in the early 1980s. Things had obviously moved on since then but I'm afraid that Peter, Gerald and Dave hadn't. It was a very sad end to a great series.

With regards to *Carry On Spying* the problem I had was that normal service had resumed. The eight weeks for *Carry On Jack* had been a one-off and they were back to shooting fifteen pages of script a day. We still had a few laughs, but my abiding memory is that it was all very quick and uncomfortable. Like standing up on an Inter-City train.

The worst thing that happened to me on that film was getting shot in the face by an overenthusiastic extra carrying a pistol, and the best thing was working with the gorgeous Barbara Windsor, who played Daphne Honeybutt. Let's start with the extra. Barbara and I were on the back of this rollercoaster-type thing travelling not very fast, and as we were going by this extra was supposed to take a shot at us from a safe distance. Instead, he ran right behind the side of this thing we were on and shot me in the face from about five yards. I don't know if you're aware of how blanks work but they're basically gunpowder and a cardboard wad and so when they're fired hundreds of pieces of cardboard are flung out very, very quickly. Because this idiot had fired it so close to my face I got a load of these bits right in my mush and, although it wasn't life threatening, if it had got me in the eye I'd have been in trouble. I complained about this and received a load of abuse for my trouble. I certainly didn't back down, though, and for the sake of the story let's just say it didn't happen again.

Working with Barbara Windsor was like a breath of fresh air. She may have been small and blonde but she didn't suffer fools and had Kenny Williams wrapped around her little finger. I'm pretty sure he ended up going on her honeymoon when she married Ronnie Knight. Imagine that! There you are in your hotel room trying to be all romantic and just before you turn out the light there's a knock at the door. ''Eeeere, put 'im down, Barbara. You don't know where 'e's been! Do you want to see my bum? Of course you do!'

That's enough to put anyone off!

She once said something very salient, did our Barbara. 'We didn't get into this business to become famous, did we, Bernie? We did it because we like fooling around and showing off a bit.' She's absolutely right. Barbara also said that I was the one person she knows in this business who just gets on with it. 'You just do your job and go fishing,' she said. 'That's the way to do it, Bernie.'

A lovely compliment from a beautiful human being.

I know Barbara's not been very well lately and as well as a huge hug I'm sending her all the luck in the world. We love you, Barbara.

CHAPTER TEN

Halt, or you will be exterminated!

You remember earlier when I made that quip about going from the sublime to the ridiculous? Well, after making *Carry On Spying* I had it in reverse because just as that was being released in the United Kingdom, I was asked by Hammer Films if I'd like to spend a few weeks in a hot country with none other than Ursula Andress. It doesn't get much more sublime than that, believe me. To top it all off we were going to be joined by Peter Cushing, John Richardson and Christopher Lee, and we'd be making a film based on a H. Rider Haggard novel called *She*. Ursula had recently appeared in *Dr No* alongside Sean Connery and as well as being one of the most beautiful women on the planet she was also one of its most sought-after actresses. The icing on the cake was that some of the filming was going to take place in the Negev Desert where I'd had lots of fun with Mr Niven. Obviously I'd forgotten about the food.

'Yes, all right then,' I said to my agent. 'If I must.'

The film was announced in May 1964 and we began shooting in August. It's all about a party of explorers (me, Peter Cushing and John Richardson) who discover an ancient African city that is ruled over by a despotic queen (Ursula), who holds the secret of eternal life. The queen believes that one of our group (not me, unfortunately, but John Richardson) is the reincarnation of her dead lover and offers him the chance to rule the kingdom with her. While all this is going on the queen's treacherous high priest (Christopher Lee – who else?) is planning to pilfer her immortality for himself. The swine!

I knew right from the off that *She* was going to be fun to make and the entire cast and crew got on like a house on fire. A few years after this, my mate Dickie Briers made a film with Raquel Welch called *Fathom*. He told me that Raquel had been a delight to work with. 'Just like one of the boys,' he told me. Well, Ursula Andress was exactly the same, and then some. She was delightful. Seriously, I've seen pantomime horses with larger egos than her, and talk about professional.

To bring me back down to earth, why don't I tell you about the time I almost had my wedding tackle blown off? OK then. One day, the delightful Mr Cushing and I were filming in the Negev Desert. We'd travelled there from our base in Eilat, which was about 25 miles away, and we were filming scenes that involved us fighting off some Bedouin people. I'm carrying a rifle, Peter a revolver, and these guys are coming at us on camels firing all kinds of everything. It was all very exciting!

The special effects guy we were supposed to have had been seconded onto another film that was shooting further north, and so we'd been left with an Israeli Army boy called Danny. He was enthusiastic, bless him, but he wasn't fully conversant with the dos and don'ts of staging a gun battle. Subsequently, when it came to putting the bullet splashes into the sand, which are meant to give the effect of gunfire, he got a bit carried away. Sometimes you'd use what's called an air line for this, which is basically just a line of plastic with holes in that gives out powerful puffs of air. It sounds quite rudimentary but put it under sand and it gives the effect that bullets are landing. Unfortunately, young Danny didn't have any air lines and so instead he used detonators that were used in plastic explosives. They look like little pencils and are set off electronically.

After Danny had set up for the first scene, we went to shoot it. Everything went fine, as far as Peter and I were concerned, but the director wasn't happy.

'No, let's do that again,' he said. 'Come on. Camels back. Effects, could you set up again, please?'

This time around, instead of laying the detonators in the same position as last time, Danny put them underneath where I was kneeling as the director shouted action. You don't have to be Sherlock Holmes to work out what happened but you do have to have quite a strong stomach.

After the director had shouted action I started firing my rifle and Danny started pressing the buttons that made his detonators detonate. Only one of them went off directly underneath me but it was enough to cause some serious damage. It was underneath my left buttock, to be exact, and, without wanting to sound too crude, it resulted in me having an extra twenty-three holes in my bum. Had I been kneeling a few inches to my left it would have blown my bits and pieces off and I wouldn't have made *The Railway Children*.

A stuntman called Gerry Crampton looked after me. I mentioned him earlier with regards to Peter Sellers's memorial service. It's hardly surprising he and I became good friends because moments after the explosion he was pulling my trousers down and ladling off the claret. Because it was so hot my blood had thinned down which meant it was flowing quite freely and the first thing I noticed, apart from the fact that my bum was rather sore, were some flies that had swarmed around my left boot. On closer inspection I realised that the detonator had blown some bits straight through my boot and the flies were feeding off the blood that was pouring out of it. I told you that you'd need a strong stomach!

While this was going on another stuntman, Terry Plummer, was sitting in a nearby chair. As Gerry was attending to me he looked at me calmly and said, 'I always knew your arsehole would go, Cribbins.'

I was speechless.

About five minutes later, Peter and I were having a smoke while I waited for an ambulance. I may have been the one in pain, but he'd been shaken badly by the accident and he was very upset.

'Don't worry, Peter,' I said, trying to reassure him. 'Once they've pulled the shrapnel out I'll be absolutely—'

Before I could finish the sentence we heard another explosion. We turned around and Danny, the Israeli boy, had blown off two of his fingers. The detonator he'd been working with wasn't wired up to anything but the heat had made it go off. It was an accident waiting to happen. Thank God he managed to move his head in time. Otherwise . . .

Without batting an eyelid Danny turned to the second assistant and said, 'Felix, I've joined the club!' He was referring to the fact that all special effects guys have bits of their body missing and so he now felt part of the team.

As soon as I got to the hospital they knocked me out with Pethidine and got to work on my bum. Although I couldn't feel any pain I could definitely hear the clink, clink, clink of the shrapnel dropping into the kidney dish. When I finally came to, I looked around and there in the next cubicle was Danny. He was spark out and had a rather large bandage on his hand. *I've joined the club*, indeed. That's just bonkers!

When I got home to Blighty the first thing I did was go and see my GP to tell him what had happened.

'I think I should take a quick look,' he said.

'I'm not an exhibit,' I replied, as I was removing my trousers. As he was having a look at my underside I suddenly felt a sharp pain. This was followed by the fuzzily familiar sound of somebody dropping a piece of metal into a bowl.

'They didn't get all the shrapnel, I'm afraid,' said the doc. 'I reckon you've got at least seven or eight bits left.'

Sure enough, after a bit more rummaging about and a bit more pain he removed a further eight pieces of metal from my posterior. I know a GP's life is a varied one but I bet he wasn't expecting that when he was munching his cornflakes. *I wonder what I'll be doing today. Pulling bits of metal out of Bernard Cribbins's arse, perhaps? Who knows . . .*

I should stress that despite the injury I had a wonderful time making *She* and the best thing to come out of it was my friendship with Peter Cushing. Just like David Niven, Peter had a reputation for being a gentleman and I can honestly say I have never heard a bad word said about him. It's quite ironic, really, given the fact that he appeared in so many horror films. You could say the same about Christopher Lee, as he was lovely too. Then again, they were only acting.

My relationship with Peter during the making of *She* was quite similar to the relationship I had with David during *The Best of Enemies*, the difference being that I spent a lot more time with Peter as I was playing his assistant. You remember I told you about going fossil hunting in the Negev with Mr Niven? Well, with Mr Cushing it was birds – of the feathered variety. Each day we would have a competition to see how many different species we could spot and I have to admit that he usually came out on top. At the end of the shoot Peter presented me with a ginormous book called *Birds of the World* and I still have it today. It weighs half a ton this thing and it's basically an avian encyclopaedia. When I first opened it there was a card inside that read, 'I wish you could be in every film I may be lucky enough to make.' Isn't that nice? I kept the card where it was and it remains there to this day.

Because I'd been to the Negev before I remembered to take my snorkelling gear with me and whenever I had some time off I'd pop for a dip. Although he was a strong swimmer Peter had never been under water with a snorkel before and, when I suggested it to him, he was all over it like a rash. 'Oh, I'd love to, Bernard,' he said. After setting him up with a snorkel, down we went. He was like an excited teenager! Once we were submerged I started pointing out different fish to him and Peter got so excited that he started telling me how wonderful it all was. This would have been fine had we been on dry land, but underwater it was slightly different. He still hadn't realised, though – he was too excited – and so as I'm pointing out fish he's doing an impression of Bill and Ben the Flowerpot Men. He genuinely was just like an excited child. It was marvellous.

Ursula and I also went snorkelling together a couple of times, just like I did with Peter. This was a slightly different experience, though, as Ursula insisted on wearing little bikini bottoms and a T-shirt. Put me right off, it did.

The funniest thing that happened back at Elstree Studios while we were making *She* took place when we were trying to film a big fight scene. The set they'd built was absolutely enormous and the people involved were the three explorers – me, Peter and John – and a tribe of men called the Amahaggers. Or the Happy Shaggers, as we christened them. Gerry Crampton was arranging the scene and everybody was being told exactly where they were expected to be. 'You, over there. You two, this way a bit, and don't you dare bloody move.' Gerry was fabulous at this sort of thing. The Amahaggers were all wearing loincloths and were carrying spears. Apart from following Gerry's directions, the only thing they had to remember to do was be loud and fierce. The scene starts when some huge doors at the back of the set open and then in pour the Happy Shaggers.

Once Gerry had finished arranging the fight the director, Robert Day, who, incidentally, had directed me in *Two-Way Stretch*, said, 'OK, action!' In ran the Happy Shaggers and the fight scene duly commenced.

About five seconds later Robert Day suddenly shouted, 'CUT! What the bloody hell are those two doing?'

Robert was pointing to the doors where the Happy Shaggers had entered and there, just emerging through said doors at a very leisurely pace, were two of them. They were smiling, holding hands, and each was carrying a joint. Whether they were shaggers or not I couldn't say, but they were definitely happy.

A few months after making *She*, the BBC asked me if I'd like to make a forty-five-minute TV special for them. You know the type of thing: sketches, songs and special guests. Sid Green and Dick Hills were going to write the script and I was told that I could even invite a guest. As long as he or she was famous.

'How about Peter Cushing?' I suggested.

'Great, if you can get him,' said Auntie. 'But what would you do with him? A sketch?'

'I was thinking of a song and dance number.'

'Song and dance? You're having us on.'

I wasn't. Peter Cushing was a huge song-and-dance fan and I thought, *What better way to surprise the public. Peter Cushing – the master of horror – singing and dancing. That's entertainment!* When I asked him he was cock-a-hoop. 'Nobody's ever asked me to do anything like that before,' he said. He wasn't the most elegant dancer on the planet but then, neither was I. He had a good voice, though, and we made a damn good stab of the number. I wish I could remember what it was!

When *She* finally opened in April 1965 Peter had just started working on a film called *Doctor Who and the Daleks*. The television series had started in 1963 and because it had been so successful a big-screen outing had been mooted almost immediately. The film was released in August 1965 and just a few weeks after that I received a telephone call asking if I'd be interested in appearing in the sequel.

'Is Peter still playing the Doctor?' I asked.

'Yes, he is,' came the reply.

'Then I'll do it.'

In the first film Roy Castle had played the Doctor's assistant and I have no idea why he didn't do the sequel. I'm so glad, though, as it was marvellous working with Peter again. We made a rather good team, he and I. The sequel's called *Daleks – Invasion Earth: 2150 AD* and joining Mr Cushing and me in the TARDIS were Jill Curzon, who played his niece, and Roberta Tovey, who played his granddaughter. Yours truly played a police constable who stumbles into the TARDIS by mistake and we all end up in the year 2150, where we save the world from the Daleks.

Speaking of which.

Despite them being thoroughly evil creatures, a Dalek gave rise to one of the biggest laughs we had on the entire film. Or rather, the chap inside working it did. Yes folks, I'm afraid it's true. Daleks are operated by humans.

The human in this instance was a lovely Australian fellow named Bob Jewell. Bob had been a Dalek operator on the television series and so he'd been poached from the BBC. Despite not having a speaking role Bob still had to deliver any lines for the Dalek he was operating, with the metallic voice we're all familiar with being dubbed over later. In *Daleks – Invasion Earth: 2150 AD*, Bob was working the chief Dalek and so he got to speak the majority of the lines. The Daleks make their first appearance when Peter and I are being taken to their spaceship. We've been collared by some stormtroopers and are being pushed along at gunpoint. As we approach the spaceship a ramp lowers and a Dalek emerges – the chief Dalek, no less. If you were watching in the cinema or at home you'd then hear the Dalek say, in a Dalek voice, 'Halt, or you will be exterminated.' Peter and I, on the other hand, heard it spoken in a voice that hailed from Australia, not the BBC Radiophonic Workshop. The difference was striking and because Bob's accent had an upward inflection that made it even worse. Just try and imagining it. 'Halt, or you will be exterminated.' Needless to say, Mr Cushing and I found this most amusing and got an attack of the giggles. The director, Gordon Flemying, who was a Scottish gentleman, didn't think there was anything funny about us being accosted by an Australian Dalek and told us, in no uncertain terms, that if we didn't pull ourselves together we'd be . . . well, exterminated!

We did as we were told.

The rest of the 1960s were an extremely happy time for me. Gill and I bought our first house, which we live in to this day, and I was being offered some fabulous jobs. One of the most interesting was a children's television series that had started in December 1965 called *Jackanory*. Created by a television producer named Joy Whitby, the format was simplicity itself: an actor or actress reading a story straight to camera with occasional illustrations, just to break things up a bit. Less was most definitely more in this case and I still think it's one of the best things I ever did. Actors and actresses used to ask me how you got on *Jackanory*! Everyone wanted a go.

The show's title comes from an old English nursery rhyme written in the eighteenth century that starts, 'I'll tell you a story, about Jack a Nory', and the first story to be broadcast was a fairy-tale called 'Cap-o'-Rushes', which was read by the actor Lee Montague. The first story I read was 'Blackbeard the Pirate' and the last, which I did in 1991, was called 'Arabel's Tree House'. That one was a bit of a comeback, though, as every other story I read was recorded between 1965 and 1979.

The best way of demonstrating the popularity of *Jackanory*, apart from citing its longevity, is to mention some of the luminaries who agreed to appear in it. I wish I could list them all as the rollcall is frighteningly impressive but just to give you a flavour: Peter Sellers, Spike Milligan, Maggie Smith, Judi Dench, Arthur Lowe, Denholm Elliott, Ian McKellen, Kenneth Williams, Victoria Wood, Michael Palin, James Robertson Justice, Alan Rickman, Margaret Rutherford, Alan Bennett, Joss Ackland, John Hurt, Prince Charles! The list goes on and on and on. They even had six Doctor Whos: Patrick Troughton, Jon Pertwee, Tom Baker, Peter Davison, Sylvester McCoy and Paul McGann. No Peter Cushing, though, alas.

Despite the multitude of storytellers only one person holds the record for the most number of episodes, and he's on the cover of this book. But shall I tell you what makes me proud of my involvement with *Jackanory*? And I mean really proud. One day in the early 1970s I was going up to London to do a voice-over. I got out at Waterloo, hailed a cab, and the chap who stopped for me was a black gentleman. After saying our hellos he asked me 'Where to', and I gave him an address in Soho. Once we were on our way the driver asked me what I was up to, as they do. 'I'm recording a promo for a programme about *Jackanory* and Roald Dahl,' I told him.

'*Jackanory?*' said the driver, smiling. 'Do you know, Mr Cribbins, that programme made me want to learn to read.'

That line still gives me shivers.

Seldom has a single sentence had such a profound effect on me. *Jackanory* had been devised specifically to stimulate an interest in reading and this was its ultimate triumph. A young lad from the East End, who'd obviously had little or no education, sees an episode of *Jackanory* and wants to pick up a book. Game, set and match to Joy Whitby and everyone who was involved in that wonderful programme.

Things were never same for me after *Jackanory* had found its feet, and I mean that in a positive way. Before that, I was just a character who'd sung a few songs and the vast majority of people who'd either seen or heard me or who recognised me were adults. Not exclusively, but mainly. After *Jackanory*, this changed and all of a sudden I became Uncle Bernard. It makes your heart leap being appreciated by a child and I will never, ever tire of it. It's the perfect tonic.

In May 1967, while I was recording a story called 'The Dark Child' for *Jackanory*, I was also working at Shepperton Studios on a film with Jerry Lewis. Just goes to show how mad this business can be. One minute I'm telling stories, and the next I'm in a film studio with a Hollywood legend. The film was called *Don't Raise the Bridge, Lower the River*, and it was being produced by Walter Shenson, who'd produced *The Mouse on the Moon*. Terry-Thomas was co-starring and despite the starry cast it had the same shooting schedule as a *Carry On* film: about five or six weeks. I played somebody called Fred Davies, although what I did I couldn't tell you. Over the years hundreds of people have asked me what it was like working with Jerry Lewis and I think they're expecting me to say either that he was difficult or he was a genius. He was neither. He was just a good actor and a nice bloke. He did have a little motorised scooter that he used to get about the studio on. I thought to myself, *If I'm very nice to him he might give me that at the end of the film*, but he never did. Jerry did introduce me to Sammy Davis Jr, though, which was nice. Sammy came to visit Jerry on the set one day and so I got to shake his hand. If that's all I can remember about *Don't Raise the Bridge, Lower the River*, it doesn't say much about the film, does it? I certainly haven't seen it since its release.

Shortly after making the film I was asked to appear in a play for Thames Television called *Another Branch of the Family*. It was part of the Armchair Theatre series and was about my character, who was a bit of an oddball, and a chimpanzee. Freddie Jones would be co-starring, which was nice, and it was to be directed by a Londoner named Kim Mills.

A week or so before we were due to start filming I got a call from Kim.

'I want you to come in and meet your co-star,' he said.

'What are you talking about? I've already met Freddie.'

'Not Freddie, you nit. The chimp! Can you get down to Thames Studios?'

To cut a long story short I went down to Thames and in the car park was a large grey lorry.

'He's in there,' said Kim.

There was an Italian man looking after him and when he opened up the back of this lorry I got the shock of my life. This chimp was a male about 3 feet high and the first thing I thought when I saw him wasn't, *Aww, come over here and give us a kiss*. It was, *You could rip my bleeding arm off, couldn't you?* The thing is, this little chap really could have done some damage if he'd wanted and I didn't feel safe at all.

As we were looking at this chimp his carer suddenly said, 'Give me your hand.'

I reluctantly agreed to his request and he pulled it forward and offered it to the chimp. The chimp then took my hand and put it in his mouth but instead of biting down on it he sucked on it.

'What's he doing?' I said, trying not to appear absolutely bloody terrified, which I was.

'He's tasting you,' said the keeper.

I didn't ask if this was with a view to eating me and when I got my hand back it went straight in my pocket.

On the first day of rehearsal the lorry arrived again, and the chimp's keeper was carrying a short iron bar.

'What's that for?' I asked, pointing at the bar.

'Oh, that. It's just to keep him under control if he gets nasty.'

Gets nasty? You could have killed somebody with this rod!

As things progressed the chimp started taking an unhealthy interest in the female production assistant. Subsequently, his keeper kept on having to pull him away from this poor girl and the chimp didn't like it. Eventually the chimp went for her and ended up ripping off her skirt. We all agreed there and then that we'd need another chimp. Not least the production assistant!

While somebody helped her out with her skirt, the keeper took the chimp back to his lorry. I couldn't help thinking that we'd all had a narrow escape.

A couple of days later, Kim called me again.

'I think we've found the right one this time. Do you want to come and have a look?'

I didn't, to be honest, but I thought I better had.

Because I knew what we might be dealing with, I decided to buy some Smarties this time as a potential sweetener and I put them in the pocket of my cardigan. There was no lorry this time, which was encouraging, and soon after parking myself in the rehearsal studios a man called Wally arrived carrying a small female chimpanzee called Lulu.

'Mr Cribbins,' said Wally. 'This is Lulu. Lulu, go and say hello to Mr Cribbins.'

Just as he said that Lulu ran across the floor, climbed straight up me, held onto my shoulders, and looked straight in my eyes. As she did that her right foot went into my pocket and pulled out the Smarties. I turned to Kim and Wally.

'I think she'll be perfect.'

Lulu and I became so close that when Freddie Jones and I had to have a heated conversation as part of the play she went for him and ended up biting his finger. She defended me. Poor Freddie had to go off and get a jab while Lulu clung to the front of me as if to say, *I saw to him, didn't I?*

I really was a busy boy in the late 1960s. I still did a bit of fishing here and there, but if a job came up I just did it and I was very grateful that people wanted to use me. Some jobs stood out far more than others, sometimes because of the people I worked alongside, sometimes because of the quality of the work and, if I was very lucky, sometimes because of both.

At the start of 1968 I received a script for a new farce by Ray Cooney and John Chapman entitled *Not Now Darling*. It had been tried out the year before at the Richmond Theatre and after making a few changes here and there it was ready to come into the West End. In the play, Arnold Crouch and Gilbert Bodley own a fur salon and while Crouch keeps everything afloat, Bodley is off philandering. After getting himself a new mistress, Bodley decides to sell her husband a fur coat at a rock-bottom price in order to keep her sweet but the husband decides to give the coat to his own mistress. After that, all hell breaks loose and the entire play is awash with plots and mistaken identities.

When I read the play I thought, *This is marvellous stuff*. It was devilishly clever and there were belly laughs all over the shop. The part they wanted me for was Arnold Crouch and the actor playing Gilbert Bodley would be Donald Sinden.

Despite Donald and I getting on well together, and despite him being a consummate farceur, he did have a touch of the Robert Morleys about him - i.e., he got bored quite easily and when that happened he too would start wandering off script and adding bits. I was now approaching forty and my tolerance for unwanted improvisation hadn't improved. After all, if you've already had Robert Morley improvising for breakfast, the last thing you need is Donald Sinden buggering about at lunch. I was, to use a rather juvenile expression, not at home to Mr Making-it-up-on-the-bloody-spot!

What I should have done was make sure my co-star aware of this prior to us opening but it just never occurred to me. I mean, how do you broach something like that? 'I just wanted

With the great James Mason in Lionel Jeffries's film *The Water Babies*.

'People don't die in television, John!' Going into battle with a very strong John Cleese.
(BBC Photo Library/Ronald Grant Archive/Mary Evans)

Booby, looking guilty!

Minnie, our last beagle.

With Helen Mirren in *The Country Wife*, part of the BBC's *Play of the Month* series. Nice work if you can get it. *(BBC Photo Library)*

What a couple of stunners! With the lovely Wilfrid Bramble in the Swedish film *The Adventures of Picasso* in 1978.

As Gertrude Stein in the strange but enjoyable *The Adventures of Picasso*.

With fellow *Jackanory*-ers Maurice Denham, Jan Francis and David Wood in 1979. This was an ensemble effort with all four of us reading J. R. R. Tolkien's *The Hobbit*. *(BBC Photo Library)*

Me and my co-star in *Dangerous Davies*.

Guys and Dolls. Left to right: Andrew Wadsworth, Betsy Brantley, *moi* and Imelda Staunton.

With my pal Elaine Paige in Cole Porter's *Anything Goes*. Like many actors and actresses, I'm most at home on the stage, and especially in a musical. *(Anthony Crickmay)*

Having a laugh with John Barrowman and Elaine Paige prior to a performance of *Anything Goes*. This was John's professional debut and we all knew that he was a big talent.

Meeting the Queen Mother backstage during my time on *Anything Goes*. I spent a whole year on that show!

The tree in Perth! I told you it was big.

With Jim Dale and Peter Richardson in the disastrous *Carry On Columbus*. The series deserved a better finale.

(above) Playing Widow Twankey at Guildford. No idea when, I'm afraid, but I look ravishing.

(right) Teeing off at the very first Cribbins Classic. I bet I sliced it.

I can't for the life of me remember what this was for, but it's a great photo, don't you think?

Having a giggle with my old pal Dickie Briers.

The cast of Ray Cooney's record-breaking farce *Run for Your Wife*. Left to right: Carol Hawkins, Peter Blake, Dickie Briers, *moi*, Bill Pertwee, Helen Gill and Royce Mills. Those smiles are all genuine, by the way.

With Dora Bryan and Roy Barraclough recording Jimmie Chinn's drama *Perfect Timing*, which is about a struggling music hall duo. I love doing a bit of radio.

A sketch of our dear dog Rosie by the multi-talented Paul Hawkyard. Gill and I adore this drawing.

Me with the lovely Rosie, our last dog. When I first went to collect her from Sussex she spent the entire journey home under my jumper, snuggled up on my belly. We had her for fifteen years. *(© John E Periam)*

Me and a very nice rainbow trout. I love a bit of fishing.

Martin Bowler and I with my best pike – 22lbs 9oz! Mr Bowler is one of the best fishermen I've ever worked with, and a thoroughly good lad to boot.

A very, very proud moment. Receiving my special BAFTA award in 2009 flanked by Dick & Dom and the wonderful Catherine Tate. *(Jo Hale/ Getty Images)*

to say how much I'm looking forward to working with you, Donald. Oh, and by the way. If you ever decide to go off-script I'll beat you to death with a rolled up copy of the *Angling Times*, OK?'

As I've already said, Ray and John's script for *Not Now Darling* was absolutely on the button which is another reason I wouldn't tolerate any kind of deviation. It was almost sacred, in a way, and I was proud to be appearing in their – emphasis on the word *their* – play.

I remember the scene where it happened vividly. It was during the second act and for reasons I won't go into now I'd just thrown a dress out of a second-floor window that had got caught on a flagpole outside. After some dialogue between me and the actress whose character owns the dress, Donald storms in and asks me what a dress is doing on the flagpole. After pausing for a second I then look at the audience, look back and say, 'waving'. It obviously doesn't seem that funny on paper but I promise you that as part of the play it got a big laugh.

About a week into the run the line failed one evening and I couldn't for the life of me work out why. Everyone had been on cue and we were all fresh. The following night I said the line again and as I'm looking back from the audience after the pause I see Donald flapping his hands from side to side – waving. He was obviously pre-empting my line which was killing it dead.

A few minutes after the show had ended I went into Donald's dressing room and asked him what he thought he was doing, or words to that effect. 'What on earth do you mean, old boy?' asked the theatrical miscreant. After explaining my complaint in slightly more detail I finished with, 'It's a perfectly good line,

Donald, which gets a perfectly good laugh and you're bloody well killing it. PACK – IT – IN!'

It didn't happen again.

This isn't simply a caveat to make us sound all chummy, but, as I said before, Donald Sinden was probably the best farceur in the country at the time and working with him wasn't simply a joy (on the whole!), it was an education. His presence alone was just incredible and it didn't matter what you were doing when he walked on stage, all eyes would gravitate immediately to him. He also possessed that almost fabled gift of timing which is so essential when playing comedy. That's something you're born with. On top of all this Donald was also a first-class raconteur so I've not done him any justice by recounting this story. The trouble is, it's the only one I can remember!

Sorry, old boy.

During the 1960s my life became invaded by a succession of small furry animals. No, I'm not talking about the Wombles. Or Barry Cryer. They came later. I'm talking about dogs.

The reason I'm putting this here is because the period I'd like to tell you about finishes in the late 1960s, so it's chronological – ish. And don't you worry. I know this book is supposed to be about me so what I'm not going to do is just waffle on about how cute they were. This is the story of how I, or Gill and I, became dog owners, and the reason it's important is because by doing so I was fulfilling a lifelong dream. As a child we'd never had one, you see (Gill had had loads, the lucky thing), and as I got older the yearning to have one simply strengthened.

While living in London we hadn't been able to have a dog as the majority of landlords wouldn't allow them. Then, in the early 1960s, we moved into a flat in a place called Claygate which is near Esher in Surrey. After getting settled in, the dog issue came up, as it always did, and we found that this time around we'd actually be able to have one. Bingo! Once Gill had managed to pull me down from the ceiling we discussed what kind of breed we'd both like and eventually settled on a beagle. They're good to look at and are rather silly. That was our reasoning.

I forget how we found them – probably through the Kennel Club or something – but after a few days of searching we finally got in touch with a breeder in South Shields and ordered ourselves a female beagle. After sorting out the money I was told I had to collect our new puppy from King's Cross, which I duly did. As you know I didn't drive in those days so I took the train up to King's Cross at the date and time specified and went down to left luggage. When I arrived, there, in the corner of the room, was a large tin box with a small inquisitive-looking animal inside. As you can imagine her box was a bit of mess (wouldn't yours be after seven or eight hours on a train?) and after picking her up I hailed a taxi and asked the driver to take us to Waterloo. Until we got back to the flat I didn't dare take her out as I had visions of her running away, so I just talked to her while we were in the taxi and on the train and told her how much Gill and I had been looking forward to meeting her. When we finally arrived at the flat I opened the box and out crept this beautiful but very messy little creature. The first thing Gill did was give our new friend a very large dog biscuit, which, after clambering up onto the sofa, she promptly buried underneath one of the cushions. Cute? You don't know the half of it!

Bessie, as we christened her, was a liver and white beagle and when she got older she became very good looking and very sexy. At least that's what she told everybody. What I mean to say is she was a very feminine dog and received an awful lot of attention. When you took her for a walk she refused to do her number ones or number twos while on the lead and so you always had to let her off for a bit. One day, while walking her on some scrubland near the flat, Gill did exactly that and while Bessie was going about her ablutions a local sheepdog appeared. After twirling his moustache a couple of times he and Bessie ran off together and by the time Gill caught up with them they were well and truly locked. After managing to manoeuvre the young lovers into a nearby stream Gill tried quite literally to throw cold water on the proceedings. That evening, when I returned home from work, I got the full story and almost fell off my chair. The little strumpet!

To be honest we didn't think anything of it (we were a bit naïve, I'm afraid) and then after a few weeks it became very clear that our Bessie was pregnant. She ended up giving birth to three puppies that we referred to as Beep Dogs. Get it? We kept the pups in a big greenhouse in the garden which acted as a kind of crèche and at about ten weeks old they waved goodbye and all went to new homes.

The following year we decided to mate Bessie with another beagle and she gave birth to six puppies: three dogs and three bitches. We decided to keep one of the bitches and so set about choosing her a name. Her kennel club name was Hawthorn

Beauty, but, as I said to Gill, 'If you think I'm shouting that in the park, you've got another think coming.' A week or so after the pups were born the actor Anton Rodgers and his family came to see them. One of his sons, who was very small at the time, couldn't say Hawthorn Beauty and kept on saying Hawthorn Booby instead. 'That's it,' said Gill. 'Let's call her Booby!' And that's exactly what we did.

A few weeks after Bessie had given birth to this litter she went off one day to stretch her legs. The pups were in a pen in the garden at the time and when she came back she went straight into the pen and dropped something out of her mouth. I'd watched Bessie come back into the garden and I had a feeling she was carrying something. As I approached the pen I saw a small bird flapping about and, on closer inspection, I realised that it was a baby thrush, completely unharmed, by the way. Bessie was obviously trying to teach her litter the ways of the world but the pups, who were a right handful, were simply bemused. *What on earth's this*, they must have thought. Just to be on the safe side I ran forward, scooped up the thrush, and took it back to where I thought it might have come from. Fortunately, I think its mum found it in the end and as far as I know it was ok. A few years later Booby was trotting around the garden one day with very swollen cheeks. 'Come here, you,' I said, and she said, 'No, I won't'. 'Yes, you will,' I said. 'Come here!' As Booby reluctantly came her mouth was pursed as if she was whistling. 'What have you got in there then?' I said. 'Come on. Let me see.' Again she refused my request so I prized open her jaws and inside was a live bank vole. What she was planning on doing with it I have no idea but once the poor little thing had got its bearings I put it back in the hedge and told it to run like hell!

The year after Bessie had given birth to Booby, she had another beagle litter and this time we ended up keeping the tri-coloured runt of the littler. Because she was so small, we called her Minnie. Now, if you have got two beagles running about the house it's not so bad, but the moment you have three they become a pack. By the time Minnie was old enough to run about with Bessie and Booby that's exactly what we had and from an entertainment point of view things changed dramatically. We used to take them up to a place called St Ann's Hill near Chertsey (the M25 runs underneath it now) and this place used to be absolutely full of rabbits. After opening the car door beagles would disappear in all directions and you could always tell when they were chasing something as they'd start yodelling. Each had a different voice: Bessie's was quite low, Booby's was quite high pitched and excitable, and Minnie's was quite squeaky. All Gill and I had to do was sit there and wait for them to get tired, which didn't take too long. It was a very easy way of exercising dogs.

You remember I said that Bessie was quite an alluring little thing? Well, one year, when she was in season, a sheepdog belonging to Charlie Drake called Boofy slept out in sub-zero temperatures just to get a chance with her. Dogs obviously know when a bitch is in season but Boofy had become such a pest that I thought I was going to have to take out an injunction against him. Charlie lived just around the corner at the time and, one morning, when I went to let the dogs out, I found Boofy fast asleep on our back doorstep. When I went to move him an indentation of his body was there surrounded by frost! That's what I call dedication. Had Boofy been a beagle then I might have let him in but unfortunately he was a sheepdog.

When Bessie came into season for the litter in which she had Minnie, Booby also came into season sympathetically. We had tried mating Booby prior to that and had found out she was barren but she obviously wanted to join in, bless her. After Bessie had given birth Booby continued copying her mum and even started producing milk. This meant that when it was time to feed the litter a fight would often break out and in the end we'd have Bessie upstairs in the bathroom feeding one half of the litter and Booby downstairs feeding the other half! Isn't that amazing? Gill and I were fascinated.

As well as doing a very good impression of being a mum, Booby also used to do an even better impression of being a small hippopotamus. Allow me to explain.

For want of a better expression, our Booby was an absolute glutton and would do anything for food. Anything! When she was old enough she discovered that, after she'd eaten, if she climbed out of the garden, which wasn't easy given that we'd put fencing all the way around to keep her and the others in, she could find second helpings. The way she made her escape was by taking a running jump and then climbing up the six or seven foot of wire mesh just like a monkey. Once at the top she'd then wobble for a few seconds, make her ascent and then go off foraging. I swear to God this is true. I'd see her start running towards the fence and I'd shout, 'Booby! Don't you dare jump over that bloody fence.' Once she'd scrambled to the top she'd look at me as if to say, 'Yeah, and what are you going to do about it, Cribbins?' She used to do this early in the morning and one day I told Gill that I'd had enough and was going to follow her and find out where she was going. After she'd escaped I got on my bike, went around the corner which I knew was the direction she was heading, and I followed her to a house that was owned by a family called Atkinson. Mr and Mrs Atkinson had five children and they obviously had a staggered breakfast time which meant Booby had anything up to seven opportunities to snaffle some grub. The first thing she'd do was run into the Atkinsons' kitchen, tell them she was starving, and then sit and have breakfast with each child as they got up. Once she'd had her fill – or once the Atkinsons had run out of food – she'd come lolloping back home with a distended stomach and start burping and farting. Seriously, she'd go out a dog, and come back a bloody hippo!

One day Gill decided to follow her – this was a lunchtime escape after she'd slept off her seven breakfasts – and she eventually found Booby sitting in front of some builders wagging her tail and saying, 'I haven't been fed for fourteen years, please help!' One by one these builders started feeding Booby bits of pie and sandwich and by the time she got home she was so fat that she couldn't even lie on her tummy or her side. She had to roll onto her back. The noises, though, were just incredible. As she walked through the door she'd be groaning like a bear with a hangover and then, once she was finally settled on the carpet, all the trumping and burping would start. It's like me after a curry.

I'm going to finish off Doggytime with a rather heart-warming little story that happened about thirty years ago featuring two dogs we adopted within just a couple of years of each other. First of all there was Bella – a King Charles Spaniel who came to us after Gill's mother died – and then Megan – a lovely little Jack Russell Corgi cross who we decided to take on when some friends of ours emigrated to America. She was a bit of a crocodile was Megan, and Gill once found her in the garden trying to eat a hedgehog! Anyway, it's probably fair to say that when Megan arrived on the scene Bella was not in favour of the new arrival. In fact, they didn't get on at all. A couple of weeks later Gill had to drive up to Scotland and, because I was away working, she had to take the dogs with her. 'But what am I going to do with them?' Gill asked. 'If I'm not free to pull them apart they'll end up killing each other.'

In the end, on the recommendation of our vet, Gill tied the two dogs up giving them each just enough lead to get within about a foot of each other. She doesn't know how on earth it happened but, by the time they arrived in Scotland, which took eight hours, Bella and Megan were best pals! They must have decided to call it quits or something. 'I just couldn't believe it,' said Gill when she arrived back. 'They got in the car sworn enemies and got out the best of friends. What a relief!' So strong was their newfound bond that, when Megan began losing her eyesight (she was already quite old when she arrived), Bella started walking just in front of her so that Megan could either smell her or feel her. She became a guide dog!

Anyway. It's time to swap these four-legged hairy animals for the two-legged one on the front of this book. Is that ok?

Not many people know this but in 1969 I had my own sketch show on ITV. It ran for two series, so it did, and the man who first approached me about it was Alan Tarrant. He was a comedy producer par excellence and had worked with everyone from Tony Hancock to Norman Wisdom. This was a completely new departure for me as I'd never had to carry my own series before, but I was completely up for the challenge. The writers were Johnnie Mortimer and Brian Cooke, who went on to write things like *Man About the House* and *George and Mildred*, and my co-stars included Bob Todd, Madeline Smith, Sheila Steafel and Tim Barrett.

Bob Todd and I used to get rather tiddly of an evening and one night in the canteen at Thames Television, which used to be based, rather appropriately, on the banks of the River Thames, we decided to hold a discus competition. We were the only ones there at the time and so we grabbed a stack of dinner plates each, took them outside, and began practising for the next Olympics. After about ten minutes we heard somebody behind us clearing their throat.

'Erm, excuse me,' said the voice. 'But what do you think you're doing?'

It was a security guard.

'Just doing a spot of discus throwing,' said Bob, lobbing one more into the Thames. 'Helps us to unwind, don't you know.'

'Well, I'd rather you didn't, if you don't mind,' said the guard.

It was obviously a rhetorical request, and I think that had we refused he'd have called the police. In the end we received a slap on the wrists and a bill from the catering company for fifty plates. The following year, Thames Television decided to move their operation from the banks of the River Thames to Euston Road, which is almost 2 miles away from water. Better to be safe than sorry, I suppose.

Good grief, we're almost at *The Railway Children*. Hasn't time flown?

Before we go to Yorkshire – the Keighley and Worth Valley Railway, to be exact, and a station called Oakworth – I'd like to tell you a little story about Roy Kinnear. We never actually worked together, Roy and I, and I only met him on a couple of occasions. The first time was memorable, however, and because it happened around this period I thought I'd slip it in.

I was walking up Charing Cross Road one day after doing a voiceover when suddenly I saw Roy walking towards me. Actors always know each other, even if they've never met. They'll say, 'Hello, mate. Are you working?' You know the kind of thing. Although I hadn't met Roy before, I obviously knew who he was and so after saying hello we stopped and had a chat. After nattering away about the business for five or ten minutes Roy suddenly said, 'Do you know what my biggest asset is, Bernard? My availability.'

Well, I'm afraid I was in stitches after that. While Roy Kinnear, star of stage and screen, was standing there calmly on Charing Cross Road, I, Bernard Cribbins, the future Mayor of Wimbledon Common, was in the process of doing myself a mischief. What a truly great line, and it was delivered with absolute comic perfection.

I wish I'd got to know Roy. Like me, he was a big rugby league fan, and the only time I saw him after that was at the

Challenge Cup final one year. Thank God he left behind so much great material. And thank you, Roy, for that wonderful line.

Speaking of rugby league, a while ago now I was invited to lead the community singing just before the start of the Challenge Cup final. I'm fairly sure it was Halifax versus St Helens. It was definitely a Yorkshire–Lancashire affair, that's for sure, so let's stick with those two. Since the end of the Second World War, the vast majority of Challenge Cup finals have taken place at Wembley Stadium and the atmosphere on that day was electric. There must have been a good eighty or ninety thousand people there and, when I walked out through the tunnel onto the hallowed turf, I felt every hair on the back of my neck stand on end. I think it was the noise that got me, not to mention all the flags flying. You couldn't help but be moved by it. Fortunately, the announcer didn't say where I was from, so as far as the majority of the crowd were concerned I was impartial. Had he said Lancashire, the atmosphere might have changed somewhat! I actually was impartial, though. I don't have a favourite team. I just enjoy the sport.

As I walked out into the middle of the pitch the two teams were lined up next to the band of the Irish Guards. As I reached the centre I tested my microphone with a couple of one-twos and then greeted the crowd.

'Good afternoon Wembley!' I said, in my least Lancastrian accent.

'Could we have a cheer for Yorkshire, please?' I shouted.

'YAAAAAAAAAAAAAAAAAAAAAAAAAAAAY.'

'And can we have a cheer for Lancashire, please?' I bellowed.

'YAAAAAAAAAAAAAAAAAAAAAAAAAAY.'

After a little bit more chat I said, 'All right, ladies and gentlemen, can you all be upstanding please for "Abide With Me"?'

The moment I'd said the word 'me' the entire stadium fell completely silent. Even the birds seemed to suddenly disappear, and the atmosphere was the most respectful I think I've ever experienced. To have so many people making such an incredible noise to then suddenly fall silent was an about-turn of biblical proportions and I really wasn't expecting it. It takes quite a lot to surprise me but as I was stood there on my own in the middle of that stadium I was dumbstruck.

After the match – I have no idea who won, surprise, surprise – I had to line up on the pitch with the players and the officials so that the guest of honour, the Duke of Edinburgh, could have a chat to us. I was standing towards the end of the line, and it was the first time I'd ever met him. When the Duke got to me he shook my hand and said, 'Hello there. I didn't know you could sing!' After that he sauntered off down the tunnel and that was that. I've met the Duke of Edinburgh several times since then and he always has a line for you. He could write comedy.

This reminds me of a little story regarding my dear mother, Ethel. You don't mind if I bring her back in for a few minutes? As I told you right at the start, she used to work in a cotton mill weaving corduroy trousers. Because of the noise of the looms going backwards and forwards, workers would have to communicate by mouthing words and reading each other's lips. Being able to communicate silently obviously had its advantages and eventually it was used almost as much outside the mills and factories as it was inside. I would watch my mother have entire conversations with women on the other side of the road and without vocalising a single word. There was hardly any traffic back then, so one could easily have walked over to the other. Instead, they used to stand on their doorstep mouthing sentences, lipreading, and, if it was needed, making the odd sign with their hands.

In the 1940s and 1950s this was used to great comic effect by the comedian Norman Evans, and later by Les Dawson. Norman used to do this skit called 'Over the Garden Wall' where, dressed as a middle-aged housewife, he'd gossip to an imaginary neighbour over a garden wall. Whenever he said something risqué, Norman would fall silent and just mouth the words. Most of you reading this will have seen either Norman or Les playing this character, and I bet it's had you in stitches. I actually remember one of the gags from *Over the Garden Wall*. Norman says, 'How's your Alice going on? Is she still in the Waffs? Oh, she's in the canteen, is she? She'll do well there. She's been in a mess before, hasn't she?' If you've never seen an 'Over the Garden Wall' sketch, I implore you to find some on the internet. You'll thank me for it.

Anyway, just after my dad had died in the mid-1970s, Mum came to stay with us for a week or two. Just to get herself together. One day we were watching a rugby league match on television and about halfway through the first half one of the big forwards started getting ticked off by the referee for something. There were obviously no pitch microphones in those days and so me and Mum were trying our best to make out what was being said. After a few minutes, the referee waved this forward away and as he walked off the forward mouthed a phrase ending with the word 'off'.

'Oooh,' said Mum, folding her arms. 'Did you see what he said?'

During Trooping the Colour, she used to be able to lipread everything the royal family were saying on the balcony. They'd all come out and the Queen would say something to Prince Philip. Seconds later, my mother would repeat what she'd just said. It was never anything risqué or embarrassing, but whatever they were saying on that balcony we were hearing via my mother. These days lipreading celebrities has become a big thing and all kinds of people seem to be getting into trouble as a result. If Mum had been around today, I could have hired her out.

Do you know, my mother was actually banned from attending rugby league matches in Oldham? This is perfectly true. She only ever went once, and she was banned on the same day. Dad was a fan and so one day he asked her if she'd like to accompany him. The story goes that Ethel got so excited that she started beating the man in front of her on his head. 'Go on,' she shouted. 'Knock him down!' The gentleman with the head took exception to it being beaten and after a frank exchange of words, Mother was asked to leave.

Well done, Ethel.

CHAPTER ELEVEN

Everybody off for Oakworth!

Before we say hello to those lovely railway children, I must tell you a very quick story. I'd forgotten all about this.

In 1965 Lionel Jeffries and I were making a film by Michael Winner called *You Must be Joking*. Lionel was playing a Scottish sergeant major and I was playing a sergeant and at one point, Lionel, who was wearing a kilt, had to pole vault out of a maze we couldn't get out of and he ended up landing on a greenhouse. They had a stunt double to do the actual pole vault, but I said to Lionel, 'Look, when you're dubbing this, as you're supposed to be pole vaulting the maze, make sure you shout, "*Póg mo thóin*" [pronounced 'pog mahone']!'

'Why on earth would I do that?' asked Lionel, looking slightly puzzled.

'Because it's Irish for kiss my arse.'

'What a bloody good idea, Bernie. I'll do just that.'

After Lionel dubbed the scene the producer of the film came up and asked him what he'd shouted. 'Oh, nothing, sir. It's just an old Gaelic war cry, that's all. It means death to the invader!'

'Oh, that's great,' said the producer. 'Thank you, Lionel.'

When the film opened in Dublin the cinema erupted and it had exactly the same effect in every cinema it was played in over there.

It was just our little contribution.

Right then, because I don't know everything, and because I want to give you the full story of *The Railway Children* and how it was made, I've had to do a bit of research. I knew bits about the backstory to the film, and about the production, of course, but learning about the origins of the film and reminding myself about some of the times we had has been a delight. While reading Lionel's obituary in the *Daily Telegraph* I read the following quote: 'But it was as the director of *The Railway Children*, one of the most enchanting films ever made for young people, that Jeffries left his mark on the history of cinema.' As amazing as Lionel was in films like *Two-Way Stretch*, *The Wrong Arm of the Law* and *Chitty Chitty Bang Bang*, I would have to agree with the person who wrote that obituary. The story of how *The Railway Children* came to light, how it became such a huge success long after it was made, and its ongoing legacy, is almost as enchanting as the film itself.

Sometime in 1968, Lionel's young daughter, Martha, came to him with a book she'd been reading. It was Edith Nesbit's Edwardian classic, *The Railway Children*; a gentle tale of three children and their adventures living alongside a Yorkshire railway line. As Martha handed the book to Lionel she said, 'Daddy, I think that would make a good film.'

In pursuit of his belief that there were more wise children in the world than wise adults, Lionel immediately spent £300 on a six-month option on the film rights and got to work on a script. Six months later, Lionel had finished his script but hadn't been able to find a backer. Undeterred, he decided to extend his option for another six months and in early 1970 he took the script to Bryan Forbes, who was then the head of production at EMI Elstree. Lionel and Bryan had first met on the set of a film called *The Colditz Story* in 1957 and had become close friends.

After agreeing to make the film, Bryan asked Lionel who he visualised as the director, to which he replied, 'I know it's a crazy idea and not on, but I've always secretly harboured a longing to direct it myself.' I obviously can't say for sure that their friendship had anything to do with Bryan Forbes agreeing to this, but handing a budget of £500,000, which is what the film would cost to make, to a first-time director was a big risk. That said, Lionel Jeffries was more than just an actor and because it had been his baby Bryan Forbes obviously had the impression that he was the right person to bring the script to life. How right he was.

When it came to casting the film . . . well, let's do me first.

One day the telephone rang. ''Ello, Bernie. It's Li here. Look darlin', I'm making a film called *The Railway Children* and I need somebody to play the station master. I think you're the man. Mind if I send you a script?'

I didn't mind at all.

You already know how well I got on with Lionel, and, as I just said, he was more than just an actor. That said, as good as the script was and as much as I was looking forward to working with my old friend again, I never thought for a moment that we might have a classic on our hands. Things like that very rarely occur to you as an actor. Some jobs you enjoy, and some jobs you don't, but at the end of the day that's what they are – jobs. You always try your best, and any plaudits that come afterwards are always gratefully received, but it's very rarely premeditated. I think that's one of the most charming things about *The Railway Children*. You had a rookie director making a film with some pals, basically. Or at least, that's how it started out. If I was directing a film for the first time, that's exactly what I would do: surround myself with people I'd worked with previously and people I trusted. Dinah Sheridan, who played the children's mother, Mrs Waterbury, had worked with Lionel before, as had a great many of the crew. That also gave the proceedings a kind of family atmosphere, which was perfect for the film we were all making.

But as well as directing the film, you also hear Lionel's voice on more than one occasion as he ended up dubbing two or three characters on it. One of these was played by a friend of ours called Paul Luty. Paul, who was from Leeds, had spent most of his adult life as an all-in wrestler and had switched to acting in the late 1960s. He played a character called Malcolm in *The Railway Children*, although I forget where he pops up. He was definitely one of Lionel's dubbing jobs. Paul used to come to our house for lunch in the 1970s and he always used to arrive with what looked like a horse's leg or something. 'Here you are, Gill, cook that,' he used to say. Gill would do her best to oblige and Paul would end up eating most of it. He was a big lad was old Paul.

The only people Lionel hadn't met before who were heavily involved in the film were the three children. Let's start with Jenny Agutter.

Two years before the film was made Jenny had appeared in a television adaptation of *The Railway Children* that had been made by the BBC. In it she'd played exactly the same role as Lionel wanted her to play in the film, the part of Roberta, or Bobbie, as she was known. At first Jenny was reluctant to accept the role as she thought it would be a step backwards. She'd recently been filming with Nicolas Roeg, who was a big director at the time, so it was completely understandable. Mr Jeffries, however, was not going to be beaten and Jenny later said that because he was such an exuberant personality, she couldn't say no. He was certainly that all right.

Now then. Let's get on to the delightful Miss Thomsett, shall we? Have a guess how old Sally was when Lionel cast her as Phyllis. Bearing in mind Phyllis was supposed to be just eleven years of age.

Well, she was actually twenty, and almost three years older than Jenny Agutter. It's hard to believe, don't you think? Apparently, Lionel called Sally back four times before giving her the job, just to make sure she looked young enough. There were conditions, though, and as well as not being allowed to reveal her real age to any members of the press, Sally wasn't allowed to see her boyfriend, drink alcohol in public or drive her new sports car. She later said that even the film crew didn't know how old she was and while they were asking Jenny how she thought a take had gone, they'd be giving poor Sally sweets!

To prevent Jenny and Sally from getting up to mischief the production company put them up in a remote hotel near Haworth, which is of course where the Brontë sisters lived. Fed up with drinking orange squash and staring out across the dark forbidding moors, Sally decided to stage a breakout one evening and ended up dragging a rather reluctant Jenny all the way to Leeds for a night out. Twenty miles away! How they managed to get there I have no idea but according to Sally they found a nightclub once they were there and, sitting on a mezzanine above them in this place, were Lionel Jeffries and the producer, Robert Lynn. Unfortunately, the two escapees were spotted by their employers and promptly escorted back to the wilds of Hawarth. I love that story.

Whether he did this consciously or not I can't say but, according to Jenny, Lionel assumed the role of an Edwardian father-figure while filming and if a take went well he'd give Jenny, Sally and young Gary Warren half a crown each. I'm afraid I can't tell you how Gary, the boy who played Peter, got the role. He was very quiet, but very pleasant. I saw him in 2014 when we had a reunion and he looked very well indeed. He'll be about sixty-four now.

Now, let's move on to the location – which, together with the trains, is really the star of the film.

After much searching, Lionel and his location manager, Richard Gill, eventually settled on the Keighley and Worth Valley Railway, which runs for 5 miles and has six stations. These days, heritage railways are commonplace, thank heavens, but back then they were a rarity and the Keighley and Worth Valley, as well as being a heritage railway, also had a tunnel, which would be needed for various scenes. The only problem was that the tunnel was a bit short for what they needed and so an extension had to be made using large canvas sheets. The station we used was Oakworth, which is obviously on the

Keighley and Worth Valley Railway. One of the advantages of using Oakworth was that it had already been restored to Edwardian condition and so it needed very little doing to it. These days, partly because of the film, I suppose, Oakworth receives many thousands of visitors every year and our heritage railways are something we should all be proud of.

I must admit that during filming, when the steam engines came into play, it put a big smile on my face. I think we used four in all, and they all had to be adorned in the livery that had been created for the fictional Great Northern and Southern Railway. It took me all the way back to the early 1930s when my pals and I used to run onto a railway bridge near our homes, and when an engine went underneath we'd all stand there inhaling the steam. Here's something else I remember. Whenever we went on holiday to Blackpool, which was always during Wakes Week, we kids would get off and go and say thank you to the engine driver. He was usually leaning out holding an oily rag or something and his face would be blackened by coal dust. 'Thanks very much, mister,' we'd shout, waving. 'My pleasure, lad. You have a nice holiday and be good for your mum.' 'I will. Bye!'

That was something very special.

I'll tell you what, though, I wouldn't have been an engine driver for all the tea in China back then. Imagine what it must have been like on the footplate going from London to Edinburgh during the winter. It must have been a hell of a job. You've got all that hot steel in front of you, yet if you put your head out for two minutes your ears freeze and fall off. No thank you. That said, the Keighley and Worth Valley Railway was maintained

225

by a lovely group of volunteers who were all steam fanatics. As well as allowing us to step onto the footplate occasionally they told us all about coal and steam and how the engines worked. It was fascinating.

The most famous location we used for *The Railway Children* was the Brontë sisters' home, Hawarth Parsonage, which was used as the doctor's house. Apart from a nearby farm that was used for the Waterburys' house, and a few other locations, everything else was filmed at Elstree where Mr Forbes could keep an eye on us.

Fortunately for Gill and me, the production company couldn't get us into the hotel outside Hawarth and so instead they found us a beautiful hotel near Bolton Abbey called the Devonshire Arms. Just behind the hotel sits a river called the River Wharfe and after filming each day I'd come back, have a large whisky, fetch my trout rod from the room and go and do some fishing. What a perfect way to unwind. It wasn't until the end of the film that I discovered I'd been poaching! I needed permission, apparently, although I don't remember catching much.

Apart from learning my lines, I obviously had to act the part of a station porter for the role of Albert Perks and that generally involved me hitting the side of trains as they came to a halt and shouting, 'OAKWORTH! EVERYBODY OFF FOR OAKWORTH!' The only thing I had to learn, so to speak, was how to change the points, but all that involved was pulling a couple of levers. Was it fun? Yes, of course it was. I especially enjoyed banging on the side of the trains bit. I've always been quite a noisy devil. You just ask Gill.

I have to say that Jenny, Sally and Gary were all wonderful to work with, and we all had a lot of fun. The lovely Jenny was not long out of ballet school so when she was standing around waiting to film a scene she'd always be in second position. Whenever I saw her doing this I'd run up, stand beside her, and do the same. 'Ready for a *pas de deux*, Miss Agutter?' 'Absolutely, Mr Cribbins. Ready when you are. And a-one, a-two, a-three, a-four.'

I keep wanting to refer to the three of them as children, but of course only Gary was. Even he was sixteen, though, so hardly a nipper. For youngsters they were all very well disciplined and I don't remember any of them ever fluffing their lines. Sally Thomsett was the most mischievous of the three. She's one of the sweetest people you could ever meet. We saw her having a sneaky fag one day and Lionel went berserk. ''Ere, madam, put that out quick. We've got a reporter coming round.' The look on her face was a picture. Silent indignation.

Shall I let you into a secret as to how they filmed what looks like a pretty dangerous scene? You remember the scene where Roberta stops the train before the landslide and then faints on the track? I'm assuming you do. Well, the engine was actually moving backwards and away from Jenny at the time and they simply reversed the film. Clever, eh? It was probably too dangerous to do it the other way.

There's also a slight continuity error I can share with you. I got this from Jenny. At the end of the film, they shot a long sequence and shortly before this took place a tree that had been concealing some telegraph lines fell down. Apparently it was too late to reshoot, so if you look carefully you can see what Jenny called 'a modern intrusion' in the background.

I think the most memorable scene in the film is definitely when Jenny – sorry, Bobbie – meets her father on the platform. If you don't shed a tear or two when she shouts, 'Daddy, my daddy,' you're made of wood. Being a bit of a sentimentalist I always well up. Jenny doesn't. Hard as nails, she is.

The film had its premiere – a royal premiere, if you please – on 21 October 1970 at the ABC cinema on Shaftesbury Avenue. This cinema had been a theatre called the Saville, and it had been converted just a few weeks before the premiere. It's a beautiful art deco building and, as far as I know, it's still a cinema today. Since the late 1960s the Saville had been used as a music venue and the last band to have appeared there prior to it being converted were a once popular combo called the Rolling Stones. I wonder what happened to them?

Anyway, that was all in the past now. On 21 October 1970, instead of Mick Jagger, Keith Richards and a few hundred groupies assailing the doors of this beautiful old building, you had me, Jenny Agutter, Sally Thomsett, Gary Warren, Dinah Sheridan and Li Jeffries, not forgetting our three guests of honour: Princess Anne, Prince Andrew and Prince Edward. Oh yes. We also had a few hundred assorted children making up the rest of the audience. Prince Andrew and Prince Edward were just young lads at the time – about ten and six respectively – and the Princess Royal was about twenty.

Jenny, Sally, Gary and I were all in costume for the premiere and after greeting the audience in character we then had to watch the film – what, again? – before meeting the young royals afterwards. This was the first time I'd ever appeared in a film that had been granted a royal premiere and I was really looking forward to the occasion. It might sound rather strange to some people but the atmosphere we'd created on the set seemed to have followed the film to the cinema and the anticipation prior to the lights dimming was almost palpable. Not just for the kids, but for us too. We were the last people to take our seats and were sitting right behind the Princess and the two Princes.

About an hour into the film, Prince Edward, who was just knee-high to a grasshopper, started losing concentration. He was only six years old, bless him, and he was probably waiting for a scene that had the steam engine in it. Just as the little Prince's attention span was really starting to wane, I suddenly appeared on the screen and for some reason he momentarily became interested again. Seconds later he was looking away once more and after looking back to his left he saw the person he'd just been looking at on the screen – i.e. me – staring straight at him. After instinctively jerking his head back towards the screen Prince Edward obviously realised what he'd seen and before he'd got halfway he suddenly yanked his head back again at a hundred miles an hour. The royal family aren't necessarily known for their double-takes, but this one was worthy of Tommy Cooper. Prince Edward's eyes almost popped out of his head. He looked at me, then back at the screen, and then at me again. I think I terrified the poor lad half to death!

In April 1971, about five months after the film had been released, I received a telephone call from Mr Jeffries.

'Bernie. Li here. Look darlin', I've got some news for you. That little film we made has been nominated for three BAFTA Awards.'

229

Naturally I was delighted.

'Congratulations, Lionel,' I said. 'You must be absolutely thrilled to bits.' I then called to Gill who was in the kitchen. '*The Railway Children* has been nominated for three BAFTAs! It's Lionel. Isn't that marvellous?'

'Hang on, hang on, I haven't finished yet,' said Li. 'Don't you want to know which awards we've been nominated for?'

To be honest that hadn't even occurred to me.

'Yes, go on then.'

'Young Sally has been nominated for best newcomer. Bit of an odd one that.'

'How do you mean?' I asked.

'Well, she made her television debut in 1964. Hardly a newcomer.'

'I think they mean the most promising newcomer to a film role, Lionel. What are the other nominations then?'

'Johnny Douglas,' said Li. 'He's up for the Anthony Asquith Award.'

I must say, this pleased me immensely. Johnny Douglas composed the music for *The Railway Children* and in my opinion it's one of the best things about the film. The main theme is very memorable and Lionel had asked Johnny to write a different piece of recurring music for each of the main characters. I thought that was very clever.

'Come on then,' I pressed. 'Who's got the other one?'

'You 'ave,' he said.

'I have?'

'Yes, you 'ave. Best supporting actor. Congratulations, darlin'.'

It honestly never occurred to me that I might have been nominated. You could have knocked me down with a feather.

'The ceremony's in March,' said Li. 'Royal Albert Hall, apparently. I'll keep you posted. Ta-ta.'

After I put down the receiver Gill walked into the living room.

'Is everything OK?' she asked. 'You look rather shocked.'

'I suppose I am,' I said finally. 'I've been nominated for a BAFTA.'

'You've been what?'

'One of those three nominations was for me. Best supporting actor.'

'My word!'

Just being associated with a film that's been nominated for a British Academy Film Award is an honour, but being nominated yourself? That conjures up even stronger emotions.

The 24th British Academy Film Awards ceremony took place on Thursday 4 March, 1971, and it was a very starry affair. The Princess Royal presented the awards and the big film that everybody was talking about that year was *Butch Cassidy and the Sundance Kid*. The competition in my category was fierce and comprised of Colin Welland, who'd appeared in *Kes*, John Mills, who'd appeared in *Ryan's Daughter*, and Gig Young, who'd put in a turn in the American film, *They Shoot Horses, Don't They?* Colin Welland ended up winning the award for his portrayal of a schoolteacher called Mr Farthing. Colin had actually been a teacher prior to becoming an actor so you could argue that he wasn't really acting. Poor old Sally also lost out to an actor from *Kes* – David Bradley, this time – and Johnny was pipped to the post by Burt Bacharach – or Burt Backache as Eric Morecambe used to call him – for his film score for *Butch Cassidy and the Sundance Kid*. Beaten by a kestrel from Yorkshire and a couple of cowboys. Oh well.

After *The Railway Children* had done the rounds at the usual cinemas it kind of disappeared. Then, about ten years later, the film was rediscovered when it was released on video. All of a sudden, people began watching it again and it's been gaining momentum ever since. If it hadn't been for video it would just have remained a nice little film that a few people saw at the end of 1970, or perhaps on television every so often.

In 2008 somebody had the bright idea of producing a stage version of the show. Then, they had the even brighter idea of putting it on at the National Railway Museum in York, which meant they could use an actual working steam engine in the show. After that it was staged at Waterloo Station, then King's Cross, and was even taken over to Canada. Gill and I went to see the production when it was on at Waterloo Station in 2010 and I was recognised right from the word go. I should have gone in disguise. The actor playing Albert Perks was Marshall Lancaster. He played Chris Skelton in *Life on Mars* and *Ashes to Ashes* and shortly before the production opened I was invited to do a photo call with him at Waterloo on the footplate of the engine they were using, a beautiful green GNR Sterling Single that had been built sometime in the late nineteenth century. The show was wonderfully inventive, and it brought back a lot of marvellous memories for me.

That same year, which was the film's fortieth anniversary, I was asked if I'd like to record an audio commentary for a new

DVD release of *The Railway Children* together with Jenny, Sally and Gary. We were also asked to attend a special screening of the film at the National Media Museum, Bradford, as part of the Bradford Film Festival. Afterwards we all took to the stage and took part in a panel discussion.

Sadly, shortly before all this happened old Lionel passed away. He'd been suffering from vascular dementia for about ten years and had died in a nursing home. It was obviously a huge pity. He'd always been such an effervescent character and it would have been fabulous to do the commentary with him. We've still got his work, though. Nobody can ever take that away from us. And I'm pleased to say that I can still recall Lionel's voice any time, and as clear as day.

''Ello darlin', Li here. Got time for a chat?'

I always had time for a chat with Lionel. He was one of life's good'ns.

CHAPTER TWELVE

There was a young lady from Trent

One of the few highlights about attending that BAFTA Awards ceremony, at which we were well and truly robbed, was seeing the great filmmaker Alfred Hitchcock collect the Fellowship Award. He was the inaugural recipient of this particular gong, which is basically a lifetime achievement award, and since then they've presented at least one of these awards every year.

When Mr Hitchcock went up to collect his award I thought to myself, *Imagine what it must be like working with him. The man's a complete legend.* I obviously associated Alfred Hitchcock with films like *Psycho* and *The Birds* – American films – and although we worked in the same industry his own branch seemed a world away from the one I inhabited.

Literally a week or two after that ceremony I received a telephone call from my agent. 'Would you like to meet Alfred Hitchcock?' he asked. What a bizarre question.

'You mean meet him as in, have a drink with him?'

'No, I mean meet him as in read for him. He's making a new film in London and he wants to talk to you about one of the parts.'

Well I never! I'm not easily shocked, as you know, but this almost had me reaching for the brandy. Just two weeks after seeing him collect that award and wondering what it must be like working with him, he's asking me out on a date.

The venue for our meeting was on Piccadilly. I turned up as requested and after having a quick chat with the great man I read the part. The film he was casting for was called *Frenzy*, which was based on a book called *Goodbye Piccadilly, Farewell Leicester Square* by Arthur La Bern. It's all about a serial killer who rapes and strangles women and the part I was up for was a landlord who is in love with one of the eventual victims. Although the character wasn't a baddie, so to speak, he was still quite a nasty so-and-so and Hitchcock himself described him as being 'particularly horrible'. It certainly wasn't my usual fare but that made the role even more attractive and, when I was finally offered it, I answered in the affirmative.

I've got two memories from this picture. One is about Mr Hitchcock's technique as a director, and the other is about his love of limericks. I think we'll do limericks first.

I was sitting next to Mr Hitchcock one day discussing a scene we were about to shoot and for some reason I happened to run off a particularly funny limerick I'd heard. I probably just thought he'd find it funny and sure enough he did. He sat there chuckling away like a good'n and I thought to myself, I've just made Alfred Hitchcock laugh! Fancy that.

The following day I arrived on set and the first person I saw was Mr Hitchcock.

'I've got something to show you, Bernard,' said Mr H. Just then, he opened a bag and pulled out a huge brown book.

'What's this?' I asked.

'It's a book featuring all of my favourite limericks. I'm potty about limericks. Didn't you know?'

It turned out Mr Hitchcock was famous for reciting saucy limericks on set and he used to do it to shock people. He hadn't done it to any of us on *Frenzy*, so I think he must have thought we were all un-shockable.

This one isn't especially rude, but apparently he recited it to Tippi Hedren while making *The Birds* (I heard this in an interview Tippi did with the BBC in 2012):

> There was a young lady from Trent
> Who said she knew what it meant
> When he asked her to dine
> Private room – lots of wine
> She knew, oh she knew – but she went!

When it came to directing Mr Hitchcock never seemed to move out of his chair. He was seventy-two or -three at the time, so not a young gentleman, and was obviously on the portly side.

There was a scene that I did with Anna Massey. First of all, we had to walk towards the camera and then, after turning to the right, the camera followed us up some stairs. All the time we were talking and we probably walked about 15 yards, so quite a way. Throughout the entire scene Mr Hitchcock didn't move once from his chair and when he shouted cut he simply said, 'Camera?'

'Yes, fine, Mr Hitchcock.'

'Sound?'

'Yes, fine, Mr Hitchcock.'

'Lighting?'

'Yes, all fine, Mr Hitchcock.'

'OK then, print it.'

He'd obviously surrounded himself with a group of techni-
cians whom he trusted implicitly, and he relied on their judgement. If they said it was OK, it was. It worked perfectly.

I had to use some extremely coarse language in that film and,
as I said, I played a pretty nasty character. While it didn't do my
career any harm in any shape or form, it certainly gave a few
people a shock. After all, I was known for appearing in comedies
and on children's television. It's all right to mix things up a bit
occasionally and mix things up it did.

Speaking of which, did you know that I once directed a television
series in Germany? It's perfectly true. This is another one of those
nice little interludes in my career. My life's been full of those. It's
what happens, you see, when you agree to do just about anything.

This happened in the autumn of 1972, which was soon after
Frenzy was released and it was the result of a show that I'd made
in Germany in July that year starring Millicent Martin. I'd
already appeared in one or two of Millie's English shows and
when she was invited to do one in Germany I was asked if I'd
go with her and direct the sketches. Sometimes when you're in
a foreign country it's nice to have a familiar face around, and
because we got on well together – and because it was a job – I
said yes. Or *ja*, as they say on the Rhine.

Speaking of familiar faces, I clocked one of these on my very
first day of filming on Millie's German show, and boy, was it a
sight for sore eyes. We were filming in Munich and, not to put
too fine a point on it, I was feeling a bit out of sorts. Why?
Well, I suppose it was because I'd never directed before. And
because I was making my debut in a foreign country and with a
crew who might not speak English. After reading that back it's

a wonder I didn't just go home! I'm glad I didn't though. And here's why.

I came out of my hotel that morning at about seven-forty-five a.m.. It was a Schlosshotel right in the middle of Munich and a car was coming to pick me up and take me to the studios. The first thing I did as I came out of the door was look to my left and there, in front of me, was an open-top bus with an advert on it saying, 'Wings Over Europe Tour, 1972'. As I looked away from the advert I saw a man walking towards me carrying a small child. He must have been about thirty or forty yards away and when he came into focus I realised, very quickly, that it was Paul McCartney. Well I never! After clocking me, a look of recognition came over his face just as it had mine and we both started smiling.

'Hey, I know you,' he said, as he walked towards me. 'You're great!' The child he was carrying was his daughter Stella, who must have been about eleven months old at the time. 'You're great too,' I replied, holding out a hand. For the next ten minutes or so young Paul and I chatted away like old pals, the main topics of conversation being our mutual friend and mentor Mr Martin, Abbey Road Studios, and a tune or two. Apparently Paul had really enjoyed my cover of 'When I'm Sixty-Four' (Phew! I thought he might have planted me one for that) and was also a big fan of both 'The Hole in the Ground' and 'Right Said Fred'. I can't remember what I said in return but it was definitely complimentary. Even old duffers like me can appreciate how incredibly talented people like Paul McCartney are – not to mention personable – and those few minutes we had together pulled me out of the doldrums and set me up for the entire shoot. Nice one, Macca!

A few weeks after that, in the autumn of 1972, I was contacted by a German comedian and entertainer there called Peter Frankenfeld, or by one of his representatives. I know Germans aren't famous for their sense of humour but this chap was the real deal and was a big star in Germany from the late 1940s until he died in the late 1970s. After the war Peter had spent a lot of time in England and while in Blackpool in the early 1960s he'd discovered a sketch written by Lauri Wylie entitled 'Dinner for One'. A two-hander, 'Dinner for One' centres on the ninetieth birthday of an aristocratic Englishwoman who hosts a celebration dinner every year for her friends. The problem is that due to her considerable age she has now outlived all of these friends and so her butler, who is of a similar vintage, has to make his way around the table impersonating them in turn – and eating their food and drinking their wine. I'm sure you can guess the rest.

Peter was so taken by the sketch that he re-created it for his television show in Germany and it's gone on to become one of the most popular comedy sketches ever written. It's televised there every New Year – without fail – and has become a seasonal staple in dozens of other countries.

Anyway, after seeing Millie's show on television, Peter Frankenfeld wanted me to go over and direct him in a series of sketch shows. This was from scratch, by the way, and with a completely German cast, so there'd be no familiar faces. On set, at least.

Looking back, it seems like a ridiculous proposition:

Dear Mr Cribbins.

Bearing in mind you don't speak German and have very little experience as a director, we wondered if you'd like to come out to Germany to direct a series of high-profile television shows, in German, and with a load of German people you've never met before. All of whom will be speaking German, incidentally.

To save you going completely mad, we advise you to bring your wife.

Yours sincerely,

Somebody in Germany having a laugh

Except they weren't, though. They were being completely serious.

The series was called *Peters Bastelstunde*, which translates roughly as 'Peter's craft lesson', and was aired on German television in January 1973.

Because some of the cast and crew had at least a smattering of English I was able to communicate well enough to avoid me having to kill anyone. But I did have to issue one or two warnings. In fact, if I hadn't had Gill there looking after me, I think I'd still be serving time in Germany. At least I'd be able to speak the language by now.

Before Gill and I escaped back to England I was presented with an antler hat rack and a card from the cast and crew saying, 'We couldn't have done it without you.' That was nice. It was a strange job and quite stressful, but I'm very glad I did it.

The moment I returned from Germany I went straight to Wimbledon Common. You know what's coming, don't you?

Underground overground, Wombley free.

Here we go! I caught them.

One Boxing Day, sometime in the late 1960s, a children's author named Elisabeth Beresford took her two children, Kate and Marcus, for a walk on Wimbledon Common as they'd been making too much noise for their grandparents. While they were running around Kate suddenly came up to Elisabeth and said, 'Mummy, isn't it wonderful being on Wombledon Common?' Elisabeth looked at Kate and said, 'That's it! The Wombles of Wimbledon!'

When she got home, Elisabeth sat down and started developing the characters (each Womble was based on a member of Elisabeth's family) and the storylines, and in 1968 a book was published by Puffin called *The Wombles*.

Some of the Wombles stories were read on *Jackanory* in 1969 and 1970 but, strangely enough, by Ronald Hines rather than me. About three years later, some bright spark at the BBC thought it might be a good idea to adapt Elisabeth's tales into a television series and they approached a stop-frame animation company called FilmFair, who were based just off Marylebone High Street. The chief animator and designer at FilmFair was called Ivor Wood and he and his colleagues had scored their first big success in 1968 with a programme called *The Herbs*. Remember Parsley the Lion? Those of a certain vintage undoubtedly will.

Although born in Leeds, Ivor had moved to Lyon in France at an early age and after studying art in Paris he'd ended up being the animator on a children's series entitled *Le Manège Enchanté*, which is better known to you and me as *The Magic Roundabout*. In 1967 Ivor had been invited to move to London and head up FilmFair and by the time the Beeb had begun badgering them about *The Wombles* they'd had further success with *Hattytown Tales* and *The Adventures of Parsley*.

When the BBC first approached FilmFair about *The Wombles*

it was with the proviso that the characters had to change their look. The illustrator for the book, a lady named Margaret Gordon, had created what looked like teddy bears crossed with rats, to be honest, and the BBC found them too scary. Giving the Wombles a new physical identity may sound like quite an easy task for an animator, but it was anything but. In fact, there was a huge amount of toing and froing.

By the second design Ivor had given the Wombles a short snout and had put them on two legs, but the BBC still wasn't happy. Finally, Ivor elongated the snout, made the ears big and floppy, and made them all a little less portly.

'Bingo!' said the BBC. 'At last, we have our Wombles.'

Once they'd agreed the design Ivor then had to set about making the puppets, which were all about 10 inches tall. He didn't have much to go on in terms of colour as the book only had one colour image, which was the cover. On that, the Wombles have dark brown fur with just a hint of gold but because the colours were both quite dark there wasn't enough of a contrast. *I know*, thought Ivor. *I'll ditch the dark brown, keep the gold, which I'll use for the faces and snouts, and cover the rest of them in white fur.* These two colours were a perfect contrast against the greens and browns of the burrow and Wimbledon Common, but what Ivor also had to take into account was that most of the viewers' television sets would have been black and white, so the clear contrast would be essential in making sure that the characters were distinguishable. He was a very clever chap, that Mr Wood.

Ivor and a lovely man called Barry Leith did the animation. It was all done by stop-frame and so even though the episodes were only five minutes long, they would take days to make.

Despite this, I think stop-frame animation has an incredible amount of charm and I much prefer it to CGI. The latter may look very flash and very detailed, but in my humble opinion it lacks something. If that makes me a bit old-fashioned – good!

Anyway, once Ivor and Barry had finished the animation I would go in to FilmFair and I'd sit there all alone with a script and with the animation in front of me on what's called a flatbed editor, which I'd operate myself.

Let's, for argument's sake, take a scene with Great Uncle Bulgaria coming out of the burrow and shouting, 'Orinoco, Orinoco. Could you come here a moment, please? I've got a job for you.' Obviously, it would be totally silent, so as it played I'd work out the voice for it. I wouldn't record it. That was done later. The purpose of this was so I could become familiar with the episodes and get everything sorted out in my head.

Because the Wombles' mouths didn't open there was no lip-syncing and that made things a lot easier. The scripts were also quite sparse, which meant I could improvise and fill in the gaps myself.

One of the things people often ask me about *The Wombles* is how I got all the voices but to be honest with you it was an absolute piece of cake. Elisabeth Beresford had written the characters so well and in such a clear pecking order that they just jumped into my mind.

Shall we have a bit of a rundown while we're here, just to refresh the old memory?

First up there's Great Uncle Bulgaria, who is the oldest and wisest of the Wombles and is very much the leader. According to my sources he's based on Beresford's father-in-law and, not surprisingly, is named after the country. Some of the younger

244

Wombles are a little bit scared of Great Uncle Bulgaria but he's really a bit of an old softie.

Next up we have Tobermory, who is an engineer and Great Uncle Bulgaria's right-hand man. Apparently he's based on Elisabeth's brother who was an inventor and is named after the capital of the Isle of Mull. He can also be a bit surly but just like Great Uncle Bulgaria he has a heart that's exactly the same colour as his face and snout. In military terms, he's like a benevolent regimental sergeant major.

Orinoco has always been my favourite Womble and I think that's the same for a lot of people. When the series started in 1973 children used to run up and tell me who their favourite was, and nine times out of ten it was Orinoco. He was based on Elisabeth's teenage son, Marcus, and was named after the river that runs through Venezuela in South America. The reason we all like Orinoco is because he's got a great hat, for starters, and because he likes eating and sleeping. He also surprises you occasionally by being brave.

Bungo was based on Elisabeth's daughter, Kate, and was named after a province in Japan. He is Orinoco's best friend but is the absolute opposite in terms of character as he's bossy and over-enthusiastic.

Tomsk is up next. I've got a funny story about him that I'll tell you in a moment. He's the athletic one, is Tomsk, and has the IQ of a dead tree. He was named after the city in Russia and loves his golf. I'm afraid I can't tell you who Tomsk is named after, as I'm not sure Elisabeth ever went public with it!

Then we have Wellington, who's basically a very sweet but very absent-minded boffin. He was named after a school in Somerset where Elisabeth's nephew went.

Last but not least we have the ravishing French temptress, Madame Cholet, who was the first female Womble and was named after a town in France. Every inch a matriarch, she was styled on Elisabeth Beresford's mother. Shall I let you into a little secret about her and Great Uncle Bulgaria? They were at it! I caught them several times. I bet you're not surprised.

There were lots of other Wombles, but if we did the whole lot we'd be here all day.

Once I'd got everything sorted in my head I would go into a place called Studio Two on Oxford Street and record a few episodes. Each one would take me about half an hour to record, so not very long. Not nearly as long as they took to animate. Wombles didn't talk a lot, you see, and there was a lot of walking about on Wimbledon Common and humming.

Looking back, what's strange is the fact that if each episode took me roughly half an hour to record and there were sixty, that means I only spent about thirty hours recording *The Wombles*, which is probably, for a lot of people, what I'm best known for. Just thirty hours out of seventy-five years. It's amazing.

The story I was going to tell you about Tomsk happened about thirty episodes in. I was due to record some more and so before I went into FilmFair I listened to the ones I'd recorded recently just to refresh my memory. When I did so I found that my voice for Tomsk had regressed from a slightly slow Womble, which he was at the beginning, to a complete imbecile! I thought, *Oh my God, I've got to regenerate him before he disappears!*

I recorded the last four or five episodes of *The Wombles* in Melbourne, Australia. This would have been in 1975 and I was appearing in a farce out there. The Guvnor at FilmFair, a man called Graham Clutterbuck, had a nephew working in a sound studio in Sydney and so at the crack of dawn one Sunday, just after I'd just done two shows on the Saturday, I got on a plane to Sydney, got picked up by a car, watched the animation, read the scripts, recorded the episodes, and then hitched a ride back to Melbourne ready to do the show again on the Monday. It wasn't that arduous, to be honest. It was just exciting.

That's the Wombles, then. I bet you'll be humming the theme tune for the rest of the day!

In October 1974, a year after *The Wombles* started, I had a rather different encounter with a furry friend, but a real one this time. I opened in a play at the Criterion Theatre in London's Piccadilly called *There Goes the Bride*. Written by Ray Cooney and John Chapman, who I'd already worked with on several different occasions, it tells the story of an underpaid and thoroughly stressed-out individual called Timothy Westerby (my character) who is having to pay for his daughter's overly lavish wedding. This eventually gives Timothy a full-on nervous breakdown, which takes the form of a voluptuous woman called Polly who thinks he's the sexiest man on earth. The problem is that Polly is just an apparition and when Timothy invites her to the wedding chaos ensues at an alarming pace. The play starred Terence Alexander, Geoffrey Sumner, Bill Pertwee and Peggy Mount, and it was a lovely play to do. Classic farce.

A lot of scenes I had were with Bill Pertwee and one night we'd just done a scene where we had to use a soda syphon. You know the kind of thing. I'm supposed to squirt it in the glass and end up getting him in the face. It was quite amusing, although Bill didn't think so.

Once I'd finished squirting him I put the soda syphon back on the drinks table and as I turned to carry on I realised that the audience were still laughing. The first thing you do in that situation is check your flies and that's exactly what Bill and I did. That just made them laugh even more and when we turned around to see what the matter was we realised that the handle on the soda syphon had jammed and there was a little jet coming out of the end, just like the *Manneken Pis* in Brussels. So there it is tinkling away and because Bill and I were now staring at this jet rather intently the audience reaction became even worse. When the soda syphon finally gave up the ghost we waited a moment for the laughter to die down and then tried to pick up the scene. Just as that happened we heard a noise coming from downstage. *What now?* I thought. We turned around, Bill and I, and there, at the foot of the stage was a woman brandishing a rolled up programme shouting, 'THERE'S A MOUSE! OH MY GOD, THERE'S A MOUSE! HELP, THERE'S A MOUSE!' As she's shouting she's whacking the front of the stage with the rolled up programme and on closer inspection I realised that there was indeed a mouse. There's no way we could carry on with the play while this woman was on a mouse hunt and so, after asking her to sit down, I decided what to do. The mouse must have eaten some poison so it wasn't going anywhere of its own accord. If I kicked it off the stage it might hit a member of the audience so I decided against that. I also thought better of stamping on the poor thing as it would have made a mess. In the end, I fetched a tumbler from the drinks table, put it over the mouse and escorted it into the wings. I then walked back on stage, got in position to carry on the scene, and before Bill could say his line, I turned to the wings and shouted, 'And sit!'

What a night that was.

CHAPTER THIRTEEN

You don't die in television, John!

Since making *The Railway Children*, I'd appeared in two episodes of *Call My Bluff*, twelve episodes of the *Val Doonican Show*, *Frenzy* for Alfred Hitchcock, *Peters Bastelstunde* for Deutschland, and as well as escorting mice off the stage at the Criterion Theatre for Ray Cooney and John Chapman, I'd started recording *The Wombles*. How's that for eclectic?

Then, in 1975, I was offered a part in one episode of a sitcom that, while not being career defining as such, has definitely become a talking point. The sitcom in question is *Fawlty Towers* and the reason John Cleese asked me to do it is because I'd recently appeared in a training video for his company, Video Arts, called *How Not to Exhibit Yourself*. John had founded Video Arts in 1972 with Antony Jay and they were already a world leader in producing training programmes for what I believe are called soft skills. This one was about how to staff an exhibition stand and as well as Mr Cleese and me it also starred the actor John Standing. It was filmed down at Olympia and my one abiding memory from making it is that John and I had to shout at each other. Given what we ended up doing in the sitcom, it could well have been a training video for appearing in that!

Three years later in the summer of 1975 John got back in touch with me and asked if I'd like to appear in an episode of a sitcom he was making with his wife, Connie Booth, called *Fawlty Towers*. After reading the script – and getting word from some friends in the industry that it was destined for great things – I said yes to Mr Cleese and told him to expect me at Television Centre – Studio TC8, to be exact – on the date he'd mentioned, which was 27 August 1975.

The episode in question, just in case some of you have never seen *Fawlty Towers* (never seen *Fawlty Towers*?!) is called 'The Hotel Inspectors' and it was the fourth episode of the first series. The owner of Fawlty Towers, mad Basil, gets wind that there are some hotel inspectors in town and becomes obsessed with identifying them. The first person he wrongly believes to be a hotel inspector is Mr Hutchinson (*c'est moi*), a cutlery salesman who specialises in spoons. Lots of schmoozing then takes place and when mad Basil discovers that Mr Hutchinson isn't a hotel inspector he inadvertently knocks him unconscious while trying to pacify him in front of the person he now thinks *is* a hotel inspector – but isn't. Are you following? When I eventually come around I beat up mad Basil behind the reception desk while he's *still* trying to schmooze the person that he thinks is a hotel inspector – but still isn't.

The entire episode is pure farce and as well as Mr Cleese putting in a barnstorming performance, the script, which he wrote with Connie, is devilishly clever. Fortunately, they let me play the part of Mr Hutchinson in a northern accent, which I suggested on account of him being a cutlery salesman, and without wanting to blow my own trumpet I think it works quite well.

I'm relying on you having seen the episode now, but when we got to the scene where I'm complaining at the lunch table about not getting a cheese salad I had to have a word with Mr Cleese. You see, as well as being about 8 feet 6 inches in bare feet, he was a very strong young man in those days (he probably still is) and during rehearsal, when he had to start gagging me and then slapping me on the back, it was a little bit too 'method'.

'Here,' I said. 'Go easy with the old chops, will you?'

'What do you mean?' he said, looking confused.

'The old one-two on the back! It's a little bit too realistic for my liking. You don't die in television, John!'

It took him a while, but he got there in the end. I think it was a combination of enthusiasm and a lack of technique.

'Oh, right!' he said, as only John can. 'Sorry, Bernard. Sorry.'

In addition to putting in a performance on that episode I also helped to arrange the fight scene at the end. You remember? The one I mentioned earlier about me going behind reception and giving Basil a good hiding. When we began rehearsing the scene, the director, John Howard Davies, had the camera in the wrong position. He had it off to one side for the first punch, and I said, 'Hang on, Herr Director, you've got to be right behind Mr Cleese for this shot so that when I come up and go bang, bang, bang, you see the punches coming but you don't see them land. When I knee him in the cobblers, *then* you shoot from the side.' As well as being a lovely chap and a terribly good director, John Howard Davies wasn't afraid to accept a bit of advice occasionally and I think it turned out very well. Basil gets his revenge, though, right at the end. You remember that bit? Just as the real hotel inspectors arrive and I'm leaving, Manuel stops me and says that Mr Fawlty wants to say *adios*. Before I can protest, mad Basil walks out and after giving me two custard pies – one in the face and one in the crotch – he puts cream in my briefcase, closes it, turns me around and sends me on my way. After that, he kisses Manuel on the forehead, goes behind reception, realises he has the real hotel inspectors standing in front of him, who've seen everything, and screams. Cut to titles. Perfect.

John, Connie, Andrew Sachs and Prunella Scales were one heck of a team of actors. To have been allowed into their gang for a day or two was a big honour, especially when you consider how well thought of *Fawlty Towers* is today. We didn't know it then, of course, but they were creating one of the best sitcoms ever made. And I was part of it. It's incredible.

People do still shout, 'SPOONS,' at me occasionally.

To which I reply, 'COBBLERS!'

I'll tell you what we haven't talked much about yet. Fishing! Over the years I've been lucky enough to make one or two programmes about the sport, which is basically my ideal job. Not everybody is into it so I won't go on and on. I've had some good times, though, and I think a story or two might just be in order.

The first one I'm going to tell you about happened just off the coast of Ireland in October 1975. I'd been asked to make a film by the Irish Fisheries Trust. We were drifting along the cliffs of Moher one day, fishing for porbeagle shark, when another fishing boat came into view. Once it was close enough the captain of this other fishing boat called out to our captain, who was called Brown.

'There's a nine or ten coming. Get back now.'

'Oh well,' said our captain, almost nonchalantly. 'We'd better go home then.'

After getting all the gear in we headed back towards the port but within minutes of us being warned about it the gale was upon us. Some of the waves were over 40 feet high – at one point you could see water both beneath you and above you – and we had water coming in absolutely everywhere.

None of us had life jackets on, by the way. We hadn't worn them while we were fishing and because they were stored down below we didn't have time to go and find them. I was sitting on a wooden bench facing the back of the boat and every time it moved – it was constant really – my coccyx took the brunt. It was agony!

While the film crew and I were all saying our prayers (nobody was sick, mind you), Captain Brown remained amazingly calm. Every time we were taken up by a wave he'd simply wait until we were down, turn us in the right direction, and then carry on coasting until it happened again. This went on for over an hour and a half and when we finally reached the harbour it was lined with what must have been well over a hundred people, all of whom were cheering. During the final stretch we'd spotted people on the cliffs and it turned out they'd been sent there to see where our boat capsized. That's what they'd been expecting to happen and they wanted to know where to pick up the bodies. Some people were actually crying when we tied up, so it was obvious that not everybody was so lucky. It was an amazing feat of seamanship and the only thing I really suffered, apart from a nervous breakdown, was a very sore coccyx. It was red raw.

Many years later, I was invited to go to Ethiopia for a Swedish fishing tackle company called Abu Garcia. I'd always wanted to go to Africa as my dad had been there during the First World War and he'd talked about it often. I used to sit there as a small boy listening to Dad's stories and thanks to him and the Tarzan films it had always been a dream destination. I wasn't disappointed. One day, we rode on ponies for about two or three hours, which resulted in me having a very sore bottom. We were riding up into the mountains to fish for rainbow trout that were living about 8000 feet above sea level. I think they'd been introduced there by some settlers, as it certainly wasn't their natural habitat.

A few days later we travelled up to Lake Chamo to fish for some Nile perch and the first thing we did was run over a hippopotamus. Not advisable, boys and girls. These animals kill more people in Africa than any other and when you see one close up it's easy to see why. It was about five o'clock in the morning and aboard we had a boatman, a cameraman, a producer and two fishermen, so six of us in all. Shortly after leaving the jetty the boat hit something and it was like going over the kerb. I was about to say what the bloody hell was that when the boatman just said, 'Hippo,' and then turned the engine to full power. It didn't give chase, thank God. When we were a bit further out another one surfaced and you could just see its ears and the top of its head. It actually wiggled its ears, this one, as if to say hello. They'd been feeding in the reed beds, apparently, and were on their way back in.

As bait, we were using some dead tilapia to try and catch these Nile perch and at one point, while we were travelling from one stretch to another, somebody had left their bait bobbing in the wake behind the boat. As we were travelling along – at some speed, it has to be said – a fish eagle suddenly came into view. It was following us about 30 or 40 feet away when all of a sudden, out came the feet. 'Watch this,' said the boatman. When he was ready, the fish eagle dived down and took this tilapia straight off a treble hook – BAM! Thanks, lads. I didn't have to fish for that one. It's still one of the most impressive things I've ever seen.

There you go. That's the fishing done. I told you it wouldn't take long.

In the summer of 1976, which was a bit of a hot one, if you remember, dear old Li Jeffries called me up and asked me if I'd like to appear in a new film he was making called *The Water Babies*. Since *The Railway Children* he'd directed two more movies: *The Amazing Mr Blunden* starring Laurence Naismith and Diana Dors, which was based on a novel called *The Ghosts* by Antonia Barber, and *Baxter!* starring Patricia Neal and Britt Ekland. Both had been well received and when he told me who my co-star would be I bit his hand off.

'It's James Mason, darlin',' he said. 'You remember him?'

Did I remember James Mason? Like David Niven, James Mason had a certain star quality that was impossible to define and I can't tell you how many films I'd seen him in over the years. He'd been a regular in Hollywood since the mid-1930s and because he was a fellow northerner – he was born 20 miles away from me in Huddersfield – I had a sneaking suspicion we might rub along OK together.

The Water Babies is based on a novel by a chap called Charles Kingsley and tells the story of a twelve-year-old chimney sweep who discovers an underwater world where young children are held prisoner by an evil shark and an eel. The underwater part was going to be animated and as well as playing Mr Masterson, James Mason's oppo, I'd also be the voice of the Eel.

In the credits, I was sandwiched in between Mr Mason and Billie Whitelaw, which wasn't a bad place to be. Even so, the film didn't seem to capture the imagination of the public somehow and didn't do as well as everyone had hoped. Unfortunately for Lionel, everything he did as a director after *The Railway Children* was immediately compared to it and he never managed to escape that. *The Amazing Mr Blunden* had done very good business, partly because it had a similar charm and simplicity to *The Railway Children*. And, while *The Water Babies* has the charm, there's a bit too much going on, I think, and the animation isn't the best ever. Anyway, it was a job, and at the time none us had any idea if it was going to be successful. We were just having some fun and trying to do the best we could.

My favourite story from this film involves a moor in North Yorkshire, James Mason and a donkey. At the time of filming, James would have been in his late sixties and although he wasn't in his pomp, exactly, he was still a legend of the silver screen. Even so there were no airs or graces with Mr Mason and everything that Lionel asked him to do, he did. James played my boss, a Mr Grimes, and he and I are basically holding this chimney sweep captive and are working him like a slave. Incidentally, the scene where he falls in the river and discovers the underwater world was filmed on the River Wharfe, not too far away from where I failed to catch many fish.

While Mr Grimes, Tom the chimney sweep and my own character were travelling from stately home to stately home, putting this poor boy to work, James had to travel by donkey. He wasn't at all fazed by this and on a road it wasn't a problem. It was on the moors that things started getting a bit wobbly.

One of the first shots we filmed on the moor had James on the donkey and me leading it. Then, we meet Billie Whitelaw, who's playing an old crone, and after we push her to one side James then rides off indignantly on the donkey. Incidentally, it was interesting hearing James Mason revert to his original Yorkshire accent for this part. Both of us had spent years being asked not to sound like northerners, and here we were both talking naturally. When Lionel shouted, 'Action,' for the shot of James riding off into the distance we all stood and watched. Not because we were expecting anything. There was just nothing else to do! The ground on which the donkey was walking was uneven to say the least and as the donkey and James waddled off into the distance I got the feeling that this might not end well. Sure enough, after they'd gone about 50 yards or so James started sliding off to the left. He was obviously doing everything in his power to make sure this didn't happen but the uneven surface and the forces of gravity were rendering him powerless. I looked at Lionel as this started happening and the look on his face was a picture. He, like all of us, was slightly in awe of Mr Mason and I think the fact that he'd had to ask him to ride a donkey in the first place had haunted Lionel.

'Oh my Gawd,' he said, stepping forward. 'Oh my Gawd, he's going to fall. Mr Mason's going to fall!'

At first, I thought James might have been attached to the donkey somehow as when he started sliding he almost went underneath it. In the end, he fell off to the side of the animal and, as the nominee of three Oscars and a handful of Golden Globes proceeded to form a nice little heap on the moor, Lionel went into meltdown.

'Jeeeeesus Christ! Mr Mason's fallen off. Call an ambulance somebody. CALL AN AMBULANCE!'

I don't think Lionel had considered the fact we might not be able to get an ambulance onto that moor but as everyone else started running to Mr Mason, Lionel carried on calling for one.

'For heaven's sake, somebody call for an ambulance! He could be dead! Speak to us, Mr Mason. Speak to us!'

The costume James was wearing included a huge black overcoat and a large black hat with a feather in it. The hat had remained on his head and so from a distance he looked like a molehill. Except this molehill was moving. Shaking, even. Perhaps he was doing the death rattle? After all, he'd fallen at least 4 feet, and onto an uneven but decidedly spongy surface!

When we reached the disaster scene, we peered over the back of James's black shaking overcoat and underneath the large black hat with the feather in it we saw a small red face. A succession of tears were running down the side of James's nose onto the heather and he was convulsing with laughter.

'Are you all right?' one of us asked.

'N-n-n-n-o,' he said, before trying to take a few deep breaths. 'Of course I'm not all right. I've just fallen off a bloody donkey!'

You can take the lad out of Yorkshire, but you can't take Yorkshire out of the lad.

Talking of Yorkshire, which I try not to do too often. The only time I've ever really formed any kind of partnership in my seventy-five years in showbusiness is when I worked with Barry Cryer on *The Good Old Days*, which I mentioned earlier. *The Good Old Days* was inspired by music hall, and in particular a show called *Ridgeway's Late Joys* that used to take place fortnightly at the Players' Theatre, where I once played a dog. Starting in 1953, *The Good Old Days* was recorded at the City Varieties Theatre in Leeds, which is the birthplace of dear Baz Cryer. The City Varieties is one of the oldest surviving music halls in the country and to make the show as authentic as possible the audience members dressed up as Edwardians. The recent repeats reveal that the show is obviously very old-fashioned – that's the idea – but it has you smiling from beginning to end. That's what music hall was all about. Having a good time.

Barry Cryer was tailormade for a programme such as this, as not only could he act, write, tell jokes and sing a song (he had a number one in Finland called 'Purple People Eater'. It's true!) but he'd also acted as chairman at the aforementioned *Ridgeway's Late Joys* at the Players'. To top it all off, Barry had made his stand-up debut at the City Varieties back in the 1860s (joke!) so together with Leonard Sachs, who was chairman on *The Good Old Days*, he was the main man.

I forget the first time I actually met Barry (it must have been during *And Another Thing*), but according to him I said something insulting, he said something insulting back, and we've been bosom buddies ever since. Our entire relationship, though, is based on laughter, pure and simple.

So how did I get to appear in *The Good Old Days*? That's easy. You remember Alfred Bradley, the man who produced all those wonderful radio plays? Well, he had an office in Leeds next door to a producer called Barney Colehan who produced *The Good Old Days*. I think Barney must have got wind through Alfred that I'd appeared in one or two musicals and he ended up asking me if I'd like to appear in an episode. I couldn't tell you what I did in that first show, but the majority of songs I sang on *The Good Old Days* were traditional music hall songs such as 'All I Want is a Proper Cup of Coffee', 'Standing at the Corner of the Street' and 'Chin Chin Cheerio'. There was always a huge amount of audience participation, which made it an absolute joy.

All together now . . .

All I want is a proper cup of coffee
Made in a proper copper coffee pot.
I may be off my dot, but I want a proper coffee in a proper copper pot.

Well done!

The double act Barry and I ended up doing on *The Good Old Days* came about by accident. We were both appearing on it in our own right one week when Barney Colehan suggested we create something.

'You're good pals. Why not give it a go?'

Why not indeed?

The first thing Barry turned us into was an incompetent fire-eating double act called Les Flambo! Barry was the straight man and I was the idiot. I can hear Leonard Sachs's introduction now.

'Parrasizmal purveyors of pyromaniac pandemonium. Ladies and gentlemen, Les Flambo!'

Most of the skit was based on us trying to light the matches and went something like this:

BARRY: Go, on, go on. Light them!

ME: These matches, Barry, they're all dead.

BARRY: They won't be alone if you don't get on with it.

ME: It's not my fault, Barry. I got these from the digs. It's Mrs Bookroyd. She keeps putting them back in the box once she's struck 'em.

BARRY: May I remind you that we're a fire-eating act?

ME: Well I know that, I'm in it!

BARRY: You're right in it. You can't have a fire-eating act without fire. It's like having a singer who can't sing.

ME: There's a few of them about, Barry.

(Cue laughter)

BARRY: I must apologise, ladies and gentlemen, but I'm saddled with an incompetent.

ME: My Uncle Arthur, he was like that.

BARRY: Like what?

ME: Well, my Uncle Arthur. He was like what you said.

BARRY: I said, IN-COM-PE-TENT

ME: Oh, I see.
(Cue more laughter.)

On another episode Barry turned us into a juggling act and his opening gag for that particular appearance was just genius. After walking on alone, Barry picks up lots of juggling clubs and starts throwing them in the air, but instead of catching them he just lets them fall on the floor. Just as that happens I walk on and Barry says, 'You're late!' I wish I had a brain like that. Do you know, Barry once christened us both Los Brillos, on account of us having hair like Brillo Pads!

Barry and I had a kind of telepathy when we worked on *The Good Old Days*, and I've never had that with anyone else either before or since. He also wrote some terrific stuff for us so we couldn't miss really. Every so often he calls me up and entertains me for a few minutes.

'Cryer here. I've got a couple of new ones for you.'

After he's finished telling his gags he says ta-ta and then hangs up, leaving me giggling away like a small child. He's the gift that keeps on giving is Mr Cryer; he's one of a kind. Thank you, Barry.

Something that doesn't befall me very often, I'm happy to say, is illness. I've always been quite fit and, because I gave up smoking and drinking many years ago, I'm hoping this will last a bit longer. The only time I've ever had to drop out of a show due to illness happened in 1979 when I came down with an acute case of Ménière's disease. Ménière's disease is a disorder of the inner ear that causes episodes in which you feel as if you're spinning. You also tend to encounter fluctuating hearing loss and, mark my words, it ain't pleasant.

I was about to open in a play called *Forty Love* at the Comedy Theatre – now the Harold Pinter Theatre – which had been written by the actor and writer, Leslie Randall. The play revolves around a Jewish couple from America who are visiting family in London and as opposed to having a holiday they're faced with a long lost cousin who is leaving his wife. My co-stars were Kenneth Connor, Diana Coupland and Stella Tanner, and it was directed by Val May. We'd opened at the Yvonne Arnaud Theatre in Guildford on 24 October and had received some terrific reviews. Then, completely out of the blue, I started having these turns and was forever having to lie down for half an hour. Dropping out of the play was obviously the last thing I wanted to do but I had no choice. Rather alarmingly, the news of my illness spawned a paragraph or two in the *Daily Telegraph* and the reason I found it alarming was because they'd put me right next to the obituaries! Whether it was anything to do with it or not I can't say, but I gave up drinking while I was having these episodes and after a few weeks it went away. Funny that.

In the late 1970s and early 1980s I spent many of my waking hours in Soho, and before you start making assumptions, no I wasn't! The reason I was there was because I was recording voiceovers for adverts and I shudder to think how many I've made over the years. It must be at least a hundred. These days a lot of voiceover artists have studios at home, so they can record an advert wearing just a dressing gown. If they want. I prefer to record them in a studio and although they're not all in Soho any more it's something to which I always look forward. Some of the ads I did that spring to mind from that period include British Telecom, of course, Tip Top Cream, Hoseasons Holidays, Jaffa Cakes, the *Sunday Times* and Vauxhall. If you can remember any others, let me know!

At the studios, I used to bump into other actors that did regular voiceover work, and the two chaps I bumped into the most were Ray Brooks and Richard Briers, which in terms of children's television equates to *The Wombles*, *Mr Benn* and *Roobarb & Custard*. Not a bad trio, even if I do say so myself.

I think I'd known Mr Briers since the early 1970s and, as well as being a fine actor, he was also terrific company. That meant when Ray Cooney asked Richard and me to appear in a new farce he'd written in 1982 we said, '*Jawohl, mein Herr!*' Actually, that's not strictly how it goes because I said, '*Jawohl, mein Herr!*' about a year before Richard. Ray had decided to take the play to Australia first to give it a test run and he asked me if I'd like to accompany him. A paid trip to Australia? Where do I sign?

The farce, incidentally, is called *Run for Your Wife* and is about a London cabbie called John Smith who happens to be a bigamist. For years he's managed to keep this fact a secret and then one day, after committing an act of heroism, the attention from both the press and the police threatens to burst his bubble. I played Stanley Gardener, John's best friend, and the rest of the cast were Australian. The play went down well over there and after returning to the UK, Ray set about preparing it for the West End. I assume he must have made some changes and on 26 October 1982 it went for another test run at the Yvonne Arnaud in Guildford. Unfortunately I couldn't do the play this time around but by the time it was ready to go into the West End in March 1983 I was back on board.

When it came to the West End, Ray knew he'd have to find a big name. The actor he cast in the role of John Smith was Dickie Briers and I have to say that when I found out about this I was slightly surprised. Richard had always claimed that he couldn't do accents – 'Just RP, love' – and he was also the best part of fifty, so a good fifteen years older than the London cabbie. About a day into rehearsals I'd realised exactly why Ray had cast Richard and although he wasn't an obvious choice – in my eyes, at least – he was superb in the role. You didn't even consider his age or the accent, you simply marvelled at his delivery – which was often rapid, to say the least – and his timing. Oh, that timing! Even so, on the opening night of the play just prior to us going on stage, Richard said to me, completely unexpectedly, 'Do you know, love? I must be the poshest fucking taxi driver in the whole of London.' You'll have to pardon the language, ladies and gentlemen, but Mr Briers liked to use naughty words every now and then. The show turned out to be one of the greatest comedy hits in West End history, and ran for nine years with a changing cast.

One Saturday during the summer, Richard and I were waiting to go on for a matinee performance and across the other side of the stage we could see that somebody had left one of the pass doors open, which went straight out onto the street. Suddenly, the sun must have come out from behind a cloud or something and a great beam of light shone in and almost blinded us.

Shielding his eyes Richard said, 'What on earth's that, Bernard?'

'It's life, Briers,' I replied. 'And we're not in it!'

That became one of Richard's favourite stories and he repeated it shortly before he died for a radio show about my career. What a truly marvellous man he was. Rest easy, sir. Rest easy.

CHAPTER FOURTEEN

Come on, Cribbins, you can do it

In 1984 I scored a double whammy when I was asked to appear as Nathan Detroit in *Guys and Dolls* at the National Theatre. This production, which had started in 1982, eventually ran for over four years at the National, on tour and in the West End. The first actor to have played Nathan in this particular production was the late Bob Hoskins. The actor who took over from Bob was Trevor Peacock, who'd written my final hit, 'Gossip Calypso', and when I took over from him in April 1984 I was joined by a predominantly new cast.

What was special about this production, apart from the music, of course, was the set. It was basically like Piccadilly Circus and the back of the stage was literally covered in neon lights. I don't know if you know the Olivier Theatre at the National, but it has an enormous stage and the seating area is fan-shaped and holds 1100 people. At the start of one scene I had to appear at the top left-hand side of the stage and walk down to front right. There was just me, and it must have been at least 20 yards. When I got to front right I had to pick up a telephone and say something like, 'Is that Louis?' but the ten or fifteen seconds prior to that were wonderful. Every single person was looking at you and, boy, did you know it. A few years ago Gill and I went to see *Oklahoma!* at the National starring Hugh Jackman and when he came on to sing 'Oh, What a Beautiful Mornin'' he appeared at the same place I had and made exactly the same journey. The hairs on the back of my neck were rigid when he started to sing.

This is a little bit left-field, but among all the acting and voiceovers, I was working with different charities. I'd like to tell you a little about some of those experiences, partly because I want to give them all a plug, but also because I've got one or two decent stories. When I say working with different charities, what I really mean is turning up to shooting days, golf days and cricket matches and having some fun. It's not difficult. The charity that I've had the most involvement with over the years is SPARKS, which stands for Sport Aiding Medical Research for Kids. I was their president for a while and I've been working with them for decades. The charity was founded by the late Jimmy Hill, among others, and, like most charities, it's indispensable.

From the mid-1980s until the mid-1990s I had my own golf day called 'The Cribbins Classic'. It was always held at Foxhills Golf Club, which is in Chertsey, and it was always in aid of two charities, one of which was a place called White Lodge Centre, which looks after children with cerebral palsy. The first time we did it, it was just a few friends really but we still managed to raise over £4,000. The last time we did it we managed to raise over £50,000 so you can see the potential of these events. Gill used to organise the whole thing and we managed to get some big old names involved. Henry Cooper always came, bless him, as did Bruce Forsyth, Ronnie Corbett, John Conteh and Colin Moynihan, the sports minister in the late 1980s. These boys did nothing *but* play golf when they weren't working, so they were a shoo-in.

After the golf we'd always have a little soirée and if any of them were feeling brave enough a celebrity or two might get up and do a turn. One year Mr Kenny Lynch played golf and afterwards he offered to sing a song. There he was, warbling merrily away, when all of a sudden a stuntman called Rocky Taylor decided that he wanted to get involved. Rocky's a legend within the film business and has appeared in about a hundred and fifty films. I think it's fair to say that young Rocky had had a few by this time and instead of picking up a microphone and accompanying Kenny, he started undressing him. Kenny never batted an eyelid and he even helped Rocky by raising a leg when he was trying to get his trousers off. Fortunately Rocky stopped at this point so we didn't have to call the police. Speaking of which.

The police used to do the scoreboard at these events and some local Boy Scouts would help out too with things such as caddying and fetching and carrying. The goodwill was quite amazing.

One year we had the top snooker players Cliff Thorburn and Kirk Stevens playing golf and afterwards I got a tap on the shoulder. It was Mr Thorburn. 'There's a snooker table through there, Bernard. Kirk and I will do an exhibition. Charge whatever you want.' That raised a few quid extra. You see, it's a team effort. Everyone turns up, everyone has a good time, and everyone helps to raise a few quid.

We had raised about £10,000 at one of these events and it was being split between a charity in Guildford, who looked after mentally handicapped children, and White Lodge Centre. The day after I went to see the lady who ran White Lodge Centre and handed her a cheque.

'There you go,' I said. 'We managed to raise £10,000, so here's a cheque for £5,000.'

'Marvellous,' she said. 'That's the new hydro pool.'

Nobody was fiddling or having a jolly with the money. It went straight to exactly where it was needed.

The man who was in charge at Foxhills Golf Club, a chap called Ian Hayton who is sadly no longer with us, called us all outside after the golf had finished one day. 'Come on,' he said. 'I've got a surprise for you.' I couldn't have been more surprised if he'd cut the moon in half. As we went out onto the balcony at the back of the club an aeroplane appeared overhead.

'What's going on?' I asked.

'Just watch,' said Ian.

It was the Red Devils parachute display team! Knowing I was once a para, Ian had arranged for them to jump as a special surprise for me. Afterwards they all lined up and I went off to inspect them. What a marvellous thing to do.

Apropos golf again, I was playing in a pro–am competition one day and none other than Sir Douglas Bader was also taking part. Douglas, as you no doubt know, lost both his legs in a plane crash but still became a famous flying ace during the war. He was playing with somebody who only had one arm so watching the two of them go around was quite something. They were playing just behind me and my golf partner for the day, and on more than one occasion they caught us up. At one hole, just after teeing off, Douglas sidled up to me. Because of his legs or lack thereof, he always used to lean on you and, after leaning on me, he said, 'Bernard. A well-developed girl of thirteen could have hit it further than that.' It was the well-developed bit that I found funny. He was a very humorous man, was Sir Douglas.

Far be it for me to blow my own golfing trumpet (I'm still going to, though), but the great Sandy Lyle once referred to me as 'Mr One Putt'. I've played with quite a few big-name players over the years – people like Brian Barnes and Lee Trevino – but Sandy was the only one who was wise enough to compliment me. To be honest, it was the only part of my game that was any good. One day, while we were halfway through a round in which I was doing particularly well and, after getting a birdie on the tenth, Sandy said, 'Here! Give somebody else a chance, Mr One Putt.'

I should have put down my putter and retired there and then.

One of the other charities I've helped out over the years is the Lord's Taverners, under the pretence that I could play cricket. The first game I played for them was in Sussex in the early 1960s and my captain that day was Sidney James. We'd been working together on something – probably *Tommy the Toreador* – and he called me up one day and asked me if I'd like to take part.

'But I've never played cricket before in my life, Sid,' I said honestly. 'I don't want to make a fool of myself.'

'Look, Bernie, it's just a bit of fun. A day out, that's all. I'll pick you up tomorrow at 9 a.m.'

Gill and I were living in Chelsea at the time and the following morning Sid and his missus arrived in an open-topped Ford Consul. 'Come on you two,' he said. 'Get in. We can get a bit of fishing in before the game, Bernie. What do you reckon?'

I was beginning to like cricket.

We arrived on the south coast with time to spare and so before we went up to the cricket ground in Hove we had two hours' fishing off the beach. We didn't catch anything but it was lovely just sitting there with Sid chatting away.

When we arrived at the cricket ground I was surprised by how many people were there. There must have been thousands. For somebody who'd never played the game before this did nothing for my nerves and, after signing a few autographs and saying hello to a few people, we went off to the changing rooms.

'Are you sure this is a good idea?' I asked Sid. 'I bet I'm the only man here who's never played before.'

'I've told you, Bernie, it's just a bit of fun. They're batting first and so you'll be fielding. You can run after a ball and throw it back, can't you?'

'I suppose so.'

Actually, that's one thing I could do, throw. I couldn't bowl, but I could certainly throw.

I'd managed to borrow some flannels and a white shirt from somebody so despite being a complete novice I didn't look too out of place.

About an hour in, I think I'd fared OK. I'd had to chase various balls and had thrown them back beautifully. In fact, I'd even enjoyed the odd round of applause here and there. I was in my cricketing comfort zone so as long as I didn't have to bowl I was going to be OK.

Just then Sid called to me.

'Right, Bernie, it's your turn to bowl. Get your backside over here, boy.'

'What do you mean, it's my turn to bowl?' I said, running over to him. 'You told me I'd be fielding. I don't want to bowl. Aww, come on, Sid. Don't make me bowl!'

Sid put his arm around me. 'Bernie, Bernie! Everybody's got to bowl. People are here to see some entertainment, so let's give it to them. You've seen them do it on the telly, haven't you?'

'Once or twice.'

'Exactly. And does it look difficult to you?'

'Yes, as a matter of fact it does.'

I think Sid had lost patience by this point as he just handed me the ball and walked away.

Come on Cribbins, I said to myself. *You can do it!*

As calmly as I could I walked away from the wicket, turned around, jogged in and bowled the ball to the man in front of me holding a piece of wood.

'Yes!' he shouted after hitting it to the off side.

They managed to get two runs but at least I'd bowled it straight.

For the next ball I went in just a bit faster but this time he hit it for a four – WHACK!

Next ball, I got the bugger middle peg. OUT!

You'd think I'd just scored the winning runs in an Ashes series the way I behaved. 'HOWZAAAAAAAAT!' I screamed, not really knowing what the hell it meant.

They wanted entertaining and, as far as I was concerned, I was giving it to 'em.

After a minute or so Sid walked over to me. 'Oi, calm down. He's an ice hockey player.'

Happy days, though!

One of the other times I played for the Lord's Taverners (yes, they invited me back) was at Wisborough Green, which is also in Sussex, and at one point I was in the middle with Trevor Howard, who was a huge cricket fan. Because I was sans equipment again I'd had to borrow a bat from a lad called David Halfyard, who played for Kent, and this thing was like a tree trunk. He was a huge fellow was David and had I been able to hit the ball properly it would have gone for miles. At it was, we had to make do with singles, although there was one occasion where I almost scored two. I could only hit the ball towards square leg, which, for those of you who are, like me, not really conversant with the game of cricket, is about a quarter-past two on a clock, unless the bowler is bowling from the other end – it's a complicated game. That was my only shot so when I went in to bat I was predictable and easy to field against. Because I was using half a tree I managed to give one of the balls quite a thump and it went straight past the first fielder. Trevor was a good fifteen years older than I was and when I called for him to go for a second run he put his hand to his chest said, 'No, Bernard. I can't. Too tired, love.' Literally a second later, Trevor was standing there right as bloody rain getting his eye in. He just wanted to bat, the old devil. I could have had two there!

Over the years I ended up playing in quite a few matches for the Lord's Taverners, although unfortunately I never got to play at Lord's. Oh well. My loss is definitely cricket's gain! I did have some fun there and as well as shaking buckets around the stands, which I used to do with Gill, I also got to go up to the commentary box. Not to commentate, of course. That would have been incredibly unwise. I just went there as a guest during a Test Match. This was a memorable half an hour and no mistake as I was in there with the legendary Fred Trueman. Christopher Martin-Jenkins was commentating alongside Farokh Engineer, and Fred and I were sitting behind them.

From a commentary point of view I had the best seat in the house because, while Chris and Farokh were commentating to the nation, Fred was commentating to me. If he didn't agree with something they said, which was often, I got his reaction first hand. The first time it happened, Derek Pringle was bowling.

'And here's Pringle,' said Chris Martin-Jenkins. 'He's coming in from the nursery end and, yes! That's a very useful delivery.'

'Useful delivery?' said Fred, nudging me. 'He couldn't deliver fucking furniture!'

He was *just* out of earshot.

A little later on I received another nudge.

''Ere, were you here yesterday?'

'No, I wasn't.'

'You won't have seen that streaker then?'

'No, I didn't!'

'Pity,' he said. 'They were the only two things that swung all day.'

Isn't that brilliant? That was Fred, though.

Many years after that I was invited to go on a golf trip by the Lord's Taverners to the West Indian island of Tobago. We raised a lot of money, but you see what I mean about it hardly being work? If anything, it's a privilege. Partly because we get treated so well, but also because we can put our fame to good use. It's the people behind the scenes who do all the proper work and who keep the charities running. We're merely helpers with familiar faces.

One day, while over in Tobago, I was booked to play nine holes of golf at the Mount Irvine Bay Resort with Tim Brooke-Taylor, Bruce Forsyth and Jimmy Hill. Tim and I were a lot less experienced than Bruce and Jimmy and so they drove off first. After that, I teed off with a five wood, which went OK, and then Tim, who was using a three iron, hit an absolute screamer! It went for miles down the fairway and all four of us just stood there speechless.

Eventually Bruce said, 'Bloody hell, Tim. What on earth did you hit?'

'I used a three iron.'

'Oh, well, you know what you did there, love. You know what you did there. You hooded the face. That's what he did there, love. Don't you agree, Jimmy? He hooded the face.'

'For God's sake, Bruce,' cried Tim. 'Don't tell me what I did!'

In 1995, the most bizarre thing happened. You wait till you read this. I'd been asked by Richard Eyre, who had directed *Guys and Dolls*, to return to the National Theatre for a play he was directing called *La Grande Magia*, which means 'The Great Magic'. Written by an Italian called Eduardo De Filippo, it tells the story of a stage magician (me) who hints at having larger, darker powers. It also starred the late actor, Alan Howard, and had opened to rave reviews. I can't remember exactly how long into the run we were – a few months, maybe – but one day, about two-thirds of the way through a performance, my mind went completely blank. It wasn't just my lines I'd forgotten. You could have asked me my name and I wouldn't have been able to tell you. I've never felt fear like that in my entire life. I was terrified. Not just in an immediate sense because we were mid-performance, but in a more general sense, i.e. *What the bloody hell's happening to me?*

The first thing I did was walk off the stage into the wings. Instinct must have reminded me to look for the prompter but, unfortunately, he or she wasn't there. In hindsight, what I should have done was just collapse, in which case they'd have brought the curtain down and would have sent for the men in the white coats. Instead, I carried on looking for the prompter and when I eventually managed to find them – or somebody who could help me – I walked back on stage and carried on. What sparked it I have no idea. It could have been a noise or something that had annoyed me. Who knows? In seven hundred years as an actor, this had never happened before and when I walked through our front door later that evening Gill immediately sensed there was something wrong.

'What on earth's the matter?' she asked, walking towards me.

'I went blank during the performance. Completely blank. I couldn't remember my lines, my name – anything.'

When something like that happens all kinds of things go through your head and you won't be surprised to learn that I didn't have the best night's sleep. What scared me most, I think, was the prospect of it happening again or, even worse, it becoming the norm. Without a memory you can't act and so I was in fear of losing my livelihood. Fortunately that didn't happen but I still get a shiver when I think about it.

The last time I did any stunt work was in 2003 for an episode of *Last of the Summer Wine*. I was seventy-four years of age at the time and played a man called Gavin Hinchcliffe who reckons that climate change is going to bring about the new ice age. In order to prepare for this I decide to learn to ski but due to a lack of snow in the Huddersfield region I attach my skis to the roof of a van driven by somebody called Miss Davenport. That sort of thing was commonplace in *Last of the Summer Wine* (people in baths with wheels on, flying down a country road) but it wasn't typical of what I'd been doing as a septuagenarian. Even so, I said I'd give it a go and so there I was, strapped to the top of an old van with my legs bent being driven around West Yorkshire.

Shortly after that I was asked if I'd like to appear in *Coronation Street* for a while. Just like *Guys and Dolls*, this provided me with yet another double whammy: it was the first time I'd appeared in a soap opera, and it was the first time I'd played a Lothario on television. Sorry, I meant ageing Lothario. He was called Wally Bannister (that's a classic *Coronation Street* name) and while pretending to be a multi-millionaire he manages to entice Tracy Barlow back to the house he claims is his but is really his employer's. If memory serves me correctly, Ken and Dierdre Barlow end up coming to this house, where I'm the gardener, just as my wife walks in after returning early from a holiday. I then get kneed in the whatsits, and everyone else ends up in the swimming pool. Ethel would have loved it!

The more I write, the more I appreciate what Roy Kinnear said to me on Charing Cross Road all those years ago. Yes, it was funny, and yes, it made me laugh, but the reason I've had such a varied career is because I've been available when I've been asked to do these things. 'Do you know what my biggest asset is, Bernard? My availability.'

You were a very astute fellow, Mr Kinnear.

CHAPTER FIFTEEN

I'm back in the TARDIS!

OK, it's Time Lord time again. Obviously, I'm going to get onto my time with David Tennant and Catherine Tate, but before I do I've got one or two other tales to tell you about me and the good Doctor. The first one took place in 1974 when the third Doctor Who, Jon Pertwee, had asked to be regenerated. The producer, Barry Letts, invited me in for an interview and it's safe to say that although we got on OK, I didn't give him the answers he was looking for.

'What are you good at, Bernard?' he asked me.

'Well, I used to be a paratrooper, so I can fight.'

'Oh, no, no, no. The Doctor doesn't fight, Bernard.'

I was just being honest.

Out of curiosity I decided to watch Tom's maiden outing and one of the very first things he did as Doctor Who was wallop somebody, tie them up and lock them in a cupboard! Isn't that just typical? My word, he was good, though.

As far as I know the first actor to be offered the role was Graham Crowden, who I'd appeared with in rep at Hornchurch. He turned it down because he didn't want to commit to three years and so in the end it went to Tom

Baker. He, David Tennant and Peter Cushing are my own favourite Doctors, so in my opinion Barry probably got the right man. Had I told him that I was a fisherman, a rambler and an occasional singer, then perhaps things might have been different. Who knows?

Thirty-two years later in 2006 I was asked if I'd like to appear in an audio production of *Doctor Who* for BBC Radio entitled, 'The Horror of Glam Rock'. They've been producing these audio episodes since the mid-1990s – or rather a company called Big Finish Productions have – and on this occasion the Doctor was being played by Paul McGann and his assistant Lucie was Sheridan Smith. The action takes place in 1974 when glam rock was all the rage. I play the manager of a band who are trying to make it big and while we're on our way to a gig one evening we're suddenly besieged by aliens at a service station on the M62. Being a fan of radio and a veteran of *Doctor Who*, I obviously jumped at the chance to do this but I never thought for a moment that I might one day complete the set and be invited to appear in the television series.

Of all the episodes in which to appear in *Doctor Who*, a Christmas special starring David Tennant and Kylie Minogue would probably be an ideal scenario for a lot of people, so when this was offered to me in the summer of 2007 I said yes before anybody could change their minds. The episode in question, entitled 'Voyage of the Damned', featured a spacecraft set on an apocalyptic collision course with Earth, a host of killer robot angels and an evil severed headed mastermind, none of which I played. In fact, my character was just a newspaper vendor who was only meant to appear in one episode. It was a lovely little part, though, and I returned home from Cardiff, which is where they film *Doctor Who* these days, a tired but happy man.

Long before my episode had even been broadcast I received a call one day from my agent. 'They're looking at making the man you played a recurring character,' he said, 'and they'd like to see you as soon as possible.'

Well I never.

What they'd decided to do with my character, Wilfred Mott, was make him the father of Sylvia Noble, who'd been popping up here and there since 2006, and the maternal grand-father of her daughter, Donna, who also made her debut in 2006 and would become one of the Doctor's companions in the 2008 series. Wilfred is a stargazer who believes in aliens so when his granddaughter goes off galivanting around the universe with the Doctor he's absolutely tickled pink. Donna was played by Catherine Tate and, due to the fact that we had so many scenes together, Catherine, David and I became as thick as thieves. The schedule was punishing, though: twelve hours a day, six days a week, and one of the best ways to cope was to keep on laughing. You won't find many funnier people than Catherine Tate, so half the time I just had to listen and laugh.

One of the many things I liked about working with Mr Tennant was that he always led by example and he's one of the most professional actors with whom I've ever worked. He was always first on set and I never once heard him raise his voice to anybody. The only thing I found difficult about working with him was when we had to run one day during one of our scenes. I don't know if you've noticed but there's a slight difference between David and I in height, build and age, and when the director shouted 'Action,' Tennant went off like a hare, whereas I went off like a dead tortoise. My knees were absolutely killing me after shooting those scenes but, even so, it was better than working.

I don't know why but everything just clicked on that show. The unit down in Cardiff was one of the best I've ever worked with and the writer, Russell T. Davies, is just talent on legs. Everyone was on the ball and everyone was doing it right. It was perfect.

My favourite episode from that series is 'Journey's End', which is the final one. The reason it's my favourite is because it has Daleks in it and, at the time of filming, I hadn't seen one of them in the flesh – or the tin, if you like – for over forty years. While we were filming this episode I had an idea one day and so I suggested it to Russell T. Davies. You'd be hard pushed to find a more amenable writer than Russell, so I knew he'd hear me out.

'The Daleks have only got one eye, right?'

'That's right, Bernard.'

'Well, why don't you give me a paintball gun? Then I can fire it and render them blind.'

'What a good idea!'

Russell took half of my idea, really, as just a few seconds after I fire the paintball gun into a Dalek's eye, it says, 'MY SIGHT IS NOT IMPAIRED,' at which point I panic and prepare to meet my maker. Fortunately for me, Billie Piper then appears and she blasts this Dalek away with a huge gun. 'Do you wanna swap?' I say, after thanking her. That was my suggestion too.

It's wonderful working with writers and directors who are open to ideas. It keeps you interested.

A few months after that series had been televised, I was sent a script for another *Doctor Who* Christmas special. It was a two-parter this time, which would be filmed in the spring of 2009, and it was going to be televised on Christmas Day 2009 and New Year's Day 2010. It was, and still is, a pleasure reading anything written by Russell T. Davies, but as I started reading the script for 'The End of Time', which is what this adventure was called, I became a tad excited.

'You'll never guess what,' I called to Gill. 'Russell has made me a companion.'

She then walked into the room looking puzzled. Heaven only knows what she must have thought.

'He's done what?'

'He's made my character Doctor Who's companion. Just like I was with Peter Cushing. It means I'm going back in the TARDIS.'

I was like a boy with a new toy and as I read on I became more and more enthusiastic. It took at least eighty years off me. The last time I'd stepped into Doctor Who's TARDIS was in 1966, the year that England won the World Cup. In fact, the film had opened just a few days after Bobby Moore lifted the trophy at Wembley. Forty-three years on, and I was about to do it all again.

Just a few moments before we came to film this scene, I said to David, 'Do you know, last time I was in the TARDIS was in 1966?' Expecting him to cry, 'Wow', or something, he just looked at me and said, 'I wasn't even born then!'

Thank you for that, David.

I won't tell you what happens in the episode as those of you who are bothered will have seen it, and those of you who aren't won't care. Suffice to say it was action-packed and because it was David's last outing as the intrepid Time Lord it was also extremely emotional.

One big difference between the television series and the film was that my character had been allowed to develop, as had his relationship with the Doctor. With the film we'd had to cram everything into just ninety minutes so any kind of development had been impossible. A bit of plot, plenty of action – done. By the time Russell started writing 'The End of Time', Wilfred and the Doctor had become like father and son, which is actually suggested once or twice in the script. Not that we *are* father and son. That would be impossible, as the Doctor is a few hundred years older that Wilfred. But that we'd like to *be* father and son. Because the base of that relationship existed as we went into those final two episodes, Russell had been able to bring it to the fore, explore it somewhat, and make it part of the storyline. Given what I think of David Tennant in real life, this made it easy for me to well up when we got to the emotional bits. And some of it is very, very emotional.

The most exciting thing I had to do while filming these episodes – even more exciting that temporarily blinding a Dalek or walking into the TARDIS again – was sitting inside a big glass ball with a laser gun sticking out of it, spinning around and shooting lots of aliens. Given my history in the Paras, I was obviously used to firing a gun. This was quite different, though, and despite it being just a model it was one of the most exhilarating things I'd done in ages. The contraption hadn't really come to life in the script – how could it? – but when I saw it for the first time and then watched somebody demonstrate it to me I felt really rather peculiar! I was in there for a good few hours and because of the way it spun around I had to take some water and a sick bag in with me, just in case. I think I was eighty at the time but I felt fifteen. Watching it back on television was just astonishing. There I was, sitting in a glass ball on the side of a spaceship travelling at 700 miles an hour, firing at aliens. It was *Boy's Own* stuff for the twenty-first century, except I wasn't a boy!

One of the biggest surprises I had while reading Russell's script was that he'd included a story I'd told him just after we first met in 2007. Because I'd asked him if I could pin my Parachute Regiment badge to my red hat – it was a hat from home, by the way – we'd started talking about my experiences and subsequently Russell had written Wilfred as a former para-trooper. This had obviously popped up from time to time in the previous episodes, but never in any detail. I was just a former paratrooper who had served in the Second World War – which I hadn't – so it was all fairly tenuous. Then, in the script, while David and I are in the TARDIS on what's supposed to be Christmas Eve, I start telling him a story. The moment I began reading this passage I knew exactly what Russell had done and I couldn't believe that he'd remembered it.

It was about my time in Haifa. On Christmas Eve in 1947, shortly before my nineteenth birthday, I was supposed to attend midnight mass in Bethlehem. There was a truck going from our barracks and, being a practising Catholic at the time, I'd put my name down. It's difficult to overestimate how much I was looking forward to this. After all, how many eighteen-year-old Christians get to attend midnight mass in such a special and significant place? Shortly before we were due to leave for Bethlehem, our platoon, which was IA Platoon, which stands for Immediate Action, were called out to a disturbance. Come midnight, instead of being in Bethlehem celebrating midnight mass, I was lying on a roof in Haifa wearing a huge overcoat to keep out the cold and, together with a few flakes of snow in the air, there were bullets flying everywhere, not to mention explosions going off all over the place.

During the show, I start telling David this story as we're above the Mediterranean and I have just spotted what is now Israel. 'I was down there in 1947,' I say to him. 'Skinny young fellow I was.' Russell had remembered every last detail and he'd written the story far better than I could ever tell it.

As well as 'The End of Time' being mine and David's final story, it was the same for Russell, Catherine and Jacqueline King, who played Sylvia Noble. David and Russell were obviously the most significant people to go. Russell had been responsible for bringing the series back to life, and David had been playing its main character for several years. In hindsight, they probably timed it perfectly as both left on a huge high.

On my very last day on *Doctor Who*, dear old Russell presented me with a picture frame that had two photos in it: one of me and Peter Cushing from 1966 with a Dalek coming out of the Thames, and one of me and David. Underneath them it said,

'To Bernard Cribbins, the Doctor's Most Faithful Companion.' Apparently I'm one of the only people to have played a companion to two different Doctors, which I think is rather special. It was a lovely thing to do.

At the 2010 National Television Awards, which were held in January at London's O2 Arena, *Doctor Who* was up for the award for most popular drama. Many of the cast had gone along to the ceremony and when it was announced that *Doctor Who* had won the award, David Tennant asked me to go up and collect the award with him. At no point did I think I would have to make a speech or anything, so when David handed *me* the award and said, 'I'm going to leave this to Bernard Cribbins. Go on, mate,' I was in danger of being left wanting.

'What a bloody cheek,' I said, as I reached the microphone. I'm pretty good at thinking on my feet so once I'd finished scolding the mischievous Mr Tennant I paid tribute to everyone who was involved with the show, which is what you're supposed to do in situations like that. Later on in the evening, David deservedly won the award for outstanding drama performance, so that sent me home with an even bigger smile on my face.

About five years ago, he and his lovely wife, Georgia, gave birth to a little boy and they ended up calling him Wilfred. Isn't that nice?

Over the years *Doctor Who* has provided me with an awful lot of work, and I'll always be very grateful for that. More importantly, though, it has gifted me some brilliant memories – Australian Daleks, anyone? – not to mention some marvellous friends; from the remarkable Peter Cushing, who I still miss, through to David, Catherine, Russell and the rest of the gang in Wales.

Diolch yn fawr!

Just when I thought things couldn't get any better I received a letter one day informing me that I'd won a lifetime achievement gong at the 2009 Children's BAFTA Awards. To win any kind of award is obviously extremely gratifying. It's like a pat on the back. This, however, was different, as it was recognition for my contribution to what I suppose I'm most associated with – children's television. Catherine Tate presented me with the award, and I couldn't think of anyone I'd rather have done it.

Afterwards, I was asked by a journalist why the Children's BAFTA Awards are important, and that's easy. The significance of children's television with regards to things such as education and development cannot be overestimated. Nor can the effort that goes into making these programmes. Because they can often seem quite simplistic, especially programmes for the tiddlers, they can often be overlooked or even denigrated, so being recognised by the British Academy is essential in my opinion. Remember that story I told you earlier about the taxi driver? If ever there was a case for the importance of children's television that's both fun and educational that's it. While I was recording *Jackanory*, I knew that as it was being televised there'd be children all over the country going, 'Just a minute, Mum. Can I just see the end?' Some will arrive at the dinner table having been entertained, and some will arrive having been inspired, just like that taxi driver. Just being part of something like that is quite incredible and more than a little gratifying.

That's why, when I was handed the award by Catherine, I accepted it on behalf of the industry. It was a 'Here's to us' kind of moment.

I'm often asked what the difference is between children and adults in terms of audience, and there are two stock-in-trade answers. First, they move about a lot more. That's the children, by the way. This makes the art of keeping them interested even more difficult and when it came to *Jackanory* it was always judged by the viewing figures. Next, children are a lot more honest than adults. If a grown-up doesn't like something they'll either keep schtum or start moaning about it, whereas a child will just start doing something else. Picking their nose or bouncing a ball. Simple. They also don't have any of the hang-ups that we adults do, so if they like something and they're in a position to tell you, they will, and vice versa. They're not rude about it. They just tell you what they think. You do get that with adults sometimes, which is quite funny. A few years ago somebody shouted to me, ''Ere, you're Bernard Cribbins, aren't you?' When I answered in the affirmative they said, 'I don't reckon you at all.' What can you say to that? Had I been in my pomp I might have clumped them one, or at least given them a gesture of some kind. As it was, I just shrugged my shoulders and wandered off. You can't please everyone all the time.

The only award I've ever won that I've claimed just for me has been my OBE. It was awarded to me in 2011 for services to drama and I had to go to Windsor Castle to collect it. Princess Anne was in charge that day and the first thing she said to me when I went up to collect the award was, 'It's a long time since the BAFTAs, Mr Cribbins.' I had to think about that for a moment, and then I realised that she must have been referring to the awards ceremony in 1971. Princess Anne had been dishing out BAFTA Awards that day, instead of knighthoods and OBEs, and although she hadn't presented me with one, we'd had a quick chat after the event. What a memory, though. I was rather impressed by that.

I have no idea who nominated me for the OBE, which is a question I'm often asked. Somebody in the appropriate office must have seen a photograph of me in the papers one day and thought, *Good God, is he still alive? We'd better give him something before he pops.* Either way, it was a lovely surprise and after the ceremony me, Gill and some friends of ours had a nice lunch to celebrate. My only regret was that my parents weren't there, as they would have been over the moon.

Avast, me hearties! We're onto the final stretch now.

The last thing I did that caused a stir was a series called *Old Jack's Boat*, which I made for the BBC just a few years ago. It's all about a retired fisherman who likes telling stories about his time at sea and is a bit like *Jackanory*. The only differences are that *Old Jack's Boat* has a setting and some additional characters. It's a bit like *Balamory* in that respect. We started making it in 2013 and we made forty-seven episodes. Another difference between this and *Jackanory* is that as opposed to using classic tales we used stories that had been written especially for us. Russell T. Davies had written us a couple, as had the former Children's Laureate Michael Rosen, so we got all the top talent.

When children recognise me these days, it's usually because of *Old Jack's Boat* and the first thing they always ask me about is my dog, Salty. When I first signed up for the show, my producer,

Dominic MacDonald, said that they'd like me to have a dog and asked me if I knew any that might be suitable. Sadly, our own dog, Rosie, had recently passed away, otherwise she'd have been perfect. I did know another dog, though, and when I mentioned her to Dominic he asked me if I'd have a word with its owner. The dog in question was a wirehaired Hungarian vizsla called Scuzz and she belonged to a pal of mine called Paul Hawkyard. Paul and I had first met back in 1992 while we were both appearing in a musical called *Lady Be Good* at the Open Air Theatre in Regent's Park. It was a damn good little show, that was, and it got fabulous reviews.

As well as being an actor, Paul is also a very talented wildlife artist and a bit of an outdoorsy type. He and I would sometimes hunt rabbits together using Scuzz as a pointer and a hawk. It would be my job to look after Scuzz and when she spotted a rabbit Paul would unhood the hawk and away it would go. Scuzz was well trained and I knew for a fact she'd work for me so, with Paul's permission, I put her forward for the job. Dominic thought she sounded perfect and so Paul and Scuzz drove up to meet Dominic and the team in Manchester. After putting Scuzz through her paces she eventually got the part and was given a contract. Paul was out of work at the time and so this was great timing. 'Bloody hell, Bernard,' he said. 'That's saved my life, that has.' Paul's from Leeds and is a good actor. Before he and Scuzz left for home that day somebody made the point that we were still looking for an actor to play a mate of Jack's called Ernie Starboard. Paul auditioned there and then and he got the role. Everyone's a winner, as they say.

Part of the show was filmed in a beautiful place called Staithes, which is on the North Yorkshire coast, and the interiors with the storytelling were shot at Halliford Studios in Shepperton. They were originally filmed in Manchester but I managed to persuade them to head south. The fact that Shepperton is about 2 miles from my home as the crow flies had nothing to do with my suggestion, by the way. Ahem.

A team of six people would come down from BBC Manchester, Paul would come up with Scuzz and stay at the Hilton Hotel in Shepperton, and we'd all have a good laugh. If they were filming just Scuzz and me, Paul would always sit just off camera in case they needed her to sit up or something. Usually she'd do it for me, but Paul's presence made her feel secure and so with him there she was more likely to behave. She's 17 now, is Scuzz, which in dog years is about 124, so she's even older than I am.

Because we made quite a few episodes of *Old Jack's Boat* they're shown regularly, and not just in the UK. As far as I know they're shown all over the world and the amount of fan mail I receive is ridiculous. Some are written by the tiddlers and some by their mums, but I always send them a postcard with Salty and me on the front. I can't think of another television programme that has given me so much exposure overseas, which means, internationally at least, I peaked at eighty-seven! Did I mention that we also won a BAFTA for *Old Jack's Boat?* That was a perfect end to a lovely job.

Next to my wonderful wife Gill, the thing I'm most grateful for in life – apart from my availability – is my health. After all, what use is having any kind of talent or ability if you're not in a position to use it? Good health has got to be your starting point, and as long as I can get about – and as long as the phone keeps ringing – I'll keep on doing what I do. What was it the old character actor, A. E. Matthews once said? 'I get up in the morning, read the obituaries, and if I'm not in them, I go to work.'

The last two big-ish jobs I've done have been playing Tom Snout the tinker in a television adaptation of *A Midsummer Night's Dream* starring Matt Lucas, Maxine Peake, John Hannah, Richard Wilson and Elaine Paige, with whom I appeared in a splendid production of *Anything Goes* back in the early 1990s or thereabouts, and a small part in a recent film called *Patrick*, which is about a very spoiled pug. How about that then? My life is just one long variety show.

This point about my health was really driven home a few years ago when I was diagnosed with having prostate cancer. My doctor, Richard, is a clever soul who is extremely good at diagnostics and one day, shortly after I'd had a blood test for something completely different, he called me back in and said there might be a problem. Sure enough, after having a few tests I was told that I had aggressive prostate cancer. Incidentally, the last time I'd had anything wrong with me was back in 1997 and I found out in exactly the same way. I went in for some routine tests, Richard spotted a problem, and the next thing I knew I was being booked in for a triple heart bypass! That was an interesting day.

'OK. What are we going to zap the cancer with then?' I asked.

'Radiotherapy,' came the reply, and over the next eight weeks I had a blast of it every single day. I did over 1200 miles in the process, which I was quite pleased with. Anyway, it got the bugger. I'm pleased to say that I've been fine ever since.

I was asked a few weeks ago if there was anything I hadn't done so far that I'd like to do, and the only thing I could think of is to appear in a Western. There used to be an American actor years ago called Walter Brennan. Some of you may remember him. He often used to play the old men in Westerns and I think I'd be a perfect replacement. Perhaps I could play Clint Eastwood's dad? Then again, he's only a year or two younger than me, so perhaps not. To be honest, though, that's nothing more than a silly dream I had years ago, and if somebody offered me a job tomorrow telling yet more stories on television for tiddlers, I'd be just as happy as I would be filming a shoot-out at the OK Corral or riding off into the sunset on a horse and cart. Genuinely I would. Life is what you make of it and, if there's one thing I've learned in my seventy-five years as an actor, it's to do your best and be grateful for every single job.

Goodbye for now.

Acknowledgements

First of all I'd like to say a very big thank you to James Hogg, not only for suggesting that I write this book, but also for helping me get it down on paper. Well done that man. I don't think we've done a bad job, have we? Others who deserve a big pat on the back are Tim Bates at Peters Fraser + Dunlop, and Andreas Campomar, Claire Chesser and Jess Gulliver at Little, Brown Book Group. We're a small team, don't you know, but we're perfectly formed.